MW00585576

365 Daily Devotions for Law Enforcement

BroadStreet
P U B L I S H I N G

BroadStreet Publishing® Group, LLC
Savage, Minnesota, USA
BroadStreetPublishing.com

BEHIND THE BADGE:
365 Daily Devotions for Law Enforcement

Copyright © 2018 Adam Davis

ISBN-13: 978-1-4245-5646-5 (faux leather)
ISBN-13: 978-1-4245-5647-2 (e-book)

Published in association with Cyle Young of the Hartline Literary Agency, LLC.

All Scripture quotations, unless noted otherwise, are taken from the Holy Bible, New International Version®, NIV® Copyright ©1973, 1978, 1984, 2011 by Biblica, Inc.® Used by permission. All rights reserved worldwide. Scripture quotations marked NKJV are taken from the New King James Version. Copyright © 1982 by Thomas Nelson, Inc. Used by permission. All rights reserved. Scripture quotations marked NLT are taken from the Holy Bible, New Living Translation, copyright © 1996, 2004, 2007 by Tyndale House Foundation. Used by permission of Tyndale House Publishers, Inc., Carol Stream, Illinois 60188, USA. All rights reserved. Scripture quotations marked TLB are taken from The Living Bible copyright © 1971 by Tyndale House Foundation. Used by permission of Tyndale House Publishers Inc., Carol Stream, Illinois 60188. All rights reserved.

Stock or custom editions of BroadStreet Publishing titles may be purchased in bulk for educational, business, ministry, fundraising, or sales promotional use. For information, please email info@broadstreetpublishing.com.

Cover design by Chris Garborg at garborgdesign.com

Typesetting by Katherine Lloyd at theDESKonline.com

Printed in China

18 19 20 21 22 5 4 3 2 1

Foreword

By Randy Sutton

I must start by telling you that I'm not a religious man. So when Adam asked me—well, honored me—by asking me to write the foreword for *Behind the Badge: 365 Daily Devotions for Law Enforcement*, I was somewhat taken aback. To be asked to write a foreword is kind of like being asked to be a godfather. It's not something to be taken lightly, and, as an author of four books myself, I understand what it means. I didn't want to commit to him until I read the book, because if it was not something I could feel good about doing, it would be hypocritical to agree. And since I am not religious, I wondered how I would feel about it.

I spent almost thirty-four years behind a badge: the first ten years as a cop in a small New Jersey community, and the next twenty-three with the Las Vegas Metropolitan Police Department. During that time, I experienced what all cops have, and that is why I understand why Adam Davis wrote this book, *Behind the Badge*. He wrote it to help those men and women who daily face cruelty, violence, the horrors of death, and some of the worst aspects of humanity, and also the deadening of the soul that accompanies bearing witness to them.

Being a cop means different things to different people, but to most who take up the badge, it is not simply a job but a calling. People who enter into it are often idealists who believe they can make a difference in the lives of others. And in reality, *they can* and *they do*. But the shear avalanche of sadness and hopelessness that envelops them during their years of service dulls their awareness of all the good they do. They develop a protective shell that is difficult to penetrate, even by those closest to them. That only serves to isolate them further from friends and family, those who truly love them and want to be part of their lives. That isolation can lead to terrible paths of destructive behavior. Drinking, drug use, infidelity, and gambling are all symptoms of a great destroyer of law enforcement officers. This is called many things: burnout, cynicism, or the "who cares syndrome." But it is in reality post-traumatic stress. It has destroyed more law enforcement officers' lives than all the physical attacks by suspects in history, because the enemy comes from within. It is insidious, and it can become so overwhelming that it can destroy both body and soul.

Post-traumatic stress can be a relentless enemy, but there are ways to combat it and defeat it. Some of the ways include therapy, and some include counseling and support from friends, family, and coworkers. But every way includes belief—belief in something greater than yourself. That is what Adam's book is all about. Belief that in the messages of each day's devotional—messages that come from someone who has been there and walked in the shoes of a law enforcement officer—there will be solace.

Readers will draw on that wisdom and the messages of hope and spiritual awareness shared by Adam each day of the year, and they will draw strength—not only from the messages, but also in the knowledge that they are not alone in their struggle. I hope you enjoy *Behind the Badge* and, perhaps more importantly, realize that none of us need to walk alone in this journey called life. God will always be by our side.

Lt. Randy Sutton (Ret.)
Author of *A Cop's Life, True Blue, To Protect and Serve,*
and *The Power of Legacy*

The Law Enforcement Code of Ethics

As a Law Enforcement Officer, my fundamental duty is to serve mankind; to safeguard lives and property; to protect the innocent against deception, the weak against oppression or intimidation, and the peaceful against violence or disorder; and to respect the Constitutional rights of all men to liberty, equality and justice.

I will keep my private life unsullied as an example to all; maintain courageous calm in the face of danger, scorn, or ridicule; develop self-restraint; and be constantly mindful of the welfare of others. Honest in thought and deed in both my personal and official life, I will be exemplary in obeying the laws of the land and the regulations of my department. Whatever I see or hear of a confidential nature or that is confided in me in my official capacity will be kept ever secret unless revelation is necessary in the performance of my duty.

I will never act officiously or permit personal feelings, prejudices, animosities or friendships to influence my decisions. With no compromise for crime and with relentless prosecution of criminals, I will enforce the law courteously and appropriately without fear or favor, malice or ill will, never employing unnecessary force or violence and never accepting gratuities.

I recognize the badge of my office as a symbol of public faith, and I will accept it as a public trust to be held so long as I am true to the ethics of the police service. I will constantly strive to achieve these objectives and ideals, dedicating myself before God to my chosen profession; Law Enforcement.[*]

---

[*] Drafted and adopted in 1957. Used by permission of the International Association of Chiefs of Police, IACP.org.

Ready to Serve

JANUARY

Ready for New Beginnings

A new year brings with it hope, excitement, optimism, and new goals. While it is not possible to predict what this year will bring, it is possible to be intentional in your walk with God and keep your heart in tune with what He is saying through His Word. Maybe last year wasn't one you care to remember, and maybe you made your share of mistakes. A new year brings with it fresh opportunities for a clean slate, new beginnings, and a time to create new habits. As a follower of Jesus Christ, every resource has been given to you to pursue your God-given destiny.

As you begin to create new habits and behaviors, you will see goals you set become realities, and even the birth of new goals after that. The previous year's disappointment will soon fade away and be forgotten. Today, if you have not planned for the new year, take time to set some small achievable goals to establish early momentum. Establish some early goals for every area of your life, and watch your outlook on life begin to change.

> *Heavenly Father, I give you my future. I lay down my past, whether good or bad, and I ask you to take my plans and make them yours. Amen.*

Therefore, if anyone is in Christ, the new creation has come: The old has gone, the new is here!

2 CORINTHIANS 5:17

Finding Success in Preparation

Preparation for duty requires more than cleaning cars, boots, uniforms, or weapons; it involves significant mental, physical, and spiritual preparation too. It means spending time firing rounds down range on a regular basis and having a plan for your family if things go bad. This type of mind-set and devotion requires sacrifice and commitment, but at the end of the day, you'll be mentally sharper and physically more prepared. Preparation and training are the cure for the onset of complacency, which is the one thing that can take you out faster than anything on the streets.

Random inspections of uniforms, vehicles, or weapons are part of many department policies. Having your gear "squared away" means you are prepared at any time for these inspections. Thankfully, our righteousness is not found in our own lives or in our own behavior or performance. We cannot do enough to make it right, but Jesus did. Our righteousness is in Him alone, and He makes our paths clear and straight. Today, go in confidence in total preparation, knowing you are well-prepared to face whatever may come your way because of the way made by your Savior.

Heavenly Father, I thank you for the freedom to spend time with you, to know you, and share your love. I know I am prepared, and I can lean on your Word and Holy Spirit. Amen.

Righteousness goes before him and prepares the way for his steps.

PSALM 85:13

Safety in Divine Boundaries

Whatever your assignment on duty, being diligent and intentional with your actions are critical to survival. The gift of boundaries and limits exists not as a means of punishment or slavery, but as a way to keep each of us free and safe. For some, knowing their personal limits gives them an excuse to overcome them, and, in certain situations, that is fine. But when it comes to being reasonable, prudent, and involving other officers or the public, we should change our thinking.

While Proverbs 21:5 may not refer to police work specifically, we can apply its principles to our work and lives. Limits and boundaries exist to give us freedom and to empower us. When we learn the true power of obedience to God's Word—His boundaries and limits—we will begin to see a tremendous change in our lives. Think about it like this: if we are in a hurry to remove our sidearm on the range, we will, at times, miss center mass on the target. Being slow to draw the weapon isn't the answer either—it's a perfect balance. Finding the sweet spot will bring tremendous freedom in your career.

Heavenly Father, I ask for your wisdom and discretion today. Bring to mind the training and instruction I have received, and help me remain vigilant and disciplined. Amen.

The plans of the diligent lead to profit
as surely as haste leads to poverty.

PROVERBS 21:5

Maintaining Poise in Adversity

Life has enough challenges of its own, but with the added stressors of a law enforcement career, it can seem overwhelming to even the strongest of people. Think back to your rookie days when you were first learning the skills needed to be successful. Often, mistakes made during those times were followed by extra physical training and maybe loud yelling from the instructors, depending on the phase of training. Those moments were preparing you to think quickly and maintain poise in the face of adversity on the streets.

Regardless of the amount of training we receive, we will make mistakes during our career. Learning to respond to adversity is determined by our mental capacity to overcome the pressure and make sound decisions. If we cannot respond in a mature manner to the slightest adversity, then our margin of error will be low. Don't focus on stumbling or mistakes today; rather, focus on being excellent through the process of each step you take. Everything you were taught was for a reason. Be intentional in all you do—in your thoughts, words, and deeds.

Heavenly Father, grant me the power to not only face but also overcome adversity today and every day. Thank you in advance for guiding my steps. Amen.

We all stumble in many ways. Anyone who is never at fault in what they say is perfect, able to keep their whole body in check.

JAMES 3:2

Benefits of Preventive Care

Anything in our life requires maintenance if we want it to last for an extended period of time. Our relationships, health, vehicles, and weapons all require us to perform preventive care so we can get the most from them. We often neglect our bodies to tend to our families, thus failing to have preventive care performed by family physicians, which often leads to more serious health issues later in life. If these were addressed sooner, appropriate treatment could likely have been a viable solution.

What level of trust would you have in your duty weapon if you never maintained the weapon or your skills? The same concept applies to every other area of life. Taking care of our bodies is a requirement if we want a long and prosperous career in law enforcement. This means we must maintain excellent fitness standards, be gallant in relationships, and be good stewards of all we possess. Today, be a good steward of God's gifts by taking the proper steps for the preventive care of your body, relationships, and even material possessions.

Heavenly Father, stir my heart to pursue you in fitness, relationships, career, finances, and spirit. Show me the importance of being a good steward of all you have given me. Amen.

After all, no one ever hated their own body, but they feed and care for their body, just as Christ does the church.

EPHESIANS 5:29

Ready to Serve

The presence of a uniformed law enforcement officer can be an intimidating show of force. In many cases, the presence of a uniformed officer will deter criminal activity from occurring and comfort those who are innocent and law-abiding citizens. Most departments still have the phrase "To Protect & Serve" on their patrol cars. This phrase is the epitome of what all law enforcement officers do, regardless of their assignment or duties.

Holding the line against evil requires proactive strategies and staying ahead of criminal activity to ensure peace and order in your community. There is a reason for those who violate the law to fear law enforcement. This is not a fear of being physically harmed, unless justified, but facing the consequences of their actions. Today, serve with honor. Protect with dignity and courage. You have been fully equipped, completely prepared, and wholly trained to face what this world has for you. Do not be afraid, but be of good courage.

> *Heavenly Father, use me as a servant for those who do good and as your agent for those who do wrong. May I be just and fair in all I do today and forever. Amen.*

For the one in authority is God's servant for your good. But if you do wrong, be afraid, for rulers do not bear the sword for no reason. They are God's servants, agents of wrath to bring punishment on the wrongdoer.

ROMANS 13:4

From the Firing Range to the Fighting Mat

Over time, there will be thousands of rounds of ammunition fired through your weapons so you can become and remain a proficient and skilled marksman. Range time is an enjoyable time, but it is to prepare us should the use of lethal force be needed. There are many areas of training we should stay up-to-date on, including firearms, ground fighting, and the law. The same skills you need to be victorious in a ground fight, using your hands and feet, are not the same skills needed to be a highly accurate sniper or accurate with any of your other weapons.

There is significance in the phrases "hands for war, fingers for battle" in Psalm 144:1. Preparing our hands for war means preparing for hand-to-hand combat, which is a ground-fighting strategy, and fingers for battle means being excellent with weapons. You are not just going to war prepared, but you are going locked and loaded, ready to walk away victorious. That is the message God has given us through His Word, a message of redemption, mercy, grace, love, and empowerment. Our power does not come from our weapons; it comes through pursuing the ways of God according to His Word.

Heavenly Father, please stir in my heart a hunger for you. Grant me wisdom to know I can only succeed in battle with you as my Lord. Amen.

Praise be to the LORD my Rock,
who trains my hands for war, my fingers for battle.

PSALM 144:1

Overcoming the Pressure to Compromise

We often find ourselves in a situation of potential compromise when we are faced with making a decision between violating our moral, religious, or ethical standards, or even our personal convictions. The fact is that we've all been directly affected by bad decisions in a moment of compromise or know someone who has. The root of every action is a result of what is in a person's heart. Compromise with sin begins with one small step that seems harmless at the time. It all begins at the heart of a person, when he or she justifies an action that is wrong.

In these moments, we are often faced with temptations based on perceived needs or desires. In these times, we choose to make the wrong decisions when we trust in our own ability rather than trust in God or trust in our timing more than God's timing. In a world where the pressure to compromise is constant, resolve today to stand firm on the principles of God's Word, to honor Him with your actions, to trust Him to supply your needs, and to strive to keep your conscience clear before both God and others.

Heavenly Father, please guide my steps today. Give me discernment and strength. Grant me willpower to overcome the temptation to compromise when it is not good for me. Amen.

So I strive always to keep my conscience clear before God and man.
ACTS 24:16

Preparing for the Tempter

reparing for duty means preparing for threats. Through the instruction of seasoned officers, we are taught the necessary skills to navigate difficult and challenging situations, many that others have faced before us. While it is not always easy or convenient to prepare, it does require tremendous mental toughness, self-discipline, and self-control. Regular training, repetition, and becoming so fluent in our skills that they become part of our natural behavior means we will be precision ready when the time comes to use those skills.

In the same manner, we should commit to preparing our hearts and minds for the day of temptation through spending time in prayer and the regular reading and studying of God's Word. This is not a means of measuring performance or another "box" to check off so we can get into heaven, but it is to equip us for those moments when we are tested and tempted to the max. Today, commit your desires to God, and commit to spending regular time in prayer and studying God's Word so you will be prepared in the moment you need it most.

Heavenly Father, lead me not into temptation. Grant me strength and grace. Prepare my heart to be victorious over and resist evil temptation. Amen.

No temptation has overtaken you except what is common to mankind. And God is faithful; he will not let you be tempted beyond what you can bear. But when you are tempted, he will also provide a way out so that you can endure it.

1 CORINTHIANS 10:13

The Power of Peace in Chaos

If everything around you seems to be falling apart, God is in control. Maybe you ask, "Why would God allow this to happen?" God doesn't cause bad things to happen, but He is with you through it. We live in a fallen world that is full of death, pain, sickness, and misery, but there is a promise: Jesus can (and will) speak to the storms in your life. One word from God can change the direction your ship is heading.

Make Him the Lord of your life, ask Him to speak to your storms, and He will. We are not promised a life of ease, but we are promised a great Comforter and a peace that surpasses all understanding. Remember who is on board your vessel. God's not asleep, and He is fully aware of what is going on in your life. All you are required to do is speak to the storm, tell it to be still. God will either calm the storm or He will give you peace through it all.

> Heavenly Father, thank you for the strength and resolve to head into the storms of life with you aboard my vessel. Secure me through these storms, and grant to me peace that surpasses all human understanding. Amen.

As they sailed, he fell asleep. A squall came down on the lake, so that the boat was being swamped, and they were in great danger.

LUKE 8:23

The Procedure of Authority

A basic principle of authority is that we must first submit to a higher authority. Officers have supervisors, chiefs of police answer to city managers, and city managers answer to the mayor and commissioners, depending on the structure of government. As believers in Christ, we know the importance of honoring those in authority and leadership and what it means to respect those positions. As law enforcement officers, we have a duty to honor our superiors, enforce the law, and honor God in all authority we operate in.

Over time, you may be treated unfairly by leaders in authority. This may lead to a jaded view of those in your command structure; however, you cannot use the excuse of being cynical to rebel against leaders who are responsible for your life. Find a way to be at peace with those you serve with, regardless of their position. Today, know the seeds you sow in submitting to authority may be reaped when you sit in higher authority; therefore, seek to honor God in all you do, regardless of who is in leadership or how they mistreat you.

Heavenly Father, give me humility to submit to those who are responsible for my life while on duty. As I honor those in authority over me, glorify your name. Amen.

Let everyone be subject to the governing authorities,
for there is no authority except that which God has established.
The authorities that exist have been established by God.

ROMANS 13:1

Ready to Clear the Building

What lurks around dark corners can be irrelevant or it can be potentially dangerous. It can make or break you, but it is best to be prepared for the worst. The problem with corners is that we lack vision of what is beyond them. Finding the courage to go into the darkest, most violent places is what sets the best apart from those who do nothing more than talk about what they would do. Cover the corners. Clear the room.

Some who read this may wonder how God can lead us, or maybe they want practical examples of how God leads us. First, He has provided each one of us with access to the best training. Second, He gives us discernment, wisdom, and insight ... if we ask Him. Third, there is supernatural protection. God speaks with a still, small voice. His leading is subtle most of the time, and if He leads the little ones, He will lead each man and woman in blue. You may find yourself on unfamiliar paths, but He will guide you.

Heavenly Father, guide my steps, and in the dark and unfamiliar places, I ask for your divine protection, discernment, and wisdom. Amen.

I will lead the blind by ways they have not known,
along unfamiliar paths I will guide them;
I will turn the darkness into light before them
and make the rough places smooth.
These are the things I will do;
I will not forsake them.

ISAIAH 42:16

Preparing for a King's Invitation

As Americans, it is difficult to understand the significance of the invitation of a king. Our form of government is different, but imagine if the president of the United States sent you an invitation to join him for dinner. While all those who ridiculed you watched with envy and in amazement, you received the favor of the most powerful person in the nation. In those moments, favor and life-changing relationships could be forged. But the uniqueness of this is that *we* did not prepare the table—*God the King did.*

In Psalm 23:5, David was referring to an enemy who watched on as he dined with the King of Glory, often a momentous occasion that took place as part of a covenant relationship. Our preparation for duty is not just training; it is also accepting the King's invitation to the table He has prepared, to dine with Him while our baffled enemies watch. Today, know you can sit at the table with the King of Kings and dine on the Bread of Life while you serve. You are in a covenant relationship with the Father, and there's nothing this world can do to break that.

Heavenly Father, thank you for the invitation to the table you have prepared for me. I humbly accept your invitation to your table in the presence of my enemies! Amen.

You prepare a table before me in the presence of my enemies. You anoint my head with oil; my cup overflows.

PSALM 23:5

Searching for Evidence

Having good evidence in a criminal investigation means the difference between the guilty going free or the innocent being convicted. For thousands of years, researchers and scientists have sought for evidence of the existence of Jesus and His resurrection, along with other miracles in the Bible. Some have sought these ancient artifacts to prove the existence of God, while others have sought them to disprove His existence. We know the truth because we believe in the Truth.

One of the most powerful statements Jesus said is found in John 14:11: "or at least believe on the evidence of the works themselves." Essentially, Jesus was saying, "If you don't believe what I am saying, at least believe the miracles you have witnessed are evidence of the existence of the Father."

Today, you may be seeking the evidence of the Truth, but it can be found all around you. The evidence you need to prove His existence or any other thing you have questions about can be found in His Word, in our hearts, and all around us.

> *Heavenly Father, help me to see, not only with my physical eyes but with my heart, the truth, the evidence of who you are. Empower and activate my faith for service to you. Amen.*

Believe me when I say that I am in the Father and the Father is in me; or at least believe on the evidence of the works themselves.

JOHN 14:11

Never Back Down

We all want an easy life, a life without conflict, trouble, or resistance. That is, unfortunately, not a reality. Every day we live, there are choices to be made—choices of good and evil, healthy or unhealthy, ethical or unethical. You may be presented with opportunities to save a life and change someone's destiny or be the consequence for another person's actions. Today, you may be tempted to take a small step down a slippery slope of immorality, unethical behaviors, and conduct unbecoming of an officer. You have the choice.

You possess the single greatest power that separates human beings from any other form of life on our planet: the gift of free will and choice. You have the power to make the decision to deny your own desires and pursue the things God has for you in life. Whether you are on duty or off duty today, you may be presented with options to cheat yourself, let up and give in to temptation, or quit on life. Deny those and pursue the greater and significantly better things God has in store for you.

Heavenly Father, when I am tempted today, give me courage and strength to make the right decision. Give me courage to do the hard things in order to please you. Amen.

Then he said to them all: "Whoever wants to be my disciple must deny themselves and take up their cross daily and follow me."

LUKE 9:23

Relentless Pursuit

If we are to experience peace and order in our communities, we must first have men and women who are willing to fight to defend and restore order when necessary. Pursuing peace means we are required to pursue the evil lurking in our world. You get out on a traffic stop and the driver bails and the chase is on, or you initiate a traffic stop and the driver speeds away at dangerous speeds. In most cases, you don't stop. There are deeper, more severe issues going on, including felonious crimes or warrants to be discovered.

Who will pursue the evil in our world so that peace is restored? There are times when violence must be embraced to restore order. To restore order, suppress evil, and seek peace, we cannot turn a blind eye to criminal activity. Be relentless in your pursuit of those who seek to do harm to those in your community. Train like you will not get another opportunity to train. Pursue the evil in your world like nobody else exists to do it.

> *Heavenly Father, grant me courage to pursue the vilest criminals. Give me boldness to chase, wisdom to know when to retreat, but, most of all, grace through it all. Amen.*

Turn from evil and do good; seek peace and pursue it.

PSALM 34:14

Divine Direction

One of the first things you teach your rookie or make sure he or she already knows is navigation of the area he or she is responsible for and how to use a map. While a GPS is beneficial, we should be able to get to our calls without having to spend precious seconds punching in locations or digging for the information. Being late to calls can not only get you in a lot of administrative trouble, but it can also be unsafe for the other officers on your shift. With clear direction on the street, you are more of an asset and don't have to explain to your partners why you were lagging on the calls.

When we depend on our natural ability to get us somewhere, we can be easily distracted. When we are guided, we are less likely to be distracted, but sometimes it takes a little extra time. Maybe you are not where you want to be in life today; maybe things haven't quite worked out the way you wanted them to. Know that you are not at the end of your rope. This is not the end for you, and your future will be blessed if you seek the direction found in God's Word. He will guide you.

Heavenly Father, guide my steps and give me direction. Provide me with supernatural discernment and wisdom. Amen.

Direct my footsteps according to your word;
let no sin rule over me.

PSALM 119:133

More Than Physical Armor

Most agencies require officers to wear body armor when on duty. Even if it is not required, we should hold each other accountable and make sure we are wearing it. While body armor reduces the likelihood of a fatal injury from a gunshot, it is not guaranteed to stop or prevent serious injury or death. There are points of weakness and limitations in our physical armor; even strongest armor in existence has areas of vulnerability. Our body armor needs to be used in conjunction with our training and skills and our knowledge of the incident; it provides us with the most support and protection possible.

Just like our physical armor requires more than just the armor, so we are to gird ourselves with the armor of God—the helmet of salvation, the shield of faith, and the belt of truth. Prepare for battle through studying God's Word today. This allows you to become strengthened in faith, encouraged in spirit, and prepared for the attacks that may come your way. God is not seeking your perfection or performance; He desires a relationship with you. You will not be disappointed.

> *Heavenly Father, thank you for giving me the training, knowledge, and wisdom to know how to effectively use the armor you provide and the armor I wear on duty. Amen.*

Therefore put on the full armor of God, so that when the day of evil comes, you may be able to stand your ground, and after you have done everything, to stand.

EPHESIANS 6:13

Strong Enough for the Shield

There is one assigned person who trains consistently with the shield, and that is his or her sole purpose. While some departments have full-time specialty response units, others may not have the manpower or resources for a full-time unit, so multiple people must be adequately trained to use the shield for high-risk entries. Without the shield, the risk of injury or death is higher. But with the shield, properly used, the likelihood of victory exponentially increases.

God's strength is immeasurable. His timetable is not the same as ours. But we can depend on His strength, support, wisdom, and protection in times of crisis. He has given us His shield of victory. The writer of Ephesians tells us the shield represents faith, which is increased by properly exercising our knowledge of God's Word. The only combatant to the arrows of the enemy, also known as his lies, is the truth of God spoken in faith. When others count you out, God has your name in the "win" column. You are more than a conqueror, but don't neglect to train with the shield! Invest your time in the truth of God's Word today.

> *Heavenly Father, I know asking for an increased level of faith is a dangerous prayer. But I know you love me. Help me to grow my faith in you. Amen.*

You have given me your shield of victory. Your right hand supports me; your help has made me great.

PSALM 18:35 NLT

Preparing a Legacy

One of the most prestigious positions on any specialty team is that of a sniper. In the book of Judges, there were seven hundred select troops who were precision-skilled. They were selected because their skills were superior to all the rest. What do you want to be known for thousands of years from now? Maybe you will be remembered for your generosity, or maybe you will be known for your service to others. If you want to leave a legacy, you need to be excellent at what you do, but to be excellent, you must first be committed.

What is your target? If you hit 50 percent of what you aim for on the range, you would not be allowed to remain on duty until you became proficient with your firearm. The greatest thoughts to take away from today is to be courageous enough to go after big goals and big dreams, and to have the guts to set a stake in the ground and decide what your legacy will be. If you go for it, be known for winning. Be excellent, be humble, and be consistent.

> *Heavenly Father, guide my hands, my mind, and my heart; give me wisdom on when to take the shot and when to holster. Amen.*

Among all these soldiers there were seven hundred select troops who were left-handed, each of whom could sling a stone at a hair and not miss.

JUDGES 20:16

The Necessity for a Proper Mind-set

There is much we can learn from mistakes, failure, pain, and loss. We are given wisdom to prepare for these types of experiences, just as we are taught to prepare for violent attacks. If we aren't careful, one "mistake" can turn into more if we let it get to us; it's best to not let these types of things get us down. For some, pride is an issue that keeps them from overcoming a simple mistake, but it should only strengthen their resolve to continue to improve, to press forward, and to strive to honor God in all they do. Quitting is not an option.

Having this type of mind-set is necessary to be successful while on duty. It would be foolish to go on duty with a soft mind-set, thinking no one wanted to bring you or your partners harm. Evil exists. The enemy wants to destroy you and your family. You know your own weaknesses. With proper perspective, you can live in a place of love that is motivated by power and not fear. Let God take the things you see as mistakes and failures of the past and use them to propel you into your divine destiny.

Heavenly Father, give me eyes to see the threats of the enemy toward me, my family, my brothers and sisters, and those around me. Amen.

But even if you should suffer for what is right, you are blessed. "Do not fear their threats; do not be frightened."

1 PETER 3:14

A Sound Strategy

Your thoughts may not be known to everyone, but eventually, if you dwell on them long enough, they will lead to behavior and action. But the circumstances of your behavior may be made known publicly. According to the National Science Foundation, our brains produce over fifty thousand thoughts per day. That is, on average, around thirty-five thoughts per *minute,* and that is if we count the hours we sleep. Naturally, all our thoughts are not going to be positive, wholesome, or just.

We experience a renewing of our mind through reading, meditating on, and studying the Scriptures found in the Holy Bible. Watch your thoughts. Identify the negative and unhealthy thoughts, and begin to act to remove those from your thought patterns. The thoughts of a righteous person are just, but the thoughts of a wicked person are full of lies. What we think about will eventually become part of our discussion, and what we talk about will eventually become part of our behavior. What will you dwell on today?

Heavenly Father, please help me to keep watch over my thoughts, and let them remain pure and holy. Give me strength to conquer my thoughts, and let them be pleasing to you. Amen.

The plans of the righteous are just,
but the advice of the wicked is deceitful.
PROVERBS 12:5

Protect Your Focus

It wasn't too long ago that I was driving and began looking at something to the right, and, without noticing, I gradually began to swerve toward the right shoulder of the roadway before I corrected my mistake. Many of us have found ourselves in this dangerous situation before. In life, where we place our focus is where our destiny becomes. If we are focused on the wrong things, we will arrive at the wrong destination. Obviously, our attention on duty is always to have roaming eyes, but there are times when our eyes must be protected from threats, temptations, or other issues.

When Jesus instructed us to seek His kingdom first, there was a reason behind it, and it has nothing to do with performance-based love or legalism. He wanted us to know the way life was *intended* to be lived, not the way the enemy has perverted it. So where is your focus? If we are not intentional about what we focus on, then we will focus on the wrong things, leading us to make bad decisions and have negative outcomes. When we keep our eyes on Jesus, however, we will be affected by His undying love.

> *Heavenly Father, keep my eyes on you amidst all the distraction in this life. Help me keep my focus on you. Amen.*

I keep my eyes always on the Lord.
With him at my right hand, I will not be shaken.

PSALM 16:8

Preparing to Engage

One quiet Sunday morning after breakfast, I noticed a man staring at me as he drove by. I was on duty, wearing my full uniform, standing next to my marked patrol car. The officer with me at the moment suggested the gentleman's actions were odd, to which I agreed, so we decided to investigate. Later on, after a vehicle pursuit, it was determined he was wanted on five outstanding felony warrants. That was a perfect explanation for why he attempted to elude us.

Think about the thousands of traffic stops you have conducted over the years. It would be odd to have a totally innocent person (with the exception of the traffic-stop violation) attempt to elude because he or she was simply afraid of law enforcement. Those who run are afraid, and they are afraid because they are evil. How we respond to those we encounter should reflect our training, but it should also reflect our everlasting God.

> *Heavenly Father, give me courage and self-control. Grant me power to conquer those who seek to destroy me and cause harm to those in my community. Amen.*

For the policeman does not frighten people who are doing right; but those doing evil will always fear him. So if you don't want to be afraid, keep the laws and you will get along well.

ROMANS 13:3 TLB

Prepared for the Journey

While we live in this world, we do not have to become like this world. While the rest of the world is trying to handle problems on their own, we depend on the strength and power of Christ and His peace to sustain us. There is significant power when we receive this revelation—it means total healing for the individual. Jesus really does change everything.

The pattern of this world is simple: hate, evil, greed, and pretty much the opposite of everything the Word of God says to be good. We must be conscious of our thoughts, be of sound mind, and meditate on the words and promises found in Scripture. When we do this, our lives will change, and we will be prepared for duty from the inside out. There is nothing in this world that the love of Jesus cannot change, and when we begin to think like Him, we speak and live according to His will. Then we are fully empowered to be victorious.

> *Heavenly Father, thank you for this day—a day to surrender my will, my thoughts, and my ways to yours. Do not let me fall into the pattern of this world, but let me honor you and please you in all I do. Amen.*

Do not conform to the pattern of this world,
but be transformed by the renewing of your mind.
Then you will be able to test and approve what God's will is—
his good, pleasing and perfect will.

ROMANS 12:2

Do You Have the *It* Factor?

The process of becoming a law enforcement officer is not an easy task. If you make it past the application process, then you have to make it past the academy and field training, followed by what is usually a one-year probationary period. But there is something that seasoned officers look for in rookies beyond a person who knows the law and can drive a patrol car. They are looking for someone with something special about them—the *it* factor. Nobody can really put a finger on what *it* is, but it produces some of the finest officers in America.

If we only focus on learning the law and being "good cops," our careers will be lackluster. Our walk with Christ is the same way. If we think we can know the Word of God and do nothing with it and live without the power of God in our lives, then we will quickly become weary in battle. The fruit of the Spirit is only possible when we allow the power of God's Spirit to produce it through profound change from the inside out. This isn't the *it* factor; this is the undefeated, immeasurable power and comfort of the Holy Spirit. And He is available to you today.

> *Heavenly Father, may my life produce the fruits of your Spirit all the days of my life. Amen.*

But the fruit of the Spirit is love, joy, peace, forbearance, kindness, goodness, faithfulness, gentleness and self-control. Against such things there is no law.

GALATIANS 5:22–23

Prepare for the Walk

It's been said that the three main things that can cost you your career in law enforcement most quickly are relationships, finances, and substance abuse. When any of these three areas are issues outside work, it causes problems at work. Most law enforcement officers will never violate the code of ethics, but many have been tested. The question is, what happens when *you* are tested? It's more than a matter of self-will or self-control; it's a matter of walking in integrity at all times, not just for your sake but to honor God.

Crisp uniforms, highly polished footwear, meticulously clean cars and weapons, and impeccable personal hygiene and grooming won't mean much if we aren't people of integrity. Temptation can come in many forms, and if we are not in constant pursuit of a relationship with Jesus, we can take a step down that infamous slippery slope. In fact, if we have the mind-set that "I'd *never* do that," we become the next to do whatever *that* is. Be intentional about integrity. Be intentional about the decisions you make, even if you believe nobody's watching.

Heavenly Father, in my moments of weakness, give me strength. In my moments of temptation, give me a clear way out and the willpower to take that way. Help me to remain a person of integrity throughout my entire career. Amen.

Whoever walks in integrity walks securely,
but whoever takes crooked paths will be found out.
PROVERBS 10:9

Primed for Success

Too often we overcomplicate the process of success. Asking God for success is usually the last thing we think about when facing a challenge. Often,we ask God to give us direction or to make life and decisions easier for us. Why not ask for total victory and a strategy for that victory? There will be many challenges in life and many obstacles to overcome, but today, don't pray *for* victory; place your flag of victory in the ground, knowing you are already victorious before you face those challenges.

Here are a few thoughts to end today with. First, success comes with us choosing to acknowledge Christ as our only Rock, our only Refuge and Hope. Second, Psalm 118:25 says, "LORD, save us! LORD, grant us success!" There is significant power in unity. When we collectively gather as one to cry out for the power of God and for Him to grant us success and victory, we can be sure He will hear our cry. Spend time dwelling on what it means to call on God individually and corporately, reflecting on the power found in both gatherings.

> *Heavenly Father, I thank you for hearing my cry for assistance, my call for victory, and I know you will grant me success in whatever I face for your glory. Amen*

LORD, *save us!* LORD, *grant us success!*
PSALM 118:25

Appearance Matters

Think about how you would respond if you saw your patrol partner in a compromising situation. Suppose you did not count money recovered from the possession of a suspect in front of a video camera and half the money was later missing, then your superiors discovered you were behind on your bills. Most of them will know you didn't take the money, but it paints you in a negative light. Avoiding the appearance of evil doesn't mean you live on eggshells, but it does mean you use wisdom and the resources at your disposal. Find a way to protect yourself before getting into a compromising situation.

Knowing the risks and threats before you hit the streets means you will be better prepared for the challenges you face. There will be numerous opportunities to engage in immoral and unethical behavior, and there will be people who take words you say and actions you do out of context to portray you as immoral and unethical. Avoid even the appearance of evil. Be intentional with your decisions, and know that you are under the microscope on duty and off duty. Today, be aware of your surroundings and the traps of the enemy. Rejecting every kind of evil means rejecting those opportunities that look enticing.

Heavenly Father, give me eyes to see temptation and the traps of the enemy; help me not be blindsided or have spiritual tunnel vision. Amen.

Reject every kind of evil.

1 THESSALONIANS 5:22

Reporting for Duty

At the end of the day, your number-one goal is to go home safe. Doing your job with excellence does not always mean everyone will be satisfied with your services. When you report for duty, go in with the goal to be the best officer on your squad—not in a competition to berate others, but to sharpen each other to be excellent in all you do. Look out for your fellow officers, for their well-being, both on and off duty. Hold each other accountable, and make sure you are all using proper and safe tactics.

Encourage your fellow officers. Guard your heart against cynicism and unhealthy, negative emotions. Be cautious against substance abuse, and if you are married and have a family, do not neglect them for your work family. Both are important, but the family you have at home is your primary responsibility. Seek to be a blessing and strive to have a positive influence, regardless of what life throws at you. When you do these, when it's time to end your shift, you can say you fulfilled your duty to your community and to God, and did it all in a good conscience.

Heavenly Father, guide my steps today. Protect not only my physical body but my emotions, my heart, and my mind. Give me success in all I do for you. Amen.

Paul looked straight at the Sanhedrin and said, "My brothers, I have fulfilled my duty to God in all good conscience to this day."

ACTS 23:1

Incident Debriefing

Many agencies offer incident debriefing following major incidents. This process allows those involved to focus on immediate issues that can be identified and addressed. One term for this process is Critical Incident Stress Management and is often offered for pre-incident preparedness as well. Understanding any potential psychological issues that may already be present or knowing how to respond to an issue in practical terms is crucial to the healing process.

As believers in Christ, our peace comes from a higher source. Furthermore, we know the burdens of life that can, as law enforcement officers, often seem too heavy to bear. The promises of God's Word for the righteous, that is those who are followers of Christ, means He will sustain them, that no burden will cause them to be shaken from their faith as long as their faith is in God. No matter what you have faced or will face today, know the burdens that you take on can be cast on the Lord and He will sustain you—you will not be shaken. Place your faith in Him totally, and watch your strength increase.

Heavenly Father, thank you for sustaining power, the unction to cast my cares on you when I want to carry them myself, and the firm foundation of faith in you so I will never be shaken. Amen.

Cast your cares on the LORD and he will sustain you;
he will never let the righteous be shaken.

PSALM 55:22

Power for Peacemakers

FEBRUARY

Standard of Excellence

There are fewer bonds that are as special as that of law enforcement officers. Many have a relationship with those on their squad, especially their partners, that no coworker relationships can compare with in another profession. Accountability, trust, and a genuine sense of belonging make up the nucleus of this bond, which inherently becomes the standard of excellence in law enforcement. While the bond between officers is unlike any other, it is the ladder of authority for accountability and for the standard of excellence, where one generation demands and expects the next to uphold and maintain a standard. This standard of excellence is unique to this family and likely not found in any other profession in the world.

The true definition of excellence is selflessness, servant-leadership, and accuracy. Being bulletproof is one thing, but being an excellent officer goes beyond what can be performed on the street and what is being performed in the hearts and lives of all you meet. Today, accept the challenge to bear the standard of excellence. Maybe your department has experienced damage to the trust and accountability in the brotherhood of law enforcement. If you are one who has experienced this, know there are people you can trust with your life. Be the leader. Be the bearer of the standard.

Heavenly Father, please open my eyes to the importance and value of proper accountability. Amen.

As iron sharpens iron,
so one person sharpens another.
PROVERBS 27:17

Love's Saving Power

From the first day you wore the badge on your chest, there's one question people always seem to ask: "Why did you become a law enforcement officer?" If you ask a hundred officers, you will likely get a hundred different answers, but the two you will hear often are, "I wanted to help people" and "I wanted to serve." The root of why we serve is simple—love. Love is the greatest motivating factor behind every law enforcement officer. It is the greatest force moving beat cops up and down the streets on the midnight shift or the drug enforcement officers pulling over cars on the interstate.

Love is a powerful force indeed. In this case, it is a force for good. Love is patient, and it is kind. You aren't expected to be babysitters or nursery-school workers, but it is possible to let love be the guiding force behind all you do as law enforcement professionals. Today, in all your efforts, let your center guide be the love of Jesus, loving others as He loved us first. When we do this through our examples, our lives have the power to change others, and one life can change a community, a state, and even a nation.

> *Heavenly Father, remind me of the greatest power known to humanity—love—when I am at my worst. Amen.*

Love is patient, love is kind. It does not envy, it does not boast, it is not proud.

1 CORINTHIANS 13:4

Assigned to a Lazy Partner

Having a partner who acts as though he or she is already retired is frustrating. If you are easily angered by your partner's lack of action, it is a poor reflection on your leadership qualities and integrity, but it is also indicative that you may not be walking in love. If you want to motivate a lazy partner, begin digging in to discover the root cause of his or her behavior. As their partner, you would rather work it out with them without the need for them to receive official counseling from a supervisor. If their laziness goes beyond not doing their job and encroaches into officer-safety issues, maybe it is time to tighten up the ratchet.

It is not right to embarrass or dishonor anyone who wears the badge with integrity, but there is a right way and a wrong way to handle the responsibility of being a sworn peace officer. Taking responsibility, no matter the rank or position, means we hold each other accountable, applying positive peer pressure, and rallying around those who are lagging behind. Commit to not only holding others accountable but also to being held accountable yourself. Bring your squad together, make a resolution, make a pact, make it official, and work to honor God.

Heavenly Father, guide me as a leader, and grant me wisdom beyond my own capability to lead. Amen.

It does not dishonor others, it is not self-seeking,
it is not easily angered, it keeps no record of wrongs.

1 CORINTHIANS 13:5

Quiet Heroes

Maybe you don't attribute quietness to a hero. Having met some of the most heroic men of our generation, I can tell you some of the most dangerous men are the quietest. They are businesslike and relaxed but extremely well trained. It isn't the person who is constantly bragging about his skills who poses the greatest threat; it is the one who is quietly serving, always striving to improve on the day before. These are the people who are often overlooked for honor because they are silently or quietly serving.

When we seek public rewards for our actions, we rob ourselves of the bountiful blessings of God. A true hero is someone who doesn't need to seek out the attention of others to reinforce his or her value. Mordecai, in the book of Esther, was a great example of a quiet hero. He fought to defend the oppressed people of God and even prevented an assassination of the king. What many did not know at the time was that Haman wanted God's people killed. What would our world look like today had Haman had his way and Mordecai not been a quiet hero?

> *Heavenly Father, may my service be done in an honorable and humble manner, not self-seeking for my own glory but to glorify your name. Amen.*

"What honor and recognition has Mordecai received for this?" the king asked. "Nothing has been done for him," his attendants answered.

ESTHER 6:3

I Owe You One

After arriving on the scene of a motor-vehicle collision, I discovered the driver experienced a medical event that led to the collision. Later, a member of this man's family contacted my superior officers and provided me with written commendations for my work—it was like they said, "Thanks, I owe you one." In our line of work, we help many people, many of whom will never be able to repay us in any way. That is the beauty of being selfless servants.

There will be many times when you or other officers will help someone, and that person will want to show their appreciation. Like those we serve, I will never forget the actions of those who have helped me and the look in the eyes of those of whom I've helped. We should never abandon our purpose to love people, regardless of what they try to do to harm us. Our service should be conducted in a manner that exemplifies love. It is because of this debt to love that we walk out our calling with excellence in law enforcement. Today, serve in such a way that others want the same love that causes you to serve with passion and excellence.

Heavenly Father, help me remember the sacrificial love you have always shown me, and help me reflect that love and sacrifice to others. Amen.

Let no debt remain outstanding,
except the continuing debt to love one another,
for whoever loves others has fulfilled the law.
ROMANS 13:8

Overtime Push

There are numerous studies supporting the relation between the lack of sleep and suicide. In fact, one recent study revealed a key indicator in suicidal tendencies is the lack of sleep or sleep-related issues.* For you as a law enforcement officer, that means you must take extra care of yourself to ensure you get adequate rest, not because you are subject or more prone to taking your own life but because you need the sharpest skills, mentally and physically, to face the ever-increasing threat on the streets.

There are many opportunities for overtime work in law enforcement, and many take advantage of this to make ends meet. Maybe you do this to save for the holidays, pay off extra bills, or save up for some special occasion or expense. There are times when working overtime is a requirement. As you strive to get in the hours, get the bills paid, save up for the holidays, or whatever it is you are working toward, take time to rest. The effects of chronic fatigue far outweigh the money you will make from overtime, and I am sure your loved ones will agree. Remember that even Jesus took time to rest.

Heavenly Father, give me strength when I must work long hours and double shifts, and give me the wisdom to know when I have reached my limits. Amen.

May the Lord direct your hearts into God's love and Christ's perseverance.

2 THESSALONIANS 3:5

---

* Rebecca A. Bernert and Thomas E. Joiner, "Sleep Disturbances and Suicide Risk: A Review of the Literature," *Neuropsychiatric Disease and Treatment*, Dove Medical Press, Dec. 2007, www.ncbi.nlm.nih.gov/pmc /articles/PMC2656315/.

Praying for the Persecutor

We've all had tasks assigned to us that we would rather delegate to someone with less seniority or rank. Everyone has their favorite duties, but as with any job, we take the good with the bad. Maybe praying for those we see as enemies is one of those assignments we'd rather pass off to someone else. But we cannot profess to be a follower of Jesus Christ and pray for only those who treat us with love and respect. This means we lead by example, not only doing the work we enjoy and love but also doing the dirty work, which includes praying for our enemies and those who persecute us.

When you pray for someone who persecutes you, you are releasing the poison of bitterness and the seeds of hatred and anger. When Jesus commanded us to pray for those who persecute us, He was telling us this for our own benefit. Not only do we operate in obedience to the words spoken by Jesus, but we are also pruning ourselves of unfruitful and poisonous elements that will prevent our growth in Christ. It may not be an easy task to do, but praying for those who hate us, persecute us, and despise us will produce marvelous results.

Heavenly Father, help me to pray for those who persecute me. Give me the heart to love my enemies and reflect you to others. Amen.

But I tell you, love your enemies
and pray for those who persecute you.
MATTHEW 5:44

The Boss Was Probably Right

A few months after I began night shift, right after graduating the academy, I was dispatched to a call where there was a large crowd of people surrounding the suspect in question. I vividly remember my shift lieutenant pulling me to the side after the call was over and, in a professional manner, scolding me for an officer-safety issue. He was right. I was wrong. As you become a more seasoned officer, you may find yourself wanting to rebut any scolding or correction, but it is probably for your well-being.

You may even want to challenge the brass on certain policies or procedures. Remember, there is a reason most of them outrank you. Your goal should be to set an example to those who answer to you or see you as a role model, and to demonstrate to those in leadership your skills and ability to lead, even if you are not bearing the rank of a leader. Take the initiative. If you absolutely cannot go without challenging the brass on something, use tact. Don't try to challenge them in front of the entire squad.

> *Heavenly Father, help me to respect my superiors, even when I believe they are wrong, because the way I treat them today is sowing seeds for how a subordinate may treat me in the future. Amen.*

Those whom I love I rebuke and discipline.
So be earnest and repent.

REVELATION 3:19

More Than Conquerors

When a foot pursuit, vehicle pursuit, or fight ends for you, the sense of relief and victory is wonderful. Almost euphoric. There couldn't be another level of victory in this lifetime than when you are in a fight for your life and you survive. But God's Word gives us a higher standard—we are "more than conquerors" through Jesus.

I don't know about you, but I want to see what this "more than conquerors" lifestyle is all about. For me, being identified by the Creator of my soul as more than a conqueror means I walk in perfect peace with Him, knowing His way is higher, His plans are better, and He has me in the palm of His hand.

Maybe it means something different to you. Life has a way of giving us different perspectives on topics, which is okay. I want to challenge you today to ask God to reveal to you what a "more than conqueror" version of you would look like. Ask Him to show you, through His Word and prayer, what your life would look like if you went from victim to victor, from conquered to more than a conqueror. It sounds like you are royalty to me.

> *Heavenly Father, reveal my true identity as it is through right relationship with you. Help me see me as you see me, as more than a conqueror through your Son, Jesus. Amen.*

No, in all these things we are more than conquerors through him who loved us.

ROMANS 8:37

As Jesus Did

In a world where race, politics, and religion create division, each person bearing a badge stands to bridge the gap between chaos and unity. Love is the motivating factor behind our service. Jesus came to suffer as a man so that He could provide salvation for all, just as your duties provide a way for the safety and protection of the innocent. He freely gave His life as payment for the sins of all humanity—it was not required. Being willing to serve in the manner you do on a daily basis has set you in high esteem with our marvelous Creator.

What resemblances of the way Jesus lived can we express today? First, be the reason peace and order are restored in lives where chaos, pain, and recklessness abound. Be the reason others have hope again for a future, which is possible if you are a consistent servant of excellence, operating in love, to serve humanity. Resolve today that you will walk in excellence, that you will commit your duties as though you were working for God, because, in reality, you are.

Heavenly Father, I commit my duties to you. I give you my calling, my profession, and every situation that may present itself. I know nothing is too big for you. Help me to serve humankind with the love Jesus did. Amen.

And walk in the way of love,
just as Christ loved us and gave himself up for us
as a fragrant offering and sacrifice to God.
EPHESIANS 5:2

Ultimate Cover

In a world where most people have smartphones, live recording of officer-involved situations creates immediate threats to the safety of officers on the scene and in future calls. In these cases, the suspect has been given your game plan. What this doesn't affect is your protection given by a true source of cover. Hatred and love of conflict are often the reasons why people are live recording you on the job, but another reason is to cover you in the event of false accusations. Many bystanders who record you while you are serving in harm's way hope you will make a mistake or let your emotions get the best of you, and they will have it recorded for the world to see.

It is not out of love that others stir up conflict or dig for past mistakes; it is out of hate or bitterness. But a person with a heart of love will strive to make things right. Don't allow the actions of hateful people affect your pursuit of justice or heart for love-driven service. The ultimate cover is love—not some weak, watered-down love. It's the love demonstrated by Jesus. As you serve and live, you are covered fully as a believer in Christ by the love He has for you.

> *Heavenly Father, renew in me a right heart, and help me to serve you with excellence. Amen.*

Hatred stirs up conflict,
but love covers over all wrongs.
PROVERBS 10:12

Do the Right Thing

One of the greatest powers any free person possesses is choice—maybe not in everything life offers, but in most cases. We have a choice most days of what we will wear, unless we work on duty all the time. We have the choice to forgive or harbor resentment. We have the choice to show mercy or judgment toward others. Doing the right thing often comes with a price tag, and that price can be determined by the choices made. Treating other people with fairness and equality isn't difficult. Being firm, fair, and equal will take you to heights in your career that many other professionals would envy.

Doing the right thing today may be difficult in the moment, with the choices presented causing conflict in your mind and heart. But at the end of the day, when you treat others as you would have them treat you, you are a man or woman of character and integrity. Being above reproach is a tall order for any person, but you were meant for this. You were created for this challenge, and you would not be in your position if you were not fully capable of fulfilling your purpose.

Heavenly Father, help me see others as you see them and realize that the way I treat others is like seed for the sower. I will reap what I sow. Amen.

Do to others as you would have them do to you.
LUKE 6:31

Do It for the Love of God

February is, for many people, all about love. This month can be rewarding or depressing. For some couples, this month is one of the rare moments where love and affection are expressed. If a card or gift is given out of tainted motives, it ruins the potential reward for the giver. It's all in the attitude and motives, which are found in the heart, which is, by nature, corrupt. For those of you who are like me, talking about "love" makes you think back to the last time you were at the range slinging lead at targets. I get it. But if you are a believer, 1 Corinthians 16:14 makes it clear—we are given a clear-cut command. It is not an easy command, but it is clear: "Do everything in love."

Maybe expressing truth or communicating in love is something you find difficult or, at the very least, not natural. Most of this month has been focused on how you deal with adversity, persecution, or other on-the-job issues as they relate to love. Will you accept the challenge today to be intentional with expressing love with your family? If you are married, remember your spouse is not a suspect and your children do not want to be interrogated. Do your duty in love, both on and off the job.

Heavenly Father, fill my heart with your love, and help me be a vessel of your love. Amen.

Do everything in love.

1 CORINTHIANS 16:14

No Greater Love

In cities across America, law enforcement officers go to work in one of the most volatile societies in human history. This is the most visible demonstration of love for humankind in our modern times. For those who pay the ultimate sacrifice, theirs is never forgotten. There is no greater love than the love a person exemplifies by giving his or her life for another human being.

What motivates you in all you do? Is it money? Is it the desire to be successful? This is a calling. Somewhere, someday, you may look back and complain about the path you took that led you to this moment. Will you regret the decision to love? Or will it be the decision to resent others?

I challenge you to not only do an immediate inventory of your heart and soul today, but to also do a regular inventory to ensure your motives are pure. Like you have heard many times before, the path down the slippery slope begins with one small innocent step. Let all you do be done in love. Even when you must become a violent warrior, let the love you have for those innocent people, your brothers and sisters in battle, and those at home, be your motivating guide.

Heavenly Father, help me to never tarnish the pure sacrifice given by those who have given their lives for the freedom and protection of others. Amen.

Greater love has no one than this:
to lay down one's life for one's friends.
JOHN 15:13

I Am My Brother's Keeper

Long after you are retired or have resigned from law enforcement, the bond you have with those in law enforcement will remain. The deepest hurt I have ever endured was saying goodbye to those who served by my side. There's something about the friendship between you and someone who made sure you went home safe every day. Yes, we are our brother's keeper. We should *want* accountability with our partners, and we should strive to see the revival of the brotherhood of the thin blue line. That bond is irreplaceable. Be the reason someone believes the brotherhood is still alive, instead of giving them a reason to believe it is fading into the pages of the past.

Regardless of what society throws at you, remember what sets you apart from any other profession in this world is the love you have for your brother and sister. No other profession has such a strong bond between its members as law enforcement. Difficult times, and changes in personnel, command, or even methods will come, but the bond of brotherhood is to never be broken. Therefore, keep loving each other, doing your due diligence to protect the line.

Heavenly Father, remind me daily that, regardless of differences, I am my brother's keeper. Amen.

*Keep on loving one another
as brothers and sisters.*

HEBREWS 13:1

Made Perfect by Love

We have the power to change the lives of complete strangers with Christlike love. Our world will never be more at peace than it was yesterday. Your service as a law enforcement officer ensures that, regardless of how bad the chaos gets, the innocent are protected. At the end of the day, your service is a tremendous act of love. In the book of Ephesians, the apostle Paul wrote to those residing in the city of Ephesus in a manner to expand their thinking. His words were not like his other letters; he wrote to edify, to encourage, and to summarize the gospel.

You will not be welcomed by all people in all places. It is important to know the place you are in right now and the work you are doing. While it may seem like an imperfect work for an imperfect people, it is exactly what God has for the people you serve, and, more importantly, probably what you need more than anything. So in all that you do, be humble, gentle, and patient, and deal with each other in love.

Heavenly Father, remind me of where I was when you rescued me. Help me reflect your perfect love to a hurting world. Amen.

Be completely humble and gentle; be patient,
bearing with one another in love.

EPHESIANS 4:2

Well-Rounded Officer

Thinking back to your academy training, you will likely remember one specific lesson more clearly than the rest. Your training covered about every area of law enforcement, from the use of force, courtroom testimony, traffic investigations, and much more. But one thing that binds all your skills, talents, and abilities together as a public servant is love. All those are bound together, preparing you as a well-rounded officer to serve your community and God's purpose.

When you dwell in unity with other people, especially other law enforcement officers, you empower morale, preparing you to successfully complete the mission before you ever begin. Divided teams fall before they ever see the battlefield. You will be a well-rounded officer, not when you complete your initial and annual training but when you conduct your duties in love for God and humanity. It would be easy to become cynical and hard-hearted in the world in which we live. But it is my opinion that when you do, you are robbing yourself of the greatest blessing of all—unity.

Heavenly Father, show me the importance of and the power of living out your expressed love as a law enforcement officer. Amen.

And over all these virtues put on love,
which binds them all together in perfect unity.
COLOSSIANS 3:14

Selfless Service

Modern culture suggests that to love self is the greatest achievement. This notion may not be directly stated, but it is strongly suggested in most advertising, social media, and other mainstream media productions. What would your life look like, as the end of it neared, if you had only loved yourself throughout your life? Lonely? That would be the best way to describe it.

While it is countercultural at the very least, loving those who cannot repay you is the most rewarding love. But on the other hand, it is not possible to love others with selfish intentions. Selfless love can only come through a heart full of passion for God and His Word and a mind that has been thoroughly renewed by God's Word. Commit yourself to studying the Bible and praying, and God will instill in you a passion to serve humanity. In turn, you will be serving God's kingdom through the service you provide.

Commit to those you serve with, to protect them, to sharpen each other's skills, and to serve your community with excellence and a selfless love. Let your legacy be that you set the path for those coming after you to serve with the love of Jesus Christ and that you served with a selfless love.

Heavenly Father, empower me to love others, on duty and off duty, like you love your children and even those who despise you. Amen.

Be devoted to one another in love.
Honor one another above yourselves.

ROMANS 12:10

A Righteous Pursuit

The only thing better than a foot pursuit or vehicle pursuit is catching the suspect. But the only reason you pursue is to apprehend. Proverbs 21:21 gives us an idea of another pursuit we should embark on: pursuing righteousness and love. Finding life, prosperity, and honor as a result of pursuing righteousness and love is a wonderful reward for the hunter. Find your way into the chase today by pursuing what will embolden you to become a more excellent version of yourself.

Finding our passion in life can be a challenge when we pursue it over pursuing what God intended for us to go after. When we lose sight of the goal we are pursuing, we lose confidence, energy, strength, and desire to continue the pursuit. Keep your eyes on the prize of righteousness and love, pursuing these through relationship with Jesus Christ. If your pursuit has grown cold, today is the perfect chance to get back in the hunt.

Heavenly Father, give me the endurance to pursue until apprehending. Grant my feet surety, and protect me as I give chase. Give me a desire to pursue you. Amen.

Whoever pursues righteousness and love finds life, prosperity and honor.

PROVERBS 21:21

Inseparable Bond

If you are new to law enforcement, then you need to know there will be other officers you will share a bond with, and this bond cannot be matched by any other relationship you have in your life. This is like the love of God in our lives. His love for us is readily available, and all we have to do is call on the name of Jesus. Some may scoff at the idea that the bond of law enforcement officers is stronger than a family bond, but I propose the notion that no other family experiences such potentially fatal threats and loss as these men and women do. Thus, the inseparable bond of law enforcement officers.

Many veteran law enforcement officers will tell you that the bond is not like it used to be. Find a way to initiate and maintain inseparable bonds with your partners. Be the first to work to make amends in conflict. Don't hold grudges. After all, we're just cops and our purpose is to protect humanity from itself.

Heavenly Father, remind me in my weakest, most difficult moments that you will never abandon me and nothing can separate me from your love. Amen.

Who shall separate us from the love of Christ?
Shall trouble or hardship or persecution
or famine or nakedness or danger or sword?

ROMANS 8:35

Power Food

If you have ever had an extended period of time without eating or gotten caught on a long detail where you had no access to food, then you know the feeling of hunger anger. It doesn't take long to learn that you need to have an emergency stash of food and water in your patrol car in case this is "one of those days." Your strength to serve is limited by the care you give your own body. The fruits of a hungry person are not pleasant, but the fruits of the Spirit are to be desired above all.

There are times when we fail to bear the fruits of the Spirit as listed in Galatians 5:22–23. However, unlike the limits on food, drinks, and other necessities in this life, there is no limit to what we can indulge on when it comes to love, peace, and the other fruits of the Spirit. Desire strongly to bear these fruits, and you will live a blessed life.

Heavenly Father, give me a hunger for the fruits of your Spirit. Show me the way to bear these fruits and pleas you. Amen.

But the fruit of the Spirit is love, joy, peace, forbearance, kindness, goodness, faithfulness, gentleness and self-control. Against such things there is no law.

GALATIANS 5:22–23

Restored to Love

There are systems in place to provide assistance if we are facing personal issues. From alcohol abuse, to marital issues, to sleeping problems, there is help for you. One of the most tragic things about law enforcement is the feeling that we can and should walk through difficult times alone. Nothing could be further from the truth. We are encouraged to restore our brothers and sisters. From a heart of love comes a sincere desire to help our own when they are down. In some cases, due to laws, regulations, and policies, there are limited options to help the career of a law enforcement officer, but we can still ensure he or she is cared for on a personal level.

Don't fall into the trap of gossiping about the lives of struggling officers. Instead, team up with others to find a way to assist them and lift them up. When we do this, we will likely see a department-wide boost in morale, and, after all, what could be more rewarding than having a positive impact on the lives of one of our own family members?

> *Heavenly Father, bring to my attention any desire I have to gossip about the situation of another officer, and give me the strength and wisdom to serve him or her when he or she needs my support the most. Amen.*

Finally, brothers and sisters, rejoice! Strive for full restoration, encourage one another, be of one mind, live in peace.

2 CORINTHIANS 13:11

Closer Than a Brother

If you have ever walked through a place in life where you needed someone to talk to—someone to listen, support, or encourage you—then you know the value of a friend. One of the greatest things about law enforcement is the bond between its officers. Many would say that this bond has changed over the years. Some say there's division in law enforcement, but let one be attacked or injured and see how divided they are. They go from being friends or friendly foes to brothers born for times of adversity.

If you've never fought for the life of another human being, then it's difficult to understand this type of love. It's more than being just a friend, more than being a coworker or zone partner. It's a family. There's a reason you were called to become part of the thin blue line. The decision is yours today: Are you going to be known as a coworker or a good friend, or will you be called brother or sister? This is your decision. This is your moment. This is your opportunity to be the uniting thread that is part of strengthening the bond of law enforcement.

> *Heavenly Father, help me to be a true brother or sister to those in need today. Amen.*

A friend loves at all times,
and a brother is born for a time of adversity.
PROVERBS 17:17

Operating from a Heart of Love

Beyond your duties as a law enforcement officer, you are a man or woman who has a family, friends, and many other people who love and care about you. There are also people you will face disagreements with, and you will need to confront them about your differences. The way you handle confrontation will determine your blessing on the other side of the issue. Finding the power to navigate through those issues in love is key to a life of peace. If you love God, you are required to love your brothers and sisters as well.

Commit yourself to intentionally dealing with others out of a heart of love, especially in situations of conflict. Even on duty, from a place of authority, you can operate from a heart of love by dealing as fairly and respectfully as possible with the community you serve. During your life, you will face many challenges as it relates to operating from a heart of love, but this will bear many rewards for you as you are faithful to the commands of God's Word.

Heavenly Father, give me the courage and power and knowledge to live and operate from a heart of love. Amen.

And he has given us this command:
Anyone who loves God must also love their brother and sister.
1 JOHN 4:21

Environmental Management

We become like those with whom we associate. Over time, if you associate with negative, hateful people, you will be affected by their words and actions. Likewise, if you associate with successful, kind, and positive people, you will be affected by their lives. At the end of the day, our thoughts are affected by the words and actions of others. Our thoughts lead to actions, and by those actions we develop habits. From there, either negative or positive circumstances are a result. Many times, we are affected without even recognizing the changes as they occur in our lives.

Our purpose is to bring a positive environment, not allowing our environment to affect our lives. For what price will you give up your peace? Use godly wisdom before you take on a soul tie with someone who will be a consistent toxic influence on your life. There are times when you will be required to partner with people who see life differently than you, which is okay, but buying into their views if they are misaligned with what God has for you, your principles, and values is a mistake you cannot afford to make. Love is a powerful gift, but use it wisely.

Heavenly Father, give me wisdom as it pertains to the relationships I have in my life, at work, socially, and at home. Help me to express your love and protect my heart. Amen.

Better a small serving of vegetables with love than a fattened calf with hatred.

PROVERBS 15:17

Forging Leaders

What an encouraging promise to know God is waiting for us to seek Him. The precedent of the student seeking the mentor was established by God thousands of years ago when He said that "those who seek me find me" (Proverbs 8:17). Of course, there are a few more caveats to that, but the principle rests easy here. If you want to grow as a law enforcement officer, invest in your career by learning as much as possible, respecting your superiors, and setting a great example for others around you. Your selfless sacrifice and initiative to be proactive and professional will take you further than bickering and backbiting. Demonstrate love, and be the example of God's love to those you meet today.

There are no guarantees any of us will live to see another day, week, or year; therefore, it is imperative we begin immediately investing in eternal values. Just as you would seek the counsel of an experienced mentor in law enforcement, so take the time to seek God through His Word. While the laws you enforce may be repealed or appealed, or fail to be upheld, God's Word never changes, and He remains the same forever.

Heavenly Father, thank you for the gift of leadership. I give you my goals and ask you to lead me as I lead others today. Amen.

I love those who love me, and those who seek me find me.
PROVERBS 8:17

Confidential Informant

As a law enforcement officer, you have access to information many citizens are not privy to. In fact, you know the personal secrets of people across your city, many of whom are in positions of power. It is wise to let love cover over the secrets you know, unless it is necessary for you to act on the information in your official duties. Don't spread rumors and useless information. On the other hand, you have access to the secrets of God's Word as you seek relationship with Him through study and prayer.

During your life, you are given a purpose that will glorify God, bring you fulfillment, and provide you with the resources you need. Seeking the wisdom of God through His Word and prayer is the most valuable action you can take on a daily basis. His wisdom and His love covers all our offenses and empowers us to fulfill our divine purpose in life.

> *Heavenly Father, thank you for the love you have for me—that it covers my faults and empowers me to serve you. Thank you for revealing your holy secrets to me as I pursue you in prayer, worship, and studying your Word. Amen.*

Whoever would foster love covers over an offense,
but whoever repeats the matter separates close friends.

PROVERBS 17:9

Undying Love

If the only people who lived were those who expressed love and lived with total love for God and others, what would this world look like? Considering the widespread evil in our world today, from paper crimes to sex crimes, murder, robbery, and everything else in the book, the pain caused to innocent people tears a little bit of their lives away. Your job is to prevent it when possible, apprehend those responsible, and protect the innocent. In all things, your duty is to essentially provide a harbor of love for humankind.

Stopping the spread of wickedness will aid in the spread of love. After all, Jesus told us in Matthew 24:12, "Because of the increase of wickedness, the love of most will grow cold." We are at the crossroads of where and when this Scripture was pointing toward. The love of most will grow cold because of discouragement and lack of justice for the wicked—it is easy to buy into the lie today. Add another reason to your "why" today. Give hope to people. They need it as much as they need fresh air and clean water.

> *Heavenly Father, help me realize the power I have to give hope to humankind. Help me realize I'm doing good for your kingdom when I apprehend criminals. Amen.*

Because of the increase of wickedness,
the love of most will grow cold.
MATTHEW 24:12

Source
of Strength

MARCH

Superior Strength

We are always taught to feed our bodies with proper nutrition so we will have fuel for our day. Adequate exercise, nutrition, and sleep are all part of building and maintaining physical conditioning and strength. But we are mere mortals, believe it or not. These bodies will wear down and give out over time. Often, when we are tired, we depend on resources that are not beneficial for our health—energy drinks and sugary foods, not to mention the exorbitant amounts of caffeine we consume.

When we lean on bad habits, old thinking, and the easy way out, we make small daily decisions that lead to terrible long-term consequences. If you want to be a man or woman with superior strength, first acknowledge your own areas of weakness. Changing nutritional habits takes time, but making small daily lifestyle changes can lead to superior strength in the long term. Depending on the wisdom of God's Word and understanding that strength comes through Him will empower each person to live at a higher level of physical energy, mental clarity, and more strength to perform your daily duties.

> *Heavenly Father, open my eyes to the bad habits that are weighing me down from achieving superior strength, and teach me to depend on you. Amen.*

I can do all this through him who gives me strength.
PHILIPPIANS 4:13

Your Secret Weapon

Your mind-set is the key to not only surviving the streets but also thriving as a law enforcement officer. Without a doubt, one of your weapons is courage. On a daily basis, law enforcement officers are faced with threats of murder, ambush, lawsuits, and complaints. Maybe you aren't afraid of dying, but would you be afraid of the financial disaster a lawsuit could cause? You will begin to experience mental and emotional fatigue if you remain in a hypervigilant state. Your secret weapon isn't on your duty belt, in your weapons locker, or in your patrol car. Your secret weapon lies in the courage, strength, and power received through the promises of God.

It is no secret, however, that you face potentially deadly situations daily. Being courageous doesn't mean you make unsafe or irrational decisions; it isn't an excuse to be reckless and act without caring for the public. Having this strength and courage through relationship with Jesus means you are an empowered, well-rounded officer with an arsenal of secret weapons at your disposal. It begins and ends with a life in pursuit of God.

> *Heavenly Father, go before me during my shift. You see all and know all, and I need your strength, your courage, and your wisdom to face the circumstances ahead of me. Grant me victory. Amen.*

Be strong and courageous. Do not be afraid or terrified because of them, for the LORD your God goes with you; he will never leave you nor forsake you.

DEUTERONOMY 31:6

More than Mere Muscle

Is it enough to be the strongest on shift? Contrary to what everyone may think, muscle isn't enough. By our own physical power, we will only be able to train to a certain max, fight to a certain limit, or run for a certain distance before fatigue sets in. Maybe you are in the best physical condition of anyone in your department, but at some point you will give out in energy. That is why we rest, that is why we have partners, and that is why we have backup.

For thousands of years, God has been providing people with supernatural strength to accomplish His divine purpose and will. Do not depend solely on your own strength to accomplish your mission today. We are all mortals and we all have limits, both physically and mentally. But by the Spirit of God and His Word, we are unstoppable. Maybe we have limits and rules on this earth, but I assure you that we serve a limitless God. When He says He will strengthen you and help you, you can bank on it.

> *Heavenly Father, help me operate within my own personal strengths and limits. Give me wisdom to know when I need to ask for help. Amen.*

So do not fear, for I am with you;
do not be dismayed, for I am your God.
I will strengthen you and help you;
I will uphold you with my righteous right hand.

ISAIAH 41:10

The Power of Two

There are very few other professions in the United States that ask people to go into the types of situations you face daily. You are required to be mentally sharp, physically fit, and emotionally sound, ready to respond in a breath to a threat to you, another officer, or a citizen. When you are dispatched to a call, you rely on the information passed along by the person reporting, the call taker, and the dispatcher to provide you with the most accurate information possible.

Knowing someone else is already handling the problem on scene causes you to experience some degree of peace. Likewise, knowing God goes before you in all you do gives peace. The power of two is significant. Two officers on scene mean the likelihood of an escalated call is decreased. Two officers on the scene of an accident means there is adequate manpower to handle the collision and traffic. Having the peace of mind that you are never alone in your duties will empower you to a place of excellence in your duties. God goes before you, but you are still responsible to prepare for the battle.

> *Heavenly Father, thank you for the peace in knowing you care enough about me to go before me and protect me; give me the insight and discernment today on every call. I am listening for you. Amen.*

For the LORD your God is the one who goes with you to fight for you against your enemies to give you victory.
DEUTERONOMY 20:4

Skeleton Crew

Some people work better under pressure, while others work better when they have significant margins. When you arrive for duty and your shift is short-staffed, it can either motivate you or demoralize you. If you want to stand out above the rest, find a way to keep a positive attitude regardless of your external circumstances, especially those you cannot control. If you are a believer in Jesus Christ and a keeper of His words, then you know the strength you receive is not from yourself or the things going on around you. In fact, your strength comes from Him alone.

When Jesus said, "My grace is all you need," He meant that in life, to get through difficult situations, all we need is the willingness to accept and receive His grace and allow it to work in our lives. Think about what that means for you today. Even if all you have is the grace of God, you've got more than a skeleton crew because you have access to the greatest source of power in creation.

Heavenly Father, I need your strength today. I need your grace and your power to cover my weaknesses. Thank you that your power is now free to work through me. Amen.

Each time he said, "My grace is all you need. My power works best in weakness." So now I am glad to boast about my weaknesses, so that the power of Christ can work through me.

2 CORINTHIANS 12:9 NLT

The Best Zone Partner

What a comforting thought it is to know that Jesus not only paid the price for our sins, but He also invites us to bring our burdens to Him. A good zone partner will jump a call for you so you can take a break or handle other police business. If you are facing an impossible task or maybe you are patrolling by yourself today, know there is someone who says, "Hey, let me grab that one. Let me help you with that one."

In fact, maybe you are burdened with anxieties, thoughts, worries, or other issues no one else knows about. Jesus knows. Right now, He is asking you if you will allow Him to help you. Don't be a call hog! Learn to accept the assistance of others. Learn to accept the competent assistance of a holy God. Today, walk in the comfort of knowing that God cares about you. Go to work knowing He loves you, He wants the best for you, and that even if your current circumstances don't reflect it, you were created to live a victorious life. But we cannot do it alone. We must have the assistance of the best zone partner any law enforcement officer could request— almighty God.

> *Heavenly Father, when I feel I am facing this world alone, remind me that you are ever present and right beside me. Amen.*

Then Jesus said, "Come to me, all of you who are weary and carry heavy burdens, and I will give you rest."

MATTHEW 11:28 NLT

March 7

Double Shift

Standing outside the door, the officer waited on his two partners to exit the apartment with the suspect in cuffs. It wasn't long, however, before the front door slammed open against the old brick, and out came the suspect and two officers in an active fight. The officer standing guard outside the apartment engaged the suspect and began to take him to the ground to place handcuffs on him. Had he been alone, those seconds and minutes would have seemed like hours until assistance arrived. He had a limited measure of strength, and it was rapidly depleted.

Just as each person has a given amount of strength, so each person is given a measure of faith. Your faith grows based on how you use it. While faith is not expendable, our physical strength is. Our physical strength will grow weak—as we age, we will naturally become weaker and more fragile. Understanding we are not equipped to fight alone and learning to battle within our own circle is critical to achieving victory and staying healthy. You may not be as young as you once were, which means you may have to depend on the assistance of others to get through difficult battles.

Heavenly Father, give me wisdom to know when I am operating outside my own limitations, both physically and mentally. Grant me strength to endure difficult situations and wisdom to know when to call for help. Amen.

The Lord is my strength and my defense;
he has become my salvation.

EXODUS 15:2

Heart of a Champion

You will encounter people who require accolades for their services for everything they do. Their motivation and intentions may be pure, but their desire for public rewards is poisoning the potential for any future return on their service. The honor of a champion servant is in the heart. One of the most effective maintenance "tasks" we can perform is asking God to search our hearts for impure motives and hidden sins, and to make us clean in His sight. The heart of a champion is not self-seeking, but it is selfless in service.

The heart of a champion is one that relentlessly pursues his or her Creator, seeking ways to serve in a way that reflects the Father in a positive light. You are a representative of God's kingdom here on earth. Your life should reflect the heart of a champion, one who is strong and places his or her hope solely in God alone. In the midst of a world of selfishness and greed, be the one who shines through with the heart of a persistent, consistent, and relentless champion. Be a law enforcement officer of excellence, reflecting the Father to the world and bringing glory to His name.

Heavenly Father, if there is any part of me that is weary, weak, or ready to quit, give me strength and fresh life. Search my heart and reveal any impure motives or hidden sins, and make me clean before you. Amen.

Be strong and take heart,
all you who hope in the Lord.

PSALM 31:24

Stop Resisting

There's a common phrase used in the middle of a fight: "Stop resisting." It's a command we are trained to give, along with a catalog of other commands, procedures, and steps to stay safe and out of internal affairs. Our efforts alone may take us a long way in life, because, after all, we were gifted by God. But when we try to resist His ultimate plan for our lives and do it all alone, we lose the power available to us through relationship with Christ.

Maybe today you hear the still, small voice of God whispering to you, "Stop resisting." His plans are better than yours; I've tested it out in my own life. When we try to live on self-sustaining power, our own efforts, and doing our own plans, we live in a place of constant struggle. Sounds familiar, right? The power of surrender is tremendous, and it cannot be adequately defined here in this devotional. Surrender your plans, your abilities, and your dreams to the one to whom they belong. At the end of the day, you will be glad you did.

Heavenly Father, I surrender my talents to you. I give you all I have, all I am, and all I ever will be. I want you to be the Lord of my life and have total control. I submit to you. Amen.

Finally, my brethren, be strong in the Lord and in the power of His might.
EPHESIANS 6:10 NKJV

Strength to Face Any Foe

If any person tells you they have no fear in life, they are saying one of two things: one, they do not know themselves well enough to properly identify the emotion of fear; or, two, they are lying. Our response to fear can be a sign of weakness, not the presence of fear alone. You have been given the power to face any enemy that may present itself to you. But to be properly prepared to address fear, you must do a few things.

First, what channel does fear move through in your life? Does it move through the filter of anger, hate, or your own plans and ideas? Or do you move fear through the filter of God's Word? When we live our lives according to His Word and filter fear through what His authority states, there is no reason to fear and there is nothing mere people can do to us. Because, after all, we are eternal beings living in temporary vessels. It's more about mind-set than it is about equipment, so make sure you have a healthy thought process going into battle today.

Heavenly Father, knowing you are for me, want the best for me, and go before me in battle gives me peace and strength, because I know that victory is mine. Grant me power to face and defeat fear in my life. Amen.

The LORD is for me, so I will have no fear.
What can mere people do to me?
PSALM 118:6 NLT

Focus on the Fundamentals

It is easy to get so focused on the desire to become more skilled and proficient that we forget about keeping brushed up on the basics. There is no benefit to building a nice mansion on a faulty foundation; the basics provide the solid foundation we need. But they also need regular refreshing and inspection. In your pursuit of Christ, don't become so focused on what you can "get" from God that you forget about seeking a relationship with Him.

One fundamental practice is continually searching God's Word for truths to apply in our lives. Even on days you don't feel like praying, whisper a prayer. On days you don't feel like reading the Bible, read just a verse. Keep your feet moving forward today while staying focused on the fundamentals of the faith. The temptation to slack off and quit will get stronger the longer you go without spending time in prayer and reading the Bible. And when you do, you will not be prepared to face the enemy on the day you encounter him. Be prepared always; don't neglect the fundamentals.

> *Heavenly Father, the basics of my salvation are faith and believing in you and the work you completed at the cross. Thank you, God, for your love and mercy. Keep my steps consistent and firm, my hands steady, and my eyes focused on you. Amen.*

Search for the LORD and for his strength;
continually seek him.
1 CHRONICLES 16:11 NLT

Repeat Offenders

Many businesses and professions depend on repeat business to grow, sustain, and even keep the doors open at times. Your business is not one of those that depends on repeat customers to stay "in business." In fact, maybe you have experienced frustration or even discouragement from seeing the same people repeatedly arrested; maybe your discouragement comes from many issues on duty. Jesus gave us a specific promise relating to this issue.

If the King of Kings said, "Here on earth you will have many trials and sorrows" (John 16:33 NLT), what more could you expect? His follow-up to that dark reminder was, "But take heart, because I have overcome the world" (John 16:33 NLT). Your repeat offenders may be causing you to experience some discouragement, or maybe you are carrying the weight of a crumbling marriage to work with you. Either way, your Father in heaven cares for you. His mercy is new every single day, and He isn't about to abandon you.

> *Heavenly Father, I want to thank you that, because you have overcome the world, I am empowered to overcome this world also. Thank you that I have peace in you regardless of the circumstances around me. Amen.*

I have told you all this so that you may have peace in me.
Here on earth you will have many trials and sorrows.
But take heart, because I have overcome the world.

JOHN 16:33 NLT

Tireless Efforts

Discouragement, frustration, family pressure, finances, health, and relationships are just a few areas that can destroy your attitude and claim your career in law enforcement—if you let them. Your tireless efforts serving as a law enforcement officer do not go unnoticed. There are many people, regardless of what you may see on the news and hear about in the media, who support you, love you, and care for you. In fact, more people support you than oppose you.

At times, it may seem like you are fighting a losing battle. It may seem like you are using a small needle to plug a hole in a dam, which will inevitably break, with you on the other side. Do not lose faith and do not be discouraged in the good service you are doing today. Somewhere there is a man, a woman, or a child who will experience the best day of their life on their absolute worst day because of you. Your harvest of blessings has not passed you by. You are not forgotten by God. He knows your name and will reward you in a handsome manner if you will persevere.

Heavenly Father, give me strength that only comes from you to serve when it is difficult. Help my unbelief, my attitude, and give me a positive outlook. Amen.

*So let's not get tired of doing what is good.
At just the right time we will reap a harvest
of blessing if we don't give up.*
GALATIANS 6:9 NLT

The Thousand-Yard Stare

Picture yourself standing on the unpaved street in the middle of two saloons. The only things moving other than your beating heart are the dry tumbleweeds blowing in the light breeze. The heat is radiating off the ground. Across the way stands another man, holding a gun, with a crazy look in his eyes. You know the look. You've seen the look in the eyes of subjects you've dealt with before. If all law enforcement officers allowed intimidation tactics to work, who would hold the peace? Who would respond to aid the innocent?

During your career, there may come a time when someone threatens you or your family. Maintaining poise and a sense of resolve in the face of individuals like this is critical to your victory. If you crumble under their intimidation, they win. However, if you remain firm and courageous, it is not only a slap in their face but it is also a demonstration of faith in what God said He would do on your behalf.

Heavenly Father, instill in me courage, unseen to any other, and wisdom to know when it is time to move out of the way. Intervene on my behalf, protect me, guide me, and direct my steps. Amen.

Don't be intimidated in any way by your enemies.
This will be a sign to them that they are going to be destroyed,
but that you are going to be saved, even by God himself.

PHILIPPIANS 1:28 NLT

Strategy for Victory

Before any shift, you are most likely required to attend a shift briefing. During the briefing, your supervisors disseminate important information regarding increased criminal activity, outstanding warrants to be served, or other details that will be addressed during the tour. Most if not all of these will require additional planning and strategy before you engage. Seldom will there be a time when the strategy does not require you to lean on your fellow officer or your fellow officer to lean on you for support.

Our source of strength as individuals is limited, and our impact as one will be minimal. But as a team, as a unified squad, well trained, with a good plan, there's nothing that can stop you. Today, may you realize that the single greatest source of strength comes from a solid relationship in Jesus Christ. Humans may fail you, but God will not. God is faithful, and He never changes. He will guard you and prepare you on the day you encounter evil.

> Heavenly Father, show me the power of unity. Reveal to me the secrets of my strength found in relationship with you, and help me to be a godly leader in all I do. Amen.

But the Lord is faithful; he will strengthen you and guard you from the evil one.

2 THESSALONIANS 3:3 NLT

Ultimate Backup

The day has come and you have been consistently training in the gym and on the range, not only preparing your body but also your mind. Today could be the day you get the call that changes your life forever. What is the game changer that gets you through it? For you, it may be extra ammo or the extra training you invested in ground fighting, or maybe the extra time spent running. But if you don't believe in yourself and have faith in all the training you invested in, what good is it?

The number-one resource you have at your disposal is faith. When the days get morbidly dark and all you can smell is the gunpowder leftover from your worst nightmare, God's peace will never leave your side. Your best backup officer cannot be with you around the clock. The good news is this: You have access to the Peacemaker, anytime, anywhere, and under any circumstances. Faith in God is the game changer that will help you through your darkest hour.

> *Heavenly Father, there will be times when I won't feel your presence, but I know there will be times I need to absolutely know you are listening. Strengthen my heart so that, in my hour of need, the enemy will not be victorious. Amen.*

But the Lord stood with me and gave me strength so that I might preach the Good News in its entirety for all the Gentiles to hear. And he rescued me from certain death.

2 TIMOTHY 4:17 NLT

Beyond the Weight Room

I f you could look back over your career, I am sure there are things you would do differently. Maybe you would have focused on better nutrition, getting more sleep, or spending more time with your family—whatever the case, there may be something you would like to change. For some of you, many days you are permitted time to train, either in the gym, at the trail, or on the range. While there is nothing wrong with training in the weight room or on the running trail, we should establish goals beyond the tangible.

One thing none of us would regret acquiring is common sense. Proverbs 8 is a unique chapter where wisdom is "speaking" to the reader. In fact, wisdom says, in Proverbs 8:14 (NLT), "Common sense and success belong to me." Today, ask God for wisdom. Obtaining wisdom is a wonderful goal, but asking God for it is the way to obtain it, because He will direct your steps. You will enjoy a substantial and fruitful career and life, seeing many rewards, if you live in the wisdom of God.

Heavenly Father, there are many things I need today. Of all the things I need, I ask for your divine wisdom in all I do. Amen.

Common sense and success belong to me.
Insight and strength are mine.
PROVERBS 8:14 NLT

When Bullets Fly

One of the most important lessons you will learn early in your career is the difference between cover and concealment. If you stand behind a telephone pole, you will not find favorable results if you are the target of gunfire. We sometimes believe that just because we don't see God, He doesn't see our actions or thoughts. Don't be fooled. He sees and knows all we do. It is a wonderful thing to serve a loving, merciful heavenly Father. The bullets may fly in life, but if you don't have adequate cover, you are in for some big trouble.

Nearly two thousand years ago, Jesus provided ultimate cover for the bullet of sin, that one thing that could bring us eternal death if we left this life without a relationship with Jesus. He didn't put a bandage over it; He provided total coverage. If you have ever been in a gunfight, then you know the comfort true cover brings. Your fortress stands ready for you today. He is ready to act on your behalf, but He desires one thing from you: relationship. Having God as your fortress when adversity comes will give you peace and remind you that He has your back.

> *Heavenly Father, thank you for the gift of salvation, the ultimate source of cover for me in the line of fire. Thank you for strength and protection. Amen.*

You are my strength, I watch for you;
you, God, are my fortress.

PSALM 59:9

No Place for Cowards

I t is almost a given that, somewhere, in most every department, there is a story of a cowardly officer. I'll be brutally honest with you: Early in my career, I was sent to a snake call. Like you, I've been in the middle of some situations most people would run from, but a snake call was not on my agenda that day. While it is something I look back on now and laugh about, I realize it was an area of weakness. Thankfully we had an officer who "loved" snakes, so he jumped the call for me.

Ducking out of a snake call is one thing, but refusing to provide aid or service to a citizen in serious danger is a different story. In the event you encounter a cowardly officer, do not humiliate him or her in front of other officers, and certainly do not confront him or her in front of the general public. Take that officer aside, counsel him or her as a brother would, and find out what the issue is. Courageous officers are needed in these times, and there is no room for cowards. Be strong. Stand firm. Be on your guard.

> Heavenly Father, my courage is a tool as a hammer is to a carpenter. Grant me the skills of a master tradesman in courage so that I may serve my community with excellence. Amen.

Be on your guard; stand firm in the faith;
be courageous; be strong.
1 CORINTHIANS 16:13

Care Package

One of the best times of the year is when school children prepare different cards and handmade gifts to express their appreciation to law enforcement. When local churches caught on, they began to randomly send food to the day- and night-shift officers. Local businesses would sponsor a meal for an entire shift as a means of expressing appreciation for the work of law enforcement. These "care packages" were gentle reminders from the community of how much they appreciated the service of our officers. The sacrifices made during the holidays did not go unnoticed.

This is a great reminder of how much of an impact it can have on others, even law enforcement officers. We should strive to reflect God's kind and caring nature and care for those who serve our communities. Think of the impact you could have on the young lives in schools in your community, and how that would affect your quality of life as you approached retirement. Jesus performed many miracles during His time on earth, but they were all preceded by compassion. Be a man or woman of compassion today. Show someone you care, because it could make a difference in their life forever.

Heavenly Father, thank you for giving me a heart of compassion, to care for those who are in need. Thank you for helping me to always maintain a heart tender toward you. Amen.

The LORD is good, a refuge in times of trouble.
He cares for those who trust in him.

NAHUM 1:7

Finish Strong

At the start of your career, you were required take a solemn oath to uphold the laws of your community, county, and state. Your promise would have been empty if you stopped at the point of the promise and never presented a fulfillment to the promise. We should rejoice in knowing that God did not stop at the point of the promise; rather, He fulfilled the promise through His Son, Jesus. But He did not stop there. God has a good purpose for your life, and He will work in and through you to fulfill it, if you are willing and allow Him to do so.

Our willingness to allow God to work in and through our lives is often made out to be a complicated process when it simply requires total surrender and submission to His plans. Don't stop with just a promise to allow God to do a work in you today, and don't stop serving your community because things may have gone bad in the past. Allow God's power to work in and through you today, and watch His good purpose for your life come to fulfillment.

> *Heavenly Father, I surrender my heart and life to you, totally and completely. From my family to career, plans, and dreams, I give them all to you. Work in me to fulfill your good purpose for my life. Amen.*

For it is God who works in you to will and to act in order to fulfill his good purpose.

PHILIPPIANS 2:13

Know Your Point Man

With a tap on the shoulder, he signaled to the point man that the team was ready to make entry. It was time to work. The point man is the first in the door, usually bearing a shield, usually the first to encounter the attacks of the enemy. In the Old Testament, before battle, musicians were sent out first. The praise of God went before His people, because they knew that their victory rested solely in the hands of God. You may be standing at the door of a dangerous situation today. Know there is real hope in God's Word just for you.

Psalm 28 is a prayer of David seeking deliverance from peril at the hands of malicious, evil, and seemingly God-defying powers. David, even in the midst of attacks and the onslaught of the enemy, declared the faithfulness of God. If we will declare God's faithfulness and protection, He will not fail us. There is a supernatural release when we declare His Word. Today, know your point man. You are not the first person in the door anymore. He goes before you in all you do.

> *Heavenly Father, thank you for being my shield and strength. I place my trust in you. My heart rejoices in you, and I praise you, for you are good. Amen.*

The LORD is my strength and my shield;
my heart trusts in him, and he helps me.
My heart leaps for joy,
and with my song I praise him.

PSALM 28:7

March 23

Know Your Enemy

I t is easy to cherry-pick verses to match our own desires. Many have done this, which has created division in the church. Luke 10:19 refers to the power of the enemy—the evil one, not the physical enemy. This can be reinforced with fact that we battle not against flesh and blood, but against principalities and powers, which is exactly what we are up against. Your enemy is not the person standing in front of you, cursing you for all you are worth. Your enemy is the one who roams this world, seeking someone to kill, steal from, or destroy. Know your enemy's strengths and weaknesses and all your enemy's habits.

Your enemy may look like a list of criminals on a wanted list, but those men and women are included in the whole package that Jesus paid for on Calvary. Like it or not, He paid the price for all who will accept and receive Him. As a servant, it is our highest duty to represent not only our agency or government well, but to represent our God well too. Be a good ambassador, but be wise and know your enemy.

> Heavenly Father, thank you for helping me identify the tactics of the enemy and giving discernment on duty. Amen.

I have given you authority to trample on snakes and scorpions and to overcome all the power of the enemy; nothing will harm you.

LUKE 10:19

Muscle Memory

Every time you train with your weapons or with your hands, you are building muscle memory. The more you train, the more natural your skill and the more proficient you become. There are times, however, when your hands may fail you. In a moment when your adrenaline is rushing through your body, your heart rate is skyrocketing, and there is imminent danger, you may do things without even thinking about them. But it may become difficult to perform at an optimum level if you have not prepared in training and physical conditioning.

What a great comfort there is in knowing we are not the first to concern ourselves with our limited strength and power. Even the psalmist acknowledged this fact. Do not neglect your training and conditioning, but also know there is one who will strengthen you when your body fails you. This is no excuse to neglect training. I am of the philosophy that if we, as mortal men and women, will do our best in training and conditioning, then when we need Him, our eternal God will supplement our weaknesses with His strength and grant us victory.

> *Heavenly Father, I place my life in your hands. Strengthen my heart and my hands, and hold me steady through every situation. Amen.*

My flesh and my heart may fail, but God is the strength of my heart and my portion forever.

PSALM 73:26

No Place to Hide

At some point in life, most of us will be required to face our darkest fears. When David was on the back side of the battlefield, before he faced Goliath, he prepared. He may not have known who or what he was preparing for at the time, but he was preparing nonetheless.

There will come a time when the only ones on the battlefield are you, your "Goliath," and whatever (and whomever) you have by your side. There will be no cover, no place to run, and no place to hide. Maybe it isn't on duty. Maybe it is behind closed doors with someone other than your spouse or after you've had too much to drink and get behind the wheel. There will come a time when you must face your giants.

The Lord is eternal and is often referred to as the "Rock." While you will be face-to-face with your giant at some point, now is the time to prepare for that battle. Gather your stones, prepare your sling, and suit up with the armor of God. Strengthen your faith in God alone and know your trust in Him is not, nor will it ever be, in vain.

> *Heavenly Father, grant me victory in every battle I face. Do not lead me into temptation today, but give me the strength, willpower, and wisdom to walk away from the lure of the evil one. Amen.*

Trust in the LORD forever, for the LORD,
the LORD himself, is the Rock eternal.

ISAIAH 26:4

Foot Pursuit

Foot pursuits are one of those things that you either love or hate. Early on, I loved foot pursuits. After catching a few clotheslines along the way, however, my love for them rapidly dissipated. There isn't a professional athlete faster than a running suspect who has warrants or is under arrest. I've seen men (and women) who wouldn't otherwise be able to walk across the street without running out of breath sprint at superhuman speeds in an attempt to elude arrest. It was in those times I depended on Habakkuk 3:19.

When we read the Scripture found in Habakkuk, it would be easy to write it off as a fairy tale or even suggest that, while it may have been true then, God doesn't work like that anymore. But I promise you that there are people out there working on duty right now who have witnessed God's intervention on the streets. Lean on God for your strength. Listen to what His Word says, and heed His guidance. If you do, He will cause you to excel in what you do, on the streets or in the office.

> *Heavenly Father, thank you for preparing my heart for victory, for strengthening my feet, and for granting me favor in your eyes and in the eyes of others. Amen.*

The Sovereign Lord is my strength;
he makes my feet like the feet of a deer,
he enables me to tread on the heights.

HABAKKUK 3:19

Dead or Alive

Listening to all the threats made by individuals or groups toward you or other law enforcement officers can cause a great deal of stress. If David was in distress because people were threatening to stone him, it wouldn't be out of the realm of possibilities for us to be stressed if people were threatening to kill us because of the badge we wear. It is human nature to respond to threats with fear, but we must find strength to be courageous and overcome those fears.

You are empowered to face your fears by the strength given through the Holy Spirit. When we spend time in prayer, reading the Bible, and keeping our focus on God's promises, we are positioned for victory instead of defeat. Do not be fooled—the enemy wants you, your family, your peace, and your life. He wants you, either dead or alive. It's up to you whether you will bow down and let him take it all or if you will find strength in God, stand, and be victorious.

Heavenly Father, thank you for the work completed by your Son, Jesus, on the cross at Calvary. I ask for your strength to face the threats made against me today. Fill me with your Spirit so I can accomplish your will. Amen.

David was greatly distressed because the men were talking of stoning him; each one was bitter in spirit because of his sons and daughters.
But David found strength in the Lord his God.
1 SAMUEL 30:6

At a Dead End

Psalm 39 is a unique chapter where David found himself dealing with illness at what he believed was the rebuke of God for his transgressions. David was asking God to grant him mercy from his present suffering. Essentially, David hit a dead end. Nothing else was working, and, for whatever reason, whether perceived or reality, he believed God was rebuking him through sickness for his sins. Psalm 39:7 is a perfect example of how David felt during his time of trouble: "But now, Lord, what do I look for?" Maybe, like David, you've hit a dead end and things don't seem to be going so well for you anymore.

Waiting on further instructions from God can cause languishing, but do not jump ahead and make your own way. It will not help you in any way to do this. If you find yourself at a dead end, waiting on God, take the time to be still and listen to what God is saying through His Word. Take the time to rest. Then once you have done all you were equipped to do, wait on God, for He will not fail you. Ask Him for direction, and He will lead you.

> *Heavenly Father, I'm not sure where to go from here. Direct my steps. Guide my feet along the path, and make my way sturdy and sure. I give my future to you. Amen.*

But now, Lord, what do I look for?
My hope is in you.
PSALM 39:7

Slow Is Smooth ...

In a culture where waiting is not acceptable, being wise, taking a little extra time along the way, and being sure of your next step can set you apart from the crowd. Waiting for God is not a pleasant place to be if you are accustomed to moving at your own pace. But it is in the season of waiting that you gain strength, wisdom, and favor in God's sight. In fact, many times, our heartaches and troubles can be avoided if we would simply be still and wait on what God wants us to do next. He still leads, regardless of what society may say. He still speaks—simply open His Word.

Being strong in God may seem like the least masculine thing you can do as a man, but your family will appreciate it. In fact, it is one of the defining factors in your becoming a man. To take heart means you are encouraged because of God's Word, His ways, and His promises. Wait on the Lord. Slow is smooth. As a law enforcement officer, you know the importance of getting it right the first time. Take a little extra time, get it right, wait on God, listen to Him, and, in the long run, you will be glad you did.

Heavenly Father, I submit to waiting on you. I will be encouraged by your promises, your Word, and the strength you provide. Amen.

Wait for the LORD; be strong and take heart
and wait for the LORD.

PSALM 27:14

Overcoming Mistakes

The first traffic stop I made as a rookie was on night shift. After I concluded the stop, I drove off. Everything seemed normal. My field training officer didn't tell me I left the spotlight on, blinding oncoming drivers; I just thought the patrol car's headlights were awesome. Eventually, he looked at me and said, "How much farther are you going to drive with the spotlight blinding oncoming drivers?" That was one of many embarrassing moments as a rookie.

When we make mistakes in training, they are easy to overcome and there is little to be embarrassed about. When we make mistakes in public, however, it can be humiliating. Being held to a high standard of excellence can take its toll on you, but knowing you will inevitably make mistakes means you have the time to develop the character to accept responsibility for them and make things right. When you are weak, it is a prime moment for the strength of Jesus Christ to shine through. And if you will trust in Him, He will direct your steps, even through the messes.

Heavenly Father, even in my mistakes, may your name to be glorified. Give me strength of character to own up to my mistakes, even when it is difficult to do. Amen.

That is why, for Christ's sake, I delight in weaknesses, in insults, in hardships, in persecutions, in difficulties. For when I am weak, then I am strong.

2 CORINTHIANS 12:10

The Power of Community Policing

During the span of a generation, we can change our world. It takes one generation to change the world for the better, but, unfortunately, it also takes one generation to destroy the world too. When we take time to invest in the younger generations, the returns and rewards can last for generations to come. Do not underestimate the value of investing in young lives. Our strength is not limited to ourselves as individuals or even as a single unit; our strength spans an entire community. The true power of community policing is relationship building, to which there are many obstacles to overcome as law enforcement officers.

Jesus was about building relationships, even when it meant reaching outside the comfort zones of His culture. Earning the trust of your community may seem like an overwhelming task, but it will help you throughout your career in law enforcement. Find a way to reach out to those who may have been forgotten in your community, and remember the value of investing in the lives of children.

Heavenly Father, our strength comes from you and you alone. Our influence lies in numbers, spanning across our agency and community. Show me the path and value of relationship building. Amen.

Through the praise of children and infants you have established a stronghold against your enemies, to silence the foe and the avenger.

PSALM 8:2

Family
Matters
for Law
Enforcement

APRIL

Be a People Builder

When you speak uplifting, positive reinforcement to another person, especially your spouse or children, you are giving him or her seeds of life. If you are a parent, your words will linger with your children well into their adulthood and have the potential to shape their perspective about God, their own self-esteem, and life in general. More important than the words, at times, is the tone in which you speak them. Be mindful today that your family is on your side. They are your haven, your place of refuge from a world in turmoil. Take time to think about the words you speak and be mindful of the way you speak them.

It is often difficult to shift from law enforcement officer to husband or Daddy, and your family deserves time with you, not the on-duty version of you. Don't expend all you have and leave those who love you most neglected. Instead, speak love and life, and the fruits will pay great dividends. Focus on investing in the relationships of your spouse, children, parents, family, and friends. You will be glad you did.

> *Heavenly Father, help me be conscious of my words and the way I speak to my family. Amen.*

So encourage each other and build each other up,
just as you are already doing.
1 THESSALONIANS 5:11 NLT

Love Is a Two-Way Street

The love and respect discussion found in Ephesians is often taken out of context and manipulated for control and power in relationship. However, let's focus on one area of marriage and relationships for today. Loving your wife as Christ loved the church means sacrificial, selfless love. That is precisely the type of love you show the people in your community every time you go in service.

Your passion to serve is to be commended, and while your spouse is certainly proud of you, your love for him or her will set the tone for your life. Selfish attitudes, poor communication, unforgiveness, and bitterness are all things we must let go if we want the best marriage God has for us. Love is a two-way street— we must love first without demanding the other person to love us in return, but allow for love if he or she gives it. This is the way Jesus loves each one of us—perfectly and sacrificially. Today, find a specific way to express love to your spouse, beginning with words of encouragement, appreciation, and love.

> *Heavenly Father, help me to be as intentional and focused on being a godly spouse as I am at being a law enforcement officer. Help me to remember the human side of my spouse and that he or she is not my enemy. Amen.*

For husbands, this means love your wives,
just as Christ loved the church. He gave up his life for her.
EPHESIANS 5:25 NLT

Poisoned Marriage

A terrible relationship with your spouse can make for a miserable life. Being selfish can ruin all your relationships and leave you desolate. Life spent alone is not how God intended it to be, whether you are married or not; He wants you to have friends and family. But no relationship is sustainable if one or both parties are selfish. One of the greatest attributes of a healthy marriage is when each spouse tries to "out serve" the other, insisting the other spouse gets his or her desires met. When we remove the focus from our own lives and shift it to the lives of others, being selfless and kind, being humble and thinking of others, our relationships will take root and grow.

Ask your spouse today if you come across as selfish. Don't get defensive and try to argue your way around it, but listen intently to what he or she says when responding. Another way to take personal inventory and determine if you are selfish is to ask a trusted friend who will tell you the truth. Being intentional about putting others first and thinking of others before yourself will position you to be a tremendous friend and an even better spouse.

Heavenly Father, remove from me any selfish attitude toward my spouse, and reveal to me any arrogant or prideful ways. I surrender them to you. Amen.

Don't be selfish; don't try to impress others.
Be humble, thinking of others as better than yourselves.
PHILIPPIANS 2:3 NLT

Captured and Cherished

For the married men reading this, your marriage is more important than your career in law enforcement. Our spouses, regardless of whether you are the husband or wife, have many hours, heartaches, and sacrifices invested in our lives, and we owe them our absolute best as it pertains to our relationships. I've often wondered why there wasn't a clear Scripture stating how much of a blessing husbands are to wives, but if you've found a good wife, you have found favor from God.

When we cherish our spouses as Jesus cherishes the church, treat them with love and respect, and love them selflessly, we align ourselves scripturally for God's divine blessings and favor, not to mention a great marriage. The statistics say that if you are married and you are in law enforcement, your marriage doesn't stand a chance. But the stats don't stand a chance—you are stronger than a number. Be intentional, love your spouse, be quick to forgive, and lean on God through difficult situations.

> *Heavenly Father, give me the wisdom to lead my family, to love my spouse the way he or she needs to be loved, and to honor you in my marriage. Help me be the best spouse I can be and to meet the needs I was created to meet in my spouse's life. Amen.*

He who finds a wife finds what is good
and receives favor from the LORD.

PROVERBS 18:22

Careful of the Company You Keep

The people you spend time with affect your character. At the end of the day, you will become more like those you allow to invest in your life. This could be detrimental to your marriage. Think about the commitment you share with those you serve with while on duty. If you associate with individuals who are battling substance abuse issues, you are exposing yourself to opportunity for error. Not only that, but you are allowing an opportunity for insecure thoughts to enter the mind of your spouse.

Keeping bad company can lead to a domino effect of negative circumstances. Just like when driving a vehicle, keeping your eyes down the road for any threats and distractions in marriage means you can avoid heartbreak, unnecessary stress, and costly mistakes. Communicate with your spouse your need for friendships outside of law enforcement, and commit to having friendships that align with the plans and goals you have as a married couple. Ask God to match you and your spouse to a like-minded couple, for this will lead you into more peaceful paths in your marriage.

Heavenly Father, give me wisdom to see and know when the company I keep is not healthy for my marriage, and give me the wherewithal to remove myself from those situations. Send my spouse and me godly couples to associate with, who will glorify your name. Amen.

Do not be misled:
"Bad company corrupts good character."
1 CORINTHIANS 15:33

Back to the Basics

Life gets messy, complicated, and busy. Getting back to the basics in marriage means we refuse to neglect one of the most important relationships in our lives. We need to be intentional about communicating with our spouse, loving them the way they need to be loved, and respecting them, not treating them like a suspect. Focusing on the basics in our marriages means we are intentional about putting our spouses first (for example, even if we can't make dinner on time, we call them to let them know). As a married believer, you are called to love your spouse before yourself.

How we love our spouses will reflect on our relationship with Christ. We cannot parade around as a hero in a uniform and abuse our spouses with our words or neglect and expect to receive God's blessings. Focus on making things right with your spouse. If that seems impossible, remember that God thrives on the impossible. Ask Him for the wisdom and guidance needed to navigate a damaged relationship with your spouse, and, above all, communicate with your spouse and pray together.

> *Heavenly Father, I cannot do this on my own. I need your guidance. Help me get back to the basics of being a great spouse; show me how my spouse needs to be loved, and bring reconciliation where division has existed. Amen.*

Dear friends, let us love one another, for love comes from God. Everyone who loves has been born of God and knows God.

1 JOHN 4:7

It Takes Two to Submit

There is always a lot of talk about the need for a wife to submit to the husband, but this is only in the context and understanding that the husband is first submitted to Christ. If both the husband and wife do not submit to one another, the seeds of selfishness eventually take root. One main cause of failed marriages includes selfishness—the "I deserve" mentality. We should strive to follow Christ and the instructions in the Word of God as it relates to marriage.

We should never treat our spouse like our enemy. If one party in the marriage refuses to work toward reconciliation or is abusive, the situation may require counseling or additional intervention. Be the first in your marriage to submit to your spouse. This drives a dagger through the heart of pride and aligns you with the Word of God. Communicating with your spouse from a place of humility instead of a place of defensiveness means you are giving room for the intervention of the Holy Spirit in your relationship. The day that both of you are fighting over who gets to serve whom is the day you have grasped the true vision of submitting to each other out of reverence for Christ.

Heavenly Father, give me a vision of my marriage where both my spouse and I are submitted to each other and you, for your glory. Amen.

Submit to one another out of reverence for Christ.
Ephesians 5:21

Is It Worth It?

The temptation to seek the affection of or have sex with another person other than your spouse may come. Maybe you are bored at home. Maybe you have grown apart from your spouse, or he or she doesn't understand you, or you just feel the need to have the attention of someone else. At the end of the day, is it worth it? You may have a rough marriage at home and your spouse may *not* "get" you or the stress you deal with, but it's an awfully selfish position to take.

If you have been down "Infidelity Drive" and survived, you know the pain others will endure. Anyone with a conscience will have internal conflict with his or her decision of sexual immorality. Therefore, it is best to remain committed to your spouse, through the good times and bad, and find ways to focus on the best in each other. Fight for love instead of finding reasons to fight. Keep it real, keep it in the marriage, and keep it in the bedroom.

Heavenly Father, thank you for the marvelous gift of sex. Please show me the beauty of this gift from your eyes and how I can fan the flames of passion between my spouse and me, and protect our relationship from infidelity. Amen.

But since sexual immorality is occurring,
each man should have sexual relations with his own wife,
and each woman with her own husband.

1 CORINTHIANS 7:2

A Time to Run Away

She comes along looking better than sin itself. He comes along flexing, talking smooth, making promises your man only wishes he could hold up. How do you respond to the seducing power of a temptress or tempter? You run for your life. At least that is what the writer of 1 Corinthians 6:18 said. There are not many situations where you are willing to run away from as a law enforcement officer, but this is one you should be willing and proud to flee from.

The price of engaging in sexual immorality goes beyond the initial contact. It brings pain to someone you love and someone who loves you deeply; it brings pain to your children, your family, your friends, and the people who look up to you. Please, heed the warnings. Do not be seduced by the temptations of those who would lure you into their destructive traps. It will claim your family, your career, and your joy, and leave you empty and destitute. Yes, you can rebound in time, but some things take a lifetime to come back from, and this decision is one of them!

> *Heavenly Father, give me the eyes to see the seductive power of the temptress and give me the guts to run from it. Amen.*

Flee from sexual immorality. All other sins a person commits are outside the body, but whoever sins sexually, sins against their own body.

1 CORINTHIANS 6:18

April 10

Passionate Partners

L et's focus on two things today: self-control and passion. If you are physically attracted to someone and are in a relationship with them, it is going to be difficult to control your emotions, and, at some point, you are going to need to set boundaries of physical contact. Someone in 1 Corinthians 7:9 thought this was important enough to include it in the Bible, so I figured, with some of the issues we have seen in our culture, it should probably be mentioned here.

For some reason, we let the passion fizzle out over time after we say our vows. But before we are married, it takes all the power and self-control we have to stay out of the bed with our significant other. During marriage, we should focus on nurturing our spouse like we did before we became husband and wife. We should never base our love on fear or on the reciprocity of love, and we should also never stop letting our spouse know just how smoking hot they are. Never stop being passionate partners! Keep the flames of your marriage bed white hot.

> *Heavenly Father, thank you for my spouse. Thank you for the beautiful gift of sex. Thank you for protecting my marriage and giving me the wisdom to nurture my spouse in love and compassion. Amen.*

But if they cannot control themselves, they should marry, for it is better to marry than to burn with passion.

1 CORINTHIANS 7:9

Take Time for Your Kids

As parents, training our children is often interpreted as either discipline, teaching, or some other external lesson. The life of a law enforcement officer is a busy life, one that requires many sacrifices. But one of the greatest things we can do for our children is to make time to be with them—to go to their events and to spend time with them. Building a healthy relationship with your child begins when he or she is an infant, but it only takes a short time to destroy that relationship.

If you aren't a parent, make it possible for those who are parents to be with their kids when possible. I am not suggesting you cancel your plans for theirs, but consider helping make the lives of their children a little bit easier along the way. The sacrifices you make are difficult, and, in the long run, they will probably help your career. But don't forget to take time to invest in your children. Starting them off the way they should go and training them right means more than just disciplining them. Quality time can do for your child more than any material possession ever could.

Heavenly Father, help me to reflect your nature to my children as a parent, and when life is busy and I get distracted, remind me of my first mission—my children. Amen.

Start children off on the way they should go,
and even when they are old they will not turn from it.
PROVERBS 22:6

They Aren't Suspects

You see the impact evil has on the lives of others. You see the impact fatherless homes have on communities, and you see the impact abandoned children have in schools. From shoplifting to drug possession, juveniles are committing more (and more violent) crimes. It may become easy as a parent to become a disciplinarian or authoritarian to your children, but the secret to the heart of our children is quality time and love.

If we are always barking orders at our children, eventually their ears will begin to tune us out. Then our voices will become harsher, and, eventually, our children will become completely discouraged and disconnected from us; they will quit trying. Holding a standard of perfection means you give no mercy or grace, and while that may work on the streets, there's hardly any place for it in the home. Walk with love and handle the hearts of your children with white gloves. Before you head home from your shift, take time to dump the things you dealt with at work at the feet of Jesus. He is strong enough to handle your burdens and willing to carry your load.

Heavenly Father, when my patience runs thin or my temper is short, remind me that my children need me to love them and discipline them, but most of all to be here for them. Help me, Lord, to be a godly parent and to not exhaust my child. Amen.

Fathers, do not embitter your children,
or they will become discouraged.
COLOSSIANS 3:21

Give Them Wisdom

As a parent of two boys and a beautiful girl, I can tell you that boys know nothing about balance. And by balance, I mean they can eat more than a horse, play for twenty-four hours a day, and never stop asking questions. There is no fear when it comes to danger and no common sense when it comes to risk. While we should strive for balance in discipline, we should not deprive our children of healthy reprimand when it is needed. This is the impartation of wisdom we are responsible for giving our children.

The wisdom of God comes to us through reading His Word and gaining knowledge and life experience, then, with all that, we pass it down to our children through correcting misaligned behavior. If you are like me, you don't like to discipline your children; it doesn't bring you pleasure. But what it does is give you peace in knowing you are passing down valuable lessons that will save them time, pain, and heartache, even if it takes them enduring a moment of suffering at the time.

Heavenly Father, as you have loved me, you have disciplined me. Help me to not become overbearing on my children because of the things I see on duty, but to love my children and impart wisdom. Amen.

A rod and a reprimand impart wisdom,
but a child left undisciplined disgraces its mother.

PROVERBS 29:15

Habits of a Good Leader

t is out of a spirit of immaturity that we attempt to lord over our families with authority or discipline. This type of behavior will only last for so long before those entrusted to us begin to rebel and buck the tyranny of our rule. Instead, each of us who have been so entrusted with a family should lead them by example. If we are overweight and out of shape, it is unwise to think we can expect those entrusted to us to behave any differently than we do.

Our habits become the habits of our children, and our spouses deal with the carnage. There are a few things we can do to change the destiny of our children, but it all begins with our personal habits. We cannot expect our unhealthy behaviors to be done in vain, because in due season, we will reap what we sow. Commit to being intentional with your decisions, changing your negative habits, creating new healthy habits, and unifying your family. Set the example, and in time your family will follow.

> *Heavenly Father, may I never abuse those entrusted to me by you. Help me in my weakness, and set before me the example of your Son as a leader to my family. Amen.*

Not lording it over those entrusted to you,
but being examples to the flock.

1 PETER 5:3

Party Killers

When it comes to parenting and discipline, there are as many schools of thought and opinions as there are brands of shoes. But I will say this: We cannot ignore the unhealthy behavior of our children. If you notice, a few days back the focus was on the other extreme—overbearing, disciplinarian parenting. The key is balance, whatever approach you have in parenting.

If you ignore your children's behavior, it only leads to death. If you are overbearing, it can lead to death too. It is time to kill the party. The relationship between you and your children is a special bond, one that no one can ever replace, but it is not the same as any friendship. Giving your children hope begins with being willing to lovingly confront them when they are wrong, but also admitting when you are wrong too. Demonstrating godly character as a parent will embed in the minds of your young protégés the necessary images to mimic as adults.

Heavenly Father, teach me the balance of healthy discipline as a parent. Help me to hang up my duty belt and badge when I come home, and to love my family like they deserve and need to be loved. Amen.

Discipline your children, for in that there is hope;
do not be a willing party to their death.
PROVERBS 19:18

Don't Raise a Fool

I have seen good parents do all they knew how to do with their children only to see their children end up in prison or even dead. They were good parents. So what went wrong? Your job, as a parent, is not to raise your children to be good children; it is to prepare your children to be successful adults. Children are not born knowing right and wrong; they are taught the difference. As such, they must be taught the correct way of living. If every person in your community caught on to this, imagine how much the schools would change and what future generations would look like.

Maybe the good parents lacked the will to discipline their children. We don't know. But at the end of the day, your children are entrusted to you. Your duty as a law enforcement officer when you are on duty is to restore order, uphold the law, and apprehend suspects. But your position and authority as a law enforcement officer has no value to your wayward child. They need the effective, present, and involved love of a parent. Today, commit to changing a generation starting with one.

> *Heavenly Father, help me to be a godly parent and to impart godly wisdom into the hearts and minds of my children. Amen.*

Folly is bound up in the heart of a child,
but the rod of discipline will drive it far away.

PROVERBS 22:15

A Compassionate Parent

Dealing with criminals daily makes you mentally tough, which can either be a good thing or a negative thing. If it costs you compassion toward your children, I'd say it is negative. This is no excuse to raise up weak kids, but it is a reminder that we should leave our police mind-set at the door when we arrive home. Loving our families with compassion is one of the ways Jesus would love them. In fact, every miracle Jesus performed was preceded by compassion.

People pray daily for miracles but often fail to see the power they possess to be the miracle to their own families or to their own children. Showing them compassion, love, and quality time are all ways to demonstrate the nature of God to our families. And as law enforcement officers, it is a good reminder that compassion for those whom we serve can go a long way.

> *Heavenly Father, give me a heart of compassion toward my spouse and children. Help me to love my family like you love me. Amen.*

*As a father has compassion on his children,
so the Lord has compassion on those who fear him.*

PSALM 103:13

Obedience Creates Breakthrough

If your parents are still living, when was the last time you called them? The older I get, the more I realize the frailty and brevity of life. We are never promised another moment. To think of some of the downright silly things we have allowed to destroy the relationships we have had with our parents, spouses, and children is mind-boggling. Today, begin with forgiveness.

Mending a relationship may not mean you begin with forgiveness if you were wronged, but you begin with forgiveness out of obedience so you can begin the narrative of relationship again with your loved one. As a law enforcement officer, it is easy to forget we were given life by someone else. Call your mom, your dad, or your family and tell them you love them. Go spend time with them. Honor them. Take the risk of mending relationships, because, after all, you are a peacemaker. You will be glad you did.

Heavenly Father, give me wisdom and a course to approach damaged relationships; help me to seek forgiveness in areas where I have wronged others and in areas I have been wronged. Amen.

Children, obey your parents in the Lord,
for this is right.

EPHESIANS 6:1

Lead Them to Life, Not Death

When my youngest son doesn't get his way, he wants to have a trial on the spot. He wants the facts laid out, and he wants to have a perfectly clear understanding of why or why not the results are the way they are. It is in those moments I have to make it clear through a patient, loving explanation that I do not have to provide him with an attorney, at eight years old, over his inability to get chicken nuggets.

Many of us are the same way when it comes to getting answers from God. We want to know the reasons why things are the way they are or why He said no. God will not lead us to death, but through His Son, Jesus, He leads us to eternal life. We should focus our efforts on leading our children in love. Even when our patience with them grows thin, remember God's love is long-suffering and He could have brought judgment on us long ago, but instead He gives us new mercies every morning. Lead your children to life daily.

Heavenly Father, help me in my moments of impatience with my children. Help me to speak words softly and with love, because I know they will remember it forever. Amen.

If anyone causes one of these little ones—
those who believe in me—to stumble, it would be better
for them if a large millstone were hung around their neck
and they were thrown into the sea.

MARK 9:42

Lifetime Warranty

New vehicles often come with extensive warranties, providing service for the vehicle according to the manufacturer's guidelines. Proverbs tells us that if we train our children, they will give us peace. Much like we are told by automobile manufacturers that if we maintain our vehicles, they will honor a warranty, so we are to properly train our children and expect peace from them as they mature. To discipline your children means to train your children to obey rules or follow a certain expected behavior, using punishment to correct disobedience.

Punishment can come in a variety of methods. For some, making their child write a five-hundred-word essay on the topic is plenty of punishment, while others need more traditional punishment or manual labor. It is your job as the parent to help your child discover the purpose, vision, and mission God has for his or her life. There is nothing more in this life that I can think of that will give a parent more peace or delight than to see his or her children living out their God-given destiny. Training them from a young age will help them realize this.

> *Heavenly Father, help me to cultivate in the heart of my children the vision you have for their lives. Help me to nurture the purpose you have for them, through properly training them as a parent. Amen.*

Discipline your children, and they will give you peace;
they will bring you the delights you desire.

PROVERBS 29:17

Take Care of Your Family

Behind the badge of every officer is the heart of a man or woman who is willing to do whatever it takes to get the job done, to serve their community, and to meet the needs of their family. There are seasons in life when it is necessary to work more than usual, and communicating with your spouse and children will help you to navigate through those seasons in a healthy manner. You should be commended for the service you provide to your community, the risks you take, and the dangers you face to put food on the table for your family.

There are few if any other professions where participants leave for work not knowing the dangers they will face that day or if they will come home at the end of their shift. Your faith in God, your strength and perseverance and consistency in service will provide for you and your family for many years to come. Do not become complacent on duty, but learn contentment at home.

Heavenly Father, thank you for the opportunity to serve my community. Give me favor in your eyes, as I seek your ways, and help me to provide for my family to meet all their needs. Amen.

Anyone who does not provide for their relatives, and especially for their own household, has denied the faith and is worse than an unbeliever.

1 TIMOTHY 5:8

Sentenced to Life

As you progress in your career, you will receive pay increases for promotions, cost-of-living increases, as well as other raises. These times may be tempting to acquire new debt. While a new house or new car may be enticing, consider saving money and paying a large down payment, or purchasing a used home or a nice used car. The burden caused by overloading yourself with debt is substantial, and you become a slave to the lender. You have no choice *but* to work, and to work as much as necessary to meet those obligations. This means more time away from your family. Some debt, like a thirty-year mortgage, can seem like a lifetime sentence to debt.

God's ways are always higher than our own plans. It may seem foolish or even out of date, but saving money and waiting to purchase big items like a house or car can save you the burden of slavery to debt and give you freedom millions of Americans do not enjoy. Today, seek to be different. If you have debt, communicate with your spouse and come up with a plan to pay off all debt and do not acquire any new debt. If you do not have any debt, avoid it at all costs. You are free indeed.

> *Heavenly Father, teach me the wisdom of proper financial stewardship and the freedom in not being slave to the lender. Amen.*

The rich rule over the poor,
and the borrower is slave to the lender.

PROVERBS 22:7

Gaining Wealth Is Not Evil

Some folks will tell you that if you are rich, then you are evil. This is far from the truth! It is the *love* of money that is the root of evil, not the possession of money. If you have excellent business aptitude, consider starting a business on the side, as long as it does not interfere with your duties as a law enforcement officer. Invest your money wisely and accumulate wealth, but do it for the right reasons. Doing any of this for the simple love of money will lead you down an evil and dark path.

Gaining financial wealth is not a bad goal, and it is not evil. But do not allow the goal to cause you to wander from your faith or become encompassed with immorality. The key to acquiring wealth is giving, because it ensures your heart remains pure of greed and that your love is not for money but for God. Keep your heart right and your pursuit pure, and your acquisitions will take care of themselves.

Heavenly Father, I know my family has needs, and they will have needs in the future. I also know I will need to retire one day. Please give me the wisdom from your Word as it pertains to building wealth the godly way, beginning with giving. Amen.

For the love of money is a root of all kinds of evil.
Some people, eager for money, have wandered from
the faith and pierced themselves with many griefs.

1 TIMOTHY 6:10

The Power of Giving

It would be foolish to believe your entire life revolved around your duties at work or that your influence ended where your jurisdiction begins and ends. Your influence can span this globe because of giving, and the benefits are not only good for your heart and soul, but they can help you in many other ways. Honoring God with your wealth may sound old-fashioned and out of date, but it is one of the best ways to keep your heart aligned with His and ensure you stay far from greed.

The power of giving is deeper and wider than giving to receive more in return. The power of giving is the freedom found in covenant with the Father through His Word. No other financial system will reward you or provide you with security, both short term and long term, the way God's financial system will. Tap into the power of giving, first locally with your home church and then with missions, and watch God's power expand in your life.

> *Heavenly Father, I give you all that I possess because it is yours. It is not mine. I am merely a steward over it. I submit to your ways and ask for your blessings on all I put my hand to and all I give. Amen.*

Honor the LORD with your wealth,
with the first fruits of all your crops;
then your barns will be filled to overflowing,
and your vats will brim over with new wine.

PROVERBS 3:9–10

Be Thankful
for What You Have

To everything, there must be order. Imagine if a new officer was made watch commander his first day on duty. The results could be disastrous. For some, patience to achieve their goals runs thin and ambition tends to put the goals before the process. However, if we will simply focus on being thankful for where we are, where we have come from, and what we have, our perspectives will shift to a much healthier vantage point.

If we cannot be entrusted with authority over our zone, area, or district, we cannot be entrusted to lead our department or city. If we cannot be trusted with little, then we cannot be trusted with much. It is a simple principle. Learn to cultivate the heart of a giver, live from a place of perpetual thankfulness, and watch your fields flourish. Thankfulness is a great virtue to have in your heart and a wonderful place from which to live.

Heavenly Father, life is not always perfect according to the standards others set. But I have all I need, and I am thankful. Remind me to come to you daily with a heart of thankfulness and not as a spoiled brat. Amen.

Whoever can be trusted with very little can also be trusted with much, and whoever is dishonest with very little will also be dishonest with much.

LUKE 16:10

Think Outside the Budget Box

If you have made some bad financial decisions and your credit record, score, and bank account have the scars to prove it, then you may need to think creatively as it pertains to addressing your situation. There are many plans and ideas when it comes to setting finances in order, but at the end of the day, the key is to spend less than you bring home in your paycheck. If you have since over-extended yourself in financial obligations, it may be time to put some creative ideas to work so you can eventually get to a working budget.

Your family needs the peace of mind in knowing you can not only lead them but also manage the finances and pass on the lessons so your children do not make the same mistakes. With the wisdom gained from God's Word, the lessons learned from others who have mastered finances, and your hard work, sacrifices, and creative ideas, you will have things rolling in the right direction in no time. It's time to think outside the budget box, get creative, and put those ideas to work.

Heavenly Father, I know you did not create me to live under stress, bound in debt to lenders. Give me creative ideas and strategies for getting all of my debt paid off in a legal, ethical, and holy manner. Amen.

All hard work brings a profit,
but mere talk leads only to poverty.
PROVERBS 14:23

Testing God

The topic of tithing is one that many people debate. However, I am of the belief that everything I have belongs to God and it all came from Him because He is my ultimate provider. Giving 10 percent is not a difficult thing to do. Not only does it keep our heart aligned with God, but it reminds us where our provisions originate from. Our nature is often to be self-reliant and self-sustaining, and there's nothing wrong with that. But at the same time, we must remember God is the source of all that we have been given.

I am issuing you a challenge today, much like the challenge we read in Malachi 3:10: Test God in the tithe. Be consistent and give from a pure, joyful heart. Do not give with an anticipation of receiving; instead, give with thankfulness for all you have been given. Your life, your family, and your career will never be the same.

Heavenly Father, you are the provider for all the needs I have in life, and all the provisions I have come from you. I commit to living out my thankfulness to you by giving back to you 10 percent of what is already yours and watching you meet every need. Amen.

"Test me in this," says the LORD Almighty,
"and see if I will not throw open the floodgates
of heaven and pour out so much blessing that
there will not be room enough to store it."
MALACHI 3:10

The Art of Balance

Sometimes the saying "less is more" bears more truth than we realize. I say this in the context of peace. If you are losing your relationship with your children and spouse, not getting proper rest, or neglecting your health, is the extra time and money worth it? There are times when overtime or callout is required, but we also know the attraction of off-duty jobs and overtime gigs and the strain those can place on families. I'm not suggesting working overtime is bad for your family; I am suggesting that if you are always in strife at home, maybe it is time to bring the focus back to your family.

With proper time balance and an understanding family, you will face less strife and division. But if you fail to communicate and make your family a priority, you will find that the cost of overtime is beyond the price you are willing to pay. It may be time to cut some expenses so you do not lose the reason you work. It's better to have less or nothing and have peace than to have it all and live with strife.

> *Heavenly Father, thank you for the wisdom of knowing that less is more. Help me to number my days, to place my relationship with you and my family above my career, and to seek you in all I do. Amen.*

Better a dry crust with peace and quiet
than a house full of feasting, with strife.

PROVERBS 17:1

Investment Officers

In a 2006 poll taken by the Consumer Federation of America and Financial Planning Association, 20 percent of Americans said they were depending on winning the lottery as their retirement plan. While winning the lottery would hardly be considered dishonest, the number of lives destroyed by lottery winnings is staggering. At the end of the day, we could hoard more money than any major country, but if we don't know how to manage it, we are wasting our time and energy.

Putting together a solid plan for your future means you have a plan for giving, a budget for expenses, and plan for saving. Dishonest money dwindles away because the heart is the issue, not the money. The one who gathers money little by little has established self-discipline and put forth hard work. Take time to think about your future today. What are you depending on for retirement? If you don't have a budget or you are not saving or giving, today is a great day to begin a new life.

> *Heavenly Father, give me wisdom above all things as it pertains to finances and accumulating wealth. Amen.*

Dishonest money dwindles away,
but whoever gathers money little by little makes it grow.
PROVERBS 13:11

Stay Focused on Your Goals

The key to reaching your goals, whether they are related to health, relationships, finances, or career, is consistency in executing a well-thought-out plan. You may, however, find yourself facing distractions along the way as you encounter growth phases. These are times when it is critical to remain focused on your goals, keep your eyes on the prize, and remain consistent. Anyone can do something for a day, but those who are focused and consistent win the prize.

What are you willing to do to have abundance in your life? Are you willing to plan, sacrifice material things, work hard, and be a committed follower of Christ? If so, then you have the characteristics of a champion, and it is time to put your hands to work. Like on many of the days you experience in law enforcement, staying focused and consistent in your goals in life aren't always easy, but they are necessary, and they are part of being a champion in life. You have what it takes—your family needs it, and you can deliver. Stay focused!

Heavenly Father, when wild ideas cross my mind, teach me to test them and see their value before pursuing them or entertaining them. Give me wisdom and strength to endure and to be consistent, and the spirit to remain focused amidst distractions. Amen.

Those who work their land will have abundant food,
but those who chase fantasies will have their fill of poverty.
PROVERBS 28:19

Integrity Matters

MAY

Imitating Greatness

For many officers, one of the leading reasons they serve is because of the positive influence a law enforcement officer had in their life when they were children. These people exemplified the characteristics that make our country great and are the reason we can wear the shield today. Following the steps of righteous leaders is something we should *all* do, by imitating their faith, finding their godly habits, and mimicking what they do. We all have a tendency to imitate bad behavior as children—it's natural. But as adults, we should imitate greatness.

As believers in Jesus Christ, the highest prize is running the race and receiving our reward in eternity. But as we serve our heavenly Father here on earth and our fellow citizens as law enforcement officers, we should strive to imitate the greatest people to ever wear a badge. Maybe they had some areas of weakness, or maybe they were great cops but their family lives were in shambles. You are on a journey to become equipped to be a well-rounded peace officer, prepared for victory and expecting nothing less.

Heavenly Father, I set my eyes on you. Give me good examples to follow, but never let me forget the example set before me by your Son, Jesus. I want to imitate greatness, which begins by pursuing you. Amen.

Remember your leaders, who spoke the word of God to you.
Consider the outcome of their way of life
and imitate their faith.
Hebrews 13:7

A Clean Conscience

Going to sleep with a clean conscience has more value than any shameful deed to shortcut success or cut a corner on the job. Maybe you read that and think, *That sounds cheesy.* But the weight of guilt can bury you. In time, it will take its toll on your mind, body, and soul … if you allow it. It all begins with one decision—a small, simple, innocent decision. Maybe the decision was to accept a bribe, which sounds really bad but in the big scheme of things it wasn't all that bad at the time.

What's the value of a clean conscience? Your past has some scars on it? That's a good sign you were living. If you made some bad decisions over the years, the good news is that there's still time to make things right, to clear your conscience, and to do the right thing. It's never too late to start doing the right thing.

Heavenly Father, like many others, my past is scarred. I ask you to forgive me, give me wisdom on how to move forward regarding my mistakes, and give me grace and mercy daily. Thank you for loving me and forgiving me. Help me live above reproach to bring glory to your name. Amen.

We reject all shameful deeds and underhanded methods.
We don't try to trick anyone or distort the word of God.
We tell the truth before God, and all who are honest know this.

2 CORINTHIANS 4:2 NLT

The Power of Your Words

Ending a traffic stop where the driver was issued a citation has always been awkward for me. Instead of saying, "Have a nice day," I always ended with, "Please travel safe." There are times when those departing words could easily be a bit saltier, but we are professionals and representatives of God's kingdom. Whether you are working with others actively on a case, a call, or on a traffic stop, they will remember for the rest of their lives the negative attitude and words you speak. They may not remember some of your positive nuances, but they will certainly recall the negative one.

This is why it is so important that we love our job and others with a pure heart and exemplify gracious speech, even in the face of hatred. Not only will we find resounding success on the streets, but we will develop relationships with people in the community and find favor in the eyes of our leaders. Today, if you are tempted to speak words that are less than gracious to another person, be it a coworker, citizen, or suspect, take a moment and think about how that affects your eternal investments.

Heavenly Father, my tongue is hard to tame. I am asking you to help me keep my mouth shut when I need to the most. When I speak, let my words be few and let them matter. Amen.

Whoever loves a pure heart and gracious speech will have the king as a friend.

PROVERBS 22:11 NLT

The Industry Standard

Every profession has a professional industry standard for doing business. Like many other professions, law enforcement agencies have a standard by which to adhere too. These operating procedures set the guidelines by which you carry out your duties, deal with most situations, and even address administrative functions. Likewise, you can be sure your conscience is clear and clean when you operate according to the procedures of God's Word. Treat others fairly and equally, be firm, do not relent in your pursuit of justice, and do not be discouraged in your service. Speak with concrete truthfulness, and love those who serve with you.

The industry standard is not some fairy-dust love; it is a love that smells of gunpowder, leather polish, and polyester. This industry standard doesn't look like the books tell you, and many may have fallen away from the tight-knit brotherhood of old, but that bond is still the standard. Jesus set the standard when He gave His life for us. The least we can do is hold each other accountable, strive to sharpen one another's skills, love our families, and serve our communities with nothing less than excellence.

> *Heavenly Father, thank you for the standard set before me today. Give me the spirit of excellence in all that I do, and let all I pursue honor your name. Amen.*

With Christ as my witness, I speak with utter truthfulness. My conscience and the Holy Spirit confirm it.

ROMANS 9:1 NLT

Integrity Lasts Forever

The number of traps that can claim your career, good reputation, character, or even your family are astounding. Maybe I sound like a broken record, but it is necessary to remember that one bad decision can change your entire life. Consequences can last a lifetime; whether that is fair or not, it is still true. My hope for you is that you will cling to righteousness and integrity, that you will always error on the side of being upright and flee from any potential immoral, unethical, or criminal decisions.

One decision can change the life of your family. Just one decision can change your career status. One decision can lead to a domino effect of terrible results that will take you to a place you never dreamed you could be—physically, emotionally, and mentally. Let others call you a holy roller or Bible thumper or boring; let them call you whatever, but be the one who is left standing at the end of the day with your character, integrity, and reputation still intact. After all, we serve our community as we are serving God, and we should do it in the spirit of excellence.

Heavenly Father, do not lead me into temptation, but deliver me from evil. Protect me from the snares of the enemy. As I place my hope in you, may integrity and uprightness protect me. Amen.

May integrity and uprightness protect me,
because my hope, LORD, is in you.
PSALM 25:21

Intangible Powers

We are trained and completely equipped to perform our duties as law enforcement officers in about any situation that could present itself. We experience the vilest hatred and threats of murder, but we also see the fruits of our labor at times too. The intangible powers we possess do not begin with the arrest powers; rather, they begin with our character, integrity, and ability to persevere through adversity.

Each of you reading this has the same access to the Holy Spirit as revealed to us in the New Testament. Jesus said He was leaving us a Comforter who would empower us to face these times in which we live. You have access to the resources you need to be successful as a law enforcement officer, regardless of your capacity. You also have access to the resources needed to be successful as a follower of Jesus Christ. Tap into the intangibles today and experience a new level of strength like you have never experienced before.

Heavenly Father, I know the gift of your Holy Spirit is something I need, and I receive it through relationship with you, through accepting your Son, Jesus. Fill me now with your precious Holy Spirit, and empower me to be victorious in life. Amen.

I know that you are pleased with me,
for my enemy does not triumph over me.
Because of my integrity you uphold me
and set me in your presence forever.

PSALM 41:11–12

Never Compromise

You may lack rank and position, and have little authority, but with time on the job and experience, the opportunity will present itself for you to climb the ranks. If, while you are laying the foundation for your career, you establish a pattern of compromise, what precedence does that set for you as a leader? What happens in the dark will always be revealed in the light. This means that what you do in private, whether good or bad, will be revealed to the world at some point. Your integrity cannot be easily repaired. Protect it and do not compromise.

Lying as a sworn peace officer causes a plethora of issues, on the street, in the department, and in the courtroom. Your credibility is ruined. No one can trust you. Never compromise your integrity for any reason, even if it means you are going to face uncomfortable confrontation. Deal with the issues of integrity early on. If you have made some mistakes, confront them. Ask God for wisdom, read and discover what His Word says, and seek godly counsel. Today is a new day, brothers and sisters. Strive for excellence in all you do, for God's glory and to honor the shield.

> Heavenly Father, let my words, my actions, and my thoughts bring you honor and glory today. Let my service be done in excellence, and do not let me bring dishonor to my shield or to your great name. Amen.

The LORD detests lying lips,
but he delights in people who are trustworthy.
PROVERBS 12:22

Whom Do You Serve?

The challenges you face in today's society are numerous and are significantly different than they were two decades ago. Mainly because of the presence of social media, the availability of live streaming through smartphones, and the various social-media platforms, any given situation can be misconstrued out of proportion before a valid response is given. While these challenges can cause you frustration and stress, it is important to remember a few key points.

First, you are serving the innocent, pursuing the criminal, and protecting those who are defenseless. They need you, and they depend on you. But most importantly, you are serving God. In everything you do, act as if your watch commander is God Himself. You may have the best leadership in the country working in your agency, but there will be things you disagree with at times. When you remember *whom* you serve and *why* you serve, discouraging times will tend to depart from you much more quickly. Set your sights on the things God has for you, and pursue His path relentlessly.

> *Heavenly Father, remind me today, as I prepare for duty, that I am serving you, working for you, and serving as a law enforcement officer for my community and to bring you glory. Amen.*

Whatever you do, work at it with all your heart, as working for the Lord, not for human masters.
COLOSSIANS 3:23

Watch Your Step

Times may come when you see evil people prospering while you seemingly struggle to get by. You see known criminals with enough money to pay your mortgage off while you work overtime to pay this month's payment on time. It can be discouraging if you think about it from that perspective. Or maybe you see the three-time felon go before the judge and get a slap on the wrist instead of being sent to prison for the crimes he or she committed. Would you rather be known as corrupt and be rich, or be blameless and poor? I'm not saying these are your choices, but if it came down to it, which would you choose?

Be the person who sticks to your guns, never compromising character, integrity, or sacrificing reputation for a few bucks. Your future, at this moment, is unsullied, and all you have to do is the right thing and avoid any stupid decisions. Remembering the reasons why you began this journey is key to making the right decisions when in such positions. Don't give it all up in one moment of bad judgment or over a short temper. Your future is bright, and you can accomplish great things. Don't let the ways of the perverse corrupt your path.

Heavenly Father, thank you for making my path straight, providing me with light in a dark world, and equipping me to accomplish my purpose in life. Amen.

Better the poor whose walk is blameless than the rich whose ways are perverse.

PROVERBS 28:6

Little White Lies

There are not many things that hurt as deeply as being betrayed by someone we love and trust. Being a person of integrity, learning to forgive, and letting God be your vindicator will set you light years ahead of many people you encounter. The past several days have dealt a lot with integrity, and it may seem a bit redundant or even elementary here. But this is the day you realize that your integrity is a weapon in your tool kit against those who would seek to bring you harm.

When you live in such a way that you can keep a clear conscience, are a person of integrity, and live and work with a spirit of excellence, you refuse to give the enemy a foothold in your life, and you refuse the enemy an opportunity to gain ammunition to use against you. While it may seem like it is basic or foolish to keep hounding on walking the line, it is for our own good and for God's glory, and so that we do not dishonor the shield we bear.

> *Heavenly Father, I submit to you my life, my plans, and my desires. Help me live in such a way that I keep a clear conscience, making good decisions, and maintaining integrity and being upright before you. Amen.*

Keeping a clear conscience, so that those who speak maliciously against your good behavior in Christ may be ashamed of their slander.

1 PETER 3:16

Crooked Corners

If you go to the bookstore, you will find several different books about success—from business success and financial success to marriage success and fitness success. There's something about success for everyone. But many of these will show you how to cut corners on the path to success, which only robs you, the lone participant, in the long run. God has a tremendous reward in store for those who remain committed and consistent in their pursuit of Him. Proverbs 2:7 says, "He holds success in store for the upright, he is a shield to those whose walk is blameless."

While we do have an eternal reward awaiting us, there are also rewards here on earth for our actions. They may not happen immediately, but they will happen. Taking shortcuts reduces your experience along the way, cheats you of potential blessings, and results in you not walking securely before God. Be consistent in your pursuit and be committed to integrity, and the rewards will come.

Heavenly Father, thank you for making my crooked paths straight and laying before me the divine direction you have for my life. Show me the way, and I will follow in it. Amen.

Whoever walks in integrity walks securely,
but whoever takes crooked paths will be found out.

PROVERBS 10:9

The Seeds of Thought

Thoughts are an intricate part of the process of us becoming who we were created by God to be. Pursuing justice and doing good do not begin with action; they begin with a thought. As you did not magically become a law enforcement officer without the thoughts, actions, and sacrifices, so other life results do not appear out of thin air without first having the mental capacity to dwell on those thoughts. We do not lose weight without putting in the work, and marriages are not improved without proper maintenance. But efforts begin somewhere deeper.

Our efforts originate with our beliefs and thoughts. What we dwell on will eventually become our actions and habits. Our actions are the fruits resulting from the seeds of thoughts, which happen over time as we tolerate negative, impure, and unholy thoughts. Through a consistent habit of reading the Bible, prayer, and healthy relationships, we can begin to develop a pattern of thinking that will lead to a life of fruitful results that honor God.

Heavenly Father, thank you for the gift of my mind. Thank you that I have the capacity to think and choose. Help me renew my mind through studying your Word, seeking you, and pursuing healthy relationships. Help me to evict negative and unhealthy thoughts. Amen.

Finally, brothers and sisters, whatever is true, whatever is noble, whatever is right, whatever is pure, whatever is lovely, whatever is admirable—if anything is excellent or praiseworthy—think about such things.

PHILIPPIANS 4:8

Pursue Justice

The qualities you possess are intangible, and many of them were in place before you took your oath to serve as a law enforcement officer. For some, the training requirements only sharpened those qualities, such as self-control, discipline, inner strength, and an even temper. In your career, one of the most influential resources you have access to is your words. The way you use your words begins with inner strength, self-control, and discipline.

From briefing to docket and your favorite spot at home, your pursuits in life will require self-discipline and strength—strength from your physical body and from within and strength from God and from His Word. Today is an opportunity for you to shift your focus to your inner strength, to be intentional with your words and actions, and to commit to a lifestyle that is self-controlled, upright, holy, and honoring to God.

Heavenly Father, thank you for the gifts you have placed inside me. Draw the best of those gifts out of me so I can serve you and your people with excellence and integrity. Amen.

Rather, he must be hospitable,
one who loves what is good, who is self-controlled,
upright, holy and disciplined.

TITUS 1:8

Maximum Sentence

It seems like a lot of people who violate the law do so because they lack a good conscience. But a matter of conscience is rooted deep in the hearts and souls of people across our nation, and many of the issues are a result in broken families, absent fathers and mothers, and the lack of structure in the home. If we want to instill morals, we first have to impart the will for a person to do right and good. But affecting the will of another person is a perilous task.

Boundaries exist to protect the health and well-being of society. Those who violate the law face consequences, some more harsh than others. Your mission is to stand guard, to hold the line between the violent criminal who may be roaming your community and the innocent man, woman, or child who may be his or her next victim. Your integrity matters well beyond the here and now. Hold strong to your principles, walk in love, but give those who seek to do harm a reason to fear the consequences of their evil decisions.

Heavenly Father, equip me in mind, body, and spirit to serve my community, even those who despise what I stand for. Help my life remain unsullied so that I live above reproach, never bringing dishonor to the badge, this profession, or, most importantly, to your name. Amen.

Therefore, it is necessary to submit to the authorities,
not only because of possible punishment
but also as a matter of conscience.

ROMANS 13:5

Immoveable Force

Your training and experience are two ways God keeps you safe on the streets. But even before that, you were given the fundamental pieces of knowledge to earn your certification and prepare you for the streets. Those experiences are rooted deep in your mind. But we lose our power and authority when we lack integrity and credibility, both of which can be found through following the principles in God's Word.

God's promises for you are many, and He never fails, even when the fruition of those promises don't always come through like you expected. With a solid foundation in faith, family, training, and brotherhood, you will be an immoveable force. Seek to be rooted in the Word of God through consistent study, prayer, and fellowship. Then He establishes our path and ordains our steps, directing us according to His will. There are times when it is tempting to go our own way and let God catch up, but we lose our security in Him when we do so. Commit your ways to Him—your words and actions—and He will secure your steps.

> *Heavenly Father, establish my feet in the ways of your Word. Let my walk be blameless before you because of your Son. Help me to become an immoveable force as I remain in you and you in me. Amen.*

The one whose walk is blameless, who does what is righteous, who speaks the truth from their heart. …
Whoever does these things will never be shaken.

PSALM 15:2, 5

The Evidence of Success

The mind-set of many law enforcement officers is to seek proof before believing anything. While that is necessary for success on the streets, the principles of God work a little differently. The keys to well-being lie in the hands of wisdom. It is when we seek the wisdom found in God's Word that we find His favor and the foundation for a life of integrity. Any other foundation is short-lived and will lead to destruction and frustration.

In five, ten, or twenty years, when you look back at your life, you should see the evidence of success being the fruits of integrity, wisdom, and well-being. When others speak of you, they will speak of your good name, and you will have significant favor in the eyes of God and others. But this does not come without a cost. You must be willing to lay aside the temptation to analyze the nature of God, seeking the evidence of His existence, and believe in Him. Pursue His wisdom. Above all the things in life that you will be tempted to pursue, pursue wisdom, and your life as a law enforcement officer will be abundantly fruitful.

Heavenly Father, thank you for the availability of your wisdom. Above all the things I could seek today, like riches and possessions, I ask for your wisdom, for in it are the keys to integrity and well-being. Amen.

Then you will win favor and a good name in the sight of God and man.

PROVERBS 3:4

Not on My Watch

Anytime there is a major operation going on, the general public wants to know all the details, but it is not tactically sound to reveal the strategies being used. This is one of the perils of twenty-four-hour live-streaming capabilities through smartphones. But at the end of the day, the motive and goal of these strategies is love. It's love for your fellow officer, for your family, for the victims and even the suspects, and even for yourself.

Whether you admit it or not, the root of all you do as a law enforcement officer is in being a servant. Your heart is that of a servant who will stop at nothing less than holding the line of peace, order, and justice. The goal of your daily command, whether as a street cop or a watch commander, is to ensure the leadership and commands you issue are all based on love for others. Serve with excellence, serve with pride, and command from a place of love.

> *Heavenly Father, remind me in all circumstances, whether in peace or in battle, that the root of all decisions involving humanity is based in love. To restore order, peace, or in pursuit of justice, I do it all for you. Amen.*

The goal of this command is love, which comes from a pure heart and a good conscience and a sincere faith.

1 TIMOTHY 1:5

Act of Honor

Leadership in law enforcement begins with you and the way you respond to your supervisors. This is a call to honor those who are responsible for your actions, safety, and well-being. Great leaders take time to develop, which begins the day you take your oath and the first time you pin your shield on your chest; it begins the first time you learn how to take an order and follow through with it, trusting the leadership and direction of your superior officers.

This is not a call to bow to dictatorship or immoral behavior; it is a call to make the job of those who rank higher than you a joy and not a burden. If your supervisor's job was a burden because of your actions, what benefit would it be to you? Acts of honor mean you may not like the person behind the badge but you respect the authority that person represents. Make your first duty an act of honor by showing confidence in your leaders today. In turn, you will honor God.

> *Heavenly Father, thank you for the gift of honor. Show me the power and purpose of honoring leaders and show me the reciprocating gift of honoring leaders on my path of development. Amen.*

Have confidence in your leaders and submit to their authority, because they keep watch over you as those who must give an account. Do this so that their work will be a joy, not a burden, for that would be of no benefit to you.

HEBREWS 13:17

Do the Right Thing, Even When No One Is Looking

We hear a lot of talk about "doing the right thing," but what exactly does that mean? Doing the right thing means we are guided by our internal conscience or integrity, our interactions with others, and also by submitting to leadership and authority and complying with the laws. We are influenced from a young age through teachings of faith, beliefs, training, and parenting, and each of these play a role in how we view what "doing the right thing" looks like.

When we base our thoughts, decisions, and actions on the standard of God's Word, we are safely placing ourselves in a position to do the right thing according to His ways. As we live in obedience to God, we live in a place of integrity and character, we bring honor to God and our leaders, and we position ourselves for earthly and heavenly rewards. Keep your eyes on the right prize, and do not be discouraged in times of difficulty. Do the right thing, even when no one is looking, for this is the measure of your character and the standard of your integrity as an officer.

Heavenly Father, thank you for the standard of what is right and just. Guide my feet and my mind, helping me to make the right decisions in your sight and in fairness to your people. Amen.

To do what is right and just is more acceptable to the LORD than sacrifice.

PROVERBS 21:3

Truth in Action

One of the first lessons you learned as a rookie was that if it isn't in the report, then it didn't happen. As long as you can articulate why you took a certain course of action, you should be okay. The definition of righteousness is "acting in accord with divine or moral law, free from guilt or sin; morally right or justifiable; a righteous decision."* While you will slip up along the way, your integrity will guide you. Your righteousness will lead you. You will not be destroyed because of the temptations you face or the mistakes you have experienced.

Truth in action is your actions being guided by God's Word, His principles instilled in your life, and the fruits they bear as a result of your consistency in pursuing Him. Truth in action is your perseverance through adversity and not being swayed at the first sign of trouble. Each of our lives are tarnished with sin, but because of Jesus we are made clean and equipped for faithful service to His kingdom.

> *Heavenly Father, let your Word be my guide and let your laws be written upon my heart so that my sins will not be seen through your eyes but through the price that Jesus paid. Guide my steps, and let the integrity I develop as I pursue you sustain me and guide me all my days. Amen.*

*The integrity of the upright guides them,
but the unfaithful are destroyed by their duplicity.*

PROVERBS 11:3

* "Righteous," *Merriam-Webster.com*, accessed October 25, 2017, https://www.merriam-webster.com/dictionary/righteous.

People of Integrity Serve the Helpless

It's no secret that policing is hard work—sometimes physically, sometimes mentally, and sometimes emotionally. And there are times it is tough on us in all three aspects. In Acts 20, Paul does not lead us to believe that serving others is a task to be taken lightly. It is tough work, and without the hearts to serve those who cannot help themselves, our world would be a darker place.

Our purpose goes beyond *just* hard work and serving others. Our purpose is to serve as a light to the rest of the world, that we can be both the line between total chaos, evil, and mayhem, and a life of peace, order, and lawfulness, all while being people of integrity, love, and purpose. As Jesus told us, "It is more blessed to give than to receive," we should strive to give our communities and the citizens who reside and visit them peace of mind, order, and safety.

Heavenly Father, thank you for the call to serve my community as a law enforcement officer, and thank you for the ability to give. I ask for your favor and blessing on all I do, as I pursue you, your purpose, and remain steadfast in integrity before you. Amen.

In everything I did, I showed you that by this kind of hard work we must help the weak, remembering the words the Lord Jesus himself said: "It is more blessed to give than to receive."

ACTS 20:35

Matters of the Heart

For some people, debating about senseless topics brings them pleasure and gratification. We as followers of Christ are to avoid foolish debates and doing things that do not advance the purpose of God's kingdom. As sworn peace officers, you often restore order in the lives of people to the way it was intended by God to be originally, but through a series of bad decisions or unfortunate events, they find themselves in the midst of total chaos, pain, or trouble.

There are things that we must decide on our own, whether they are good for us or bad for us. In Romans 14:14, the "unclean" thing referred to was food. We are not, as Christians, prohibited from eating food, but we are exhorted to eat using self-control. There are many issues that are not plainly listed in the Bible as sin, but there are matters of the heart or matters of your own personal convictions. You must decide what those convictions are, and, basing them on what the Bible says and on the foundation of a relationship with Jesus Christ, find the best practices in doing so.

> *Heavenly Father, thank you for giving me personal convictions based on my relationship with you. Give me the strength to stand by those convictions in difficult and trying times. Amen.*

I am convinced, being fully persuaded in the Lord Jesus, that nothing is unclean in itself. But if anyone regards something as unclean, then for that person it is unclean.

ROMANS 14:14

The Keys to Freedom

Like many of you, I have often found myself perplexed at some of the decisions people make. While at times these decisions are made under the influence of narcotics, illegal or abused prescription medications, many people make dumb decisions all on their own without the aid of any substance. One of the root causes of the downward spiral of our nation's moral status is the lack of fear of God, the lack of a moral conscience, and a lack of integrity. That is where you come into the picture.

When we fear God—meaning when we revere Him, the self-existing, holy, true God—we then find the knowledge of God because we enter into fellowship with Him. The true keys to freedom lie in having a reverent, holy fear of God, pursuing relationship with Him, and being filled with the knowledge of God—not just the knowledge but the understanding also. These are the keys to freedom. Take your keys and help someone else find freedom.

> *Heavenly Father, show me through your Word the benefits of reverently fearing you before I learn through life lessons, so I may find favor in your eyes, and the understanding and knowledge of who you are. Amen.*

Then you will understand the fear of the LORD and find the knowledge of God.

PROVERBS 2:5

Lay It All on the Table

Getting a call from dispatch to provide security for Jesus and getting there only for Him to refuse the escort—that's what John 2:24 sounds like. Jesus knew all the people around Him and didn't want any of them to handle Him. That may be off theologically, but the notion that He knows everything about us, including our thoughts, intentions, and motives, can be disconcerting. While our outward actions may look good and pure, what are our motives and intentions?

It's time we put all our hidden baggage at the feet of the one who has called us to give Him our burdens. God already knows what we need and what we are battling, but He desires a relationship with us and wants us to come to Him with thanksgiving. If you are burdened, know there is someone who cares, who desires you to bring your issues to Him. He knows everything you are carrying, secretly or known, and is willing to give you peace and strength for the journey.

> *Heavenly Father, I lay my burdens before you. I know you see and know all that is going on in my life, and you know my heart. I ask you to search me. As I draw near to you, draw near to me. Amen.*

But Jesus would not entrust himself to them,
for he knew all people. He did not need any testimony
about mankind, for he knew what was in each person.

JOHN 2:24–25

The Weight of Justice

From misdemeanors to felonies, having good cases is essential to keeping criminals off the street and providing relief to victims. It's also important for keeping the justice system balanced. But you are only responsible to have good cases; to write good, factual reports; and to gather evidence. When you become frustrated because someone doesn't receive the punishment you believe he or she deserves, it can cause you to become demotivated and lose interest in proactive police activity. However, it is important to remember that the weight of justice is not on your shoulders. You only enforce the law, protect the community, and serve those who need you.

You are part of God's divine plan for the people in your area. Your service, heart, and integrity are all pieces that God uses to reach the hearts and lives of people across our country. God is the one who bears the weight of justice and the balances of life, not you or me. Do not be discouraged if it seems like the scales are in favor of the evil or the corrupt, because soon enough things will be brought to balance by the Weight Keeper.

Heavenly Father, you control it all. Sometimes I don't understand it, but I trust you nevertheless. Help me to serve as a good and righteous piece of your force for good and for justice. Amen.

Honest scales and balances belong to the LORD;
all the weights in the bag are of his making.
PROVERBS 16:11

A Dependable Person Is a Blessing

Veteran officers, many who are now retired, talk about "hot-seating" patrol cars. This means that officers share cars from one shift to the next. If you ever had an officer who was a slob, leaving trash in the vehicle, not cleaning the vehicle interior or exterior, or not filling up the fuel tank, then you know the frustration of a person who is not dependable. Maybe they were not reliable when it came to keeping a patrol car clean, but if you needed them on a street, they could always be counted on. It's the nature of dependability that we look at, not just the circumstances surrounding the officer.

I'd rather have an officer who kept a nasty patrol car but was my best backup officer and first to jump in a fight if I needed help. A dependable person is a true blessing, and he or she will receive rich blessings in life. If you want to find dependable friends or dependable officers to back you up, then make sure that is what you exude toward others. Focus on who you want to be tomorrow, be dependable to those who need you, remain faithful to the Father and your community, and watch God honor your commitment.

> *Heavenly Father, thank you for your rich blessings in my life as I pursue you and as I am dependable to those whom I serve and serve with. Amen.*

A faithful person will be richly blessed.
PROVERBS 28:20

True Power of Humility

Mature people of excellence do not walk around telling others how good they are; their actions speak for themselves. Boasting about your own skills and accomplishments is one of the quickest ways to alienate yourself from others. If we feel the need to boast about our accomplishments, it is easy to stop the process when we remember our own success is nothing compared to the work Christ has done for us, and we can do nothing good apart from His power.

There is much required of us as law enforcement officers, but at the end of the day the essential requirements are that we act justly, love mercy, and walk humbly with God. There are many expectations on us from our agencies and from the public, but when we align ourselves with the expectations and standards of God's Word and walk in humility, we will find ourselves living in a place of favor and blessing with our colleagues. Strive to encourage those around you, build morale, and help those who serve with you and who may be facing difficult times.

Heavenly Father, in all I do today, with much power or little power, help me to do it in humility, knowing you hold the keys to heaven and earth, life and death, and power and success in your hands. Amen.

He has shown you, O mortal, what is good.
And what does the LORD require of you?
To act justly and to love mercy
and to walk humbly with your God.
MICAH 6:8

Willful Wrong

Blatantly committing wrong against your code of ethics is exponentially worse than an honest mistake, just to know to do good and do not do it is a sin. In some cases, when someone commits a crime in a heinous manner, where their actions are willful and they knowingly harmed someone, the consequences are much harsher than if the crime was under other circumstances. If you know to do good, then why would you choose not to do it? The answer to this question is rooted in integrity.

There is no doubt you, as a person of integrity, will never turn your head to a crime or person in need, and your heart for service will change the course of the lives of many people. Today, you know what needs to be done. You are required to place yourself in the face of danger for those who cannot defend themselves— the domestic-violence victims, the child-abuse victims, and the motorist in a vehicle collision. To them, you are an angel sent from heaven. Never turn a blind eye to an opportunity to change someone else's life. In so doing, there you will find significant blessings on the other side of the challenges that await.

Heavenly Father, show me what good I ought to do today, and give me the mindfulness, strength, and courage of heart to do it. Amen.

If anyone, then, knows the good they
ought to do and doesn't do it, it is sin for them.

JAMES 4:17

The Power of Integrity

I t is often said that if you are not generating complaints, then you are not doing your job correctly as a law enforcement officer. What this statement means is that if you are dealing a blow to the criminals on the streets, they will eventually fight back in more ways than one, including filing formal complaints against you. If you are a person of integrity with a pristine record, then you have little to be concerned about as it relates to frivolous complaints. Complaints will come—that is part of the profession—but vindication is sweet when you are found to be innocent of any wrongdoing.

The way we respond to adversity will have an impact on the duration of the process involving our situation. Let those who want to complain and fuss have their way, as long as we know we are doing right according to the law, according to the Constitution, and in the eyes of God. We have nothing to be worried about. Cover yourself and make sure you remain a person of integrity so you have access to the power of integrity when you need it most.

> *Heavenly Father, thank you for the vindication that comes as I pursue relationship with you and as I remain a person of integrity in my career. Guide my steps and my actions. Amen.*

Let the LORD judge the peoples. Vindicate me, LORD,
according to my righteousness,
according to my integrity, O Most High.

PSALM 7:8

Path to Victory

For nearly every situation you face, there is a plan or a strategy for victory. In fact, there are contingency plans for many issues you face on the street, and much preparation is required on your part. You know it is unreasonable to expect success as a law enforcement officer in any capacity without having clear direction, integrity, and character. But you also need significant planning and split-second decision-making abilities. Your path to victory may seem like a tricky one, but it is not impossible.

The role of integrity in your daily duties is like the role of your heart in living—without it, you cannot exist as a law enforcement officer. Your righteousness, your integrity, and your record as a peace officer may not be spotless—there may be baggage and there may be some skeletons in your closet—but when you turn your focus to pursuing Christ and accepting His sacrifice and payment for your sins, then He will make your path straight in all you do, giving you the direction for victory, every day and on every tour of duty.

> Heavenly Father, thank you for giving me total clarification and complete confidence in who you are and the direction you are taking me. I submit my life to your leading. Amen.

The righteousness of the blameless makes their paths straight, but the wicked are brought down by their own wickedness.

PROVERBS 11:5

Rewarded as Royalty

If you were thoroughly rewarded based on your performance on the job, you would likely receive numerous commendations and medals, maybe a promotion and even a raise. You did not take your oath to serve as a law enforcement officer because of the money. You did it out of a heart of service. But let's be real for a moment: It would be nice to see the treasures you have laid up because of the good you do on a daily basis, wouldn't it?

We are made clean only by the perfect sacrifice of Jesus. Because of Him, we have access to the Father and are empowered by the Holy Spirit. Therefore, when we are dealt with according to our righteousness, the Father sees His Son's payment for our sins and not our filthy past. Therefore, if we hold true to Psalm 18:20, when the Lord deals with us according to *our* righteousness, He sees Jesus and we are rewarded as royalty. This is only possible through a relationship with Jesus Christ. Now that's a commendation I'd like to receive!

> *Heavenly Father, thank you for the gift of salvation made possible only through the sacrifice of your Son, Jesus. Let my life be seen through the lens of what Jesus did for me and not my own filthy rags. Accept me as your own, Father God. Amen.*

The LORD has dealt with me according to my righteousness; according to the cleanness of my hands he has rewarded me.

PSALM 18:20

Fit
for Duty

JUNE

Training Time

There are many reasons why we should invest in keeping our bodies in excellent physical condition. From fights and pursuits to the daily stress of carrying the weight of the duty belt, we have added reasons and incentives to take good care of our bodies. But what about the stress of the job? If we take great care of our bodies, we will respond better to stressful situations. We know the importance of taking care of our physical bodies, but how much more important is it to take care of our spiritual person?

Dear friends, make it a priority to take good care of your spiritual being, as it is much more valuable than taking care of your physical body. You should train our spirit by exercising faith, meditating on God's marvelous words, and serving Him in love. Your bodies are temporary, and it is the only physical body you and I will have. Take good care of it to be a good steward of the gift you've been given. Training goes beyond qualifying on the range or getting new certifications. Training our skills is great, and staying physically fit is good, but training our spiritual person is what matters most.

Heavenly Father, give me proper perspective on the importance of taking care of my mind, body, and spirit to honor you. Amen.

Physical training is good, but training for godliness is much better, promising benefits in this life and in the life to come.

1 TIMOTHY 4:8 NLT

Take Care of Yourself

It is easy to develop negative and destructive habits to face the stress of policing, such as alcoholism, smoking, smokeless tobacco, overeating, not eating enough … well, you get the drift. If you break the smokeless tobacco habit but replace it with drinking fifteen sodas a day, have you really made any improvements? Or if you quit the tobacco and sodas but worry all the time, where is the improvement?

At the end of the day, it is your choice to take good care of your body. Even if you are not a believer in God's Word, you should have a desire to maintain good health, not only for optimum performance on duty but for better quality of life and longevity. I challenge you to look beyond the typical habits, look beyond the physical bad habits, and seek the deeper reason why they became habits to begin with. Take care of yourself, not only your physical body but your mental health and spiritual well-being too. As iron sharpens iron, challenge those around you to do the same.

Heavenly Father, guide my hands and feet. Reveal to me the unhealthy habits in my life, and give me strength to change them. Help me make taking care of my body a priority. Amen.

Don't you realize that all of you together are the temple of God and that the Spirit of God lives in you?
1 CORINTHIANS 3:16 NLT

Body Blows

It is easy to talk about getting up after being hit in the mouth, if you have never been in a fight. In fact, it is easy to talk about anything, but actually doing it is another issue. This is one of the reasons why we train diligently, not only to learn the skills but to become familiar with fighting. We want to know how to respond in an actual fight. Physical punishment can be discussed on a number of levels, whether it is the physical punishment we give our children as parents or the physical punishment our bodies endure in extreme weather conditions as we serve our communities. Or it could mean the physical punishment God sent in the Old Testament.

God doesn't send sickness, but we live in a fallen world. Thankfully, Jesus took the only physical punishment we ever have to pay. The punishment He bore for us paid the price for all our sins. Yes, your instructor or superiors may enforce physical training on you that may seem like punishment at times, but it is to prepare you to face evil in the streets. Body blows aren't always a bad thing. Prepare for battle!

Heavenly Father, thank you for strength to endure, power to win, and wisdom to know when to retreat. Amen.

Physical punishment cleanses away evil;
such discipline purifies the heart.
PROVERBS 20:30 NLT

Trembling Knees

You don't have to admit it, but there are times in the daily work of policing when fear could get the best of you. It results in a host of additional issues. The way I see it, we could allow fear to motivate us or debilitate us. Either way, it is our choice how we respond to it. If you have ever been in a situation when you knees shook, your hands trembled, your heart raced, and you felt like you were going to lose your last meal, then you know the importance of strengthened hands and knees.

If you are dealing with issues in your life today, know that while the fear may be present and real, it does not have control over you … unless you give it control. Hebrews 12:1–11 begins with a discussion about spiritual discipline and the correlation between physical discipline and discipline from God. Therefore, Hebrews 12:12 was likely speaking to those who had been dealt with by God. Walk in boldness today, even if your past, no matter how recent, was not pleasing to God. Today is a new day. Your future is going to be beautiful.

Heavenly Father, thank you for courage to face the vilest of enemies. Thank you in advance for victory in every battle. Amen.

So take a new grip with your tired hands and strengthen your weak knees.
HEBREWS 12:12 NLT

Soul Ties

Medical research has shown the correlation between negative emotions and physical sickness.* Maybe you have internalized anger or secret fears or unforgiveness stuffed away deep in your heart. Most of us relate healthy bodies to nutrition and exercise, but it goes deeper than those two categories. Sometimes we have to break ties with our past, whether it is failure to forgive ourselves of past mistakes or forgive someone else for something they may have done to us. Maybe it is time to move on and let the past fade away into history. Or maybe you need to confront the issues in a different and more direct way.

There are no easy answers in dealing with the negative emotions we harbor. It is possible, however, to be free from these emotions, which, in many cases, are the single barriers between where we are in life and where we desire to be. Negative emotions are faith inhibitors. I encourage you to strive for a 3 John 2 mentality. Begin breaking negative soul ties between your soul and negative emotions, and the rest of your health and wellness will fall in line.

> *Heavenly Father, reveal to me any negative emotions I am harboring that you want me to surrender to you. I know you want the best for me. Amen.*

Dear friend, I hope all is well with you and that you are as healthy in body as you are strong in spirit.

3 JOHN 2 NLT

---

* "Anxiety and Physical Illness," *Harvard Health*, June 2008, accessed July 27, 2017, http://www.health.harvard.edu/staying-healthy/anxiety _and_physical_illness.

In It to Win It

There are similarities between the analogy of a single runner winning a prize in a race of a bunch of people and the "narrow is the way" statement in the New Testament. Many people want the prize at the end of the race, but only a few will achieve it. What are you doing to ensure your completion of the race? Thankfully, we have been given everything we need to be victorious in this life. But just like a runner, we have to be mindful of a few things to give ourselves the best chance of success.

First, keep your heart guarded. There are many things vying for your passion, but only one who is worthy. Second, be sure to stay in your lane. If you cross over into another lane, you will cause great distraction, pain, and setback for another participant. Finally, pace yourself. If you begin the race by exhausting your limits, then you may not have enough power to finish strong. We are called to be more than conquerors in this life. Help someone else find victory and you will enjoy your victory much more.

> *Heavenly Father, keep watch over my heart, and help me keep my heart guarded in this race. Help me to finish better than I started and to gain strength and not grow tired. Amen.*

Don't you realize that in a race everyone runs, but only one person gets the prize? So run to win!

1 CORINTHIANS 9:24 NLT

For the Sake of Honor

There are times when it seems the work you do is endless and that holding the line is an overwhelming, unbearable task to do. At times, it may even seem to be a useless effort. Brothers and sisters, this is a lie. The work you do is not only needed, but it is also an act of honor to those brave souls who have paid the ultimate sacrifice. Those who gave their lives for others paved the way for you to serve with excellence. Do not allow discouragement to pin you down.

If for no other reason, serve for the sake of honor. Serve for the sake of those people who stood watch before us, walked the beat we walk today, and wore the badge we bear. Let us strip off the weight of discouragement that slows us down! Let us remove the weight of worry and serve with vigor and excellence. This is the day we have waited for and the moment we have all prepared for. For the sake of honor we serve.

> *Heavenly Father, embed in my spirit the culture of honor, and show me the significance of honoring leaders and those who have gone before me. Amen.*

Therefore, since we are surrounded by such a huge crowd of witnesses to the life of faith, let us strip off every weight that slows us down, especially the sin that so easily trips us up. And let us run with endurance the race God has set before us.

HEBREWS 12:1 NLT

A Winning Battle Plan

What good are your tools and training if you have no strategy when they are needed? Your purpose as a sworn peace officer is specific: you are to uphold the law and protect lives and property. Being precise with your aim is critical, not only to stopping the threat but for protecting life. Criminals would not take you seriously if you were fighting with the air.

There are a few things to keep you on target when you are running the race or fighting the good fight. First, remember your goals. Knowing what you are pursuing is good when you are in the trenches. Second, remember your training. Having the knowledge and skills to get the job done are essential to your success. Last, have passion. Passion will be the thing that pushes you that last hundred yards after you have run six miles. Giving you the boost you need to get to victory, passion will take you further than pursuit alone. Get the job done but have a plan, have the training, and never stop tweaking your skills.

> *Heavenly Father, I ask that you help me be prepared to hold the line between the evil that exists in this world and the innocent who do not know it exists. Give me the fire I need to get through the race and the grit to get through the fight with victory. Amen.*

Therefore I do not run like someone running aimlessly;
I do not fight like a boxer beating the air.
1 CORINTHIANS 9:26

Fit to Fight

The first time you engaged in a fight for your life on the streets, you didn't have to sit down and think about the training you received; it came to you naturally, much like second nature. It was because the knowledge and skills for hand-to-hand combat and other necessary techniques were deposited into you through classroom teaching and hands-on training. Much like the way your training was deposited in you, so faith is deposited in you through a relationship with Jesus Christ.

You are only fit to fight the good fight of faith through having first received the deposit of faith and keeping the faith and being a good steward of your gifts. You are not only commanded to keep and preserve the faith given to you, but you are challenged to stretch your faith. Anyone can pick a fight and anyone can start a race, but only those who are equipped, prepared, and properly trained can finish well. That takes a stretch of faith.

Heavenly Father, thank you for the deposit of faith, for the gifts and power to accomplish the mission you have placed me here to do. Thank you for victory. Amen.

I have fought the good fight, I have finished the race, I have kept the faith.

2 TIMOTHY 4:7

June 10

The Toll of Worry

Worry is something we often don't think about as a major issue because it has often been with us so long that it is deeply embedded in our thought processes. But when you leave for your duty, you don't want to take the pressures of your family life, finances, or other issues to work with you. Not only are you placing yourself at greater risk, but you are also placing those who depend on you at greater risk too.

The toll of worry is significant. It is mental and physical, internal and external. It affects us as individuals and those we love, care about, and work with. The toll of worry can be life-changing because it divides our attention and focus. When we are holding the line on duty, that is not something we need to deal with. Take inventory of the worries you are harboring. You don't have to discuss them with anyone if you don't want to, but talk to God about them. He's listening, and He's ready to give you peace. Tomorrow will come, but focus on the task at hand for today.

Heavenly Father, I confess my issue with worrying. You do not want me to worry but to have total confidence in you. Today, I place my situations, circumstances, and other worries in your hands. Help me to focus on the work at hand today. Amen.

Therefore do not worry about tomorrow, for tomorrow will worry about itself. Each day has enough trouble of its own.

MATTHEW 6:34

A Hero's Courage

When the world thinks of a hero, one of the first things many think about are people just like you. The reason they picture you as a hero is because you are willing to place yourself in the face of imminent danger, making split-second decisions to save lives, stop violence, reduce crime, and serve the public. The courage you possess is not in vain and it is not used foolishly.

One of your greatest assets is your relationship with God, especially in difficult times. It is in those times when you can rely on your relationship with God, His Word, and prayer to sustain you. A hero's courage is not blazon and boastful, nor is it careless and reckless. A hero's courage is perfectly balanced with faith, training, and confidence in self, God, skills, and your team. It is because of a hero's courage that our world is not in total and utter chaos today. Hold the line, hold the faith, and cling to the promises of God. He will not fail you.

> *Heavenly Father, thank you for your promises that you will not fail me, that I can cast my fears at your feet, and that you will strengthen me in the time of need. Give me righteous courage in the moment of fear. Amen.*

So do not fear, for I am with you;
do not be dismayed, for I am your God.
I will strengthen you and help you;
I will uphold you with my righteous right hand.

ISAIAH 41:10

The Power of a Healthy Mind-set

Having the right mind-set can mean the difference between going home in one piece or not going home at all. It is critical to have a healthy mind-set, but it is also necessary to know what the root of a negative mind-set is. The negative mind-set is governed by our natural desires to rebel against the nature of God. We can develop a healthy mind-set only when we focus on the things God speaks to us through the Bible, through healthy eating and exercise, and through healthy relationships.

We give power to defeat instead of victory and life when we focus on the negative circumstances we see with our eyes. As believers, we are called to walk by faith, which is a critical part of having a healthy mind-set. Be challenged to check your mind-set today. Are you focused on the right things? Are you dwelling on the past? Are you worried about the future? If you can answer yes to the last two questions, then take your problems to Jesus in prayer. Through studying the Bible and prayer, you can experience a new mind-set today.

Heavenly Father, thank you for a clear mind, a mind focused on the tasks at hand, a mind that is governed by the Spirit and not the flesh. I submit my mind to your power and not my own. Amen.

The mind governed by the flesh is death, but the mind governed by the Spirit is life and peace.

ROMANS 8:6

The Spirit of an Officer

There's a lot of talk about decisions that affect morale by administration or supervisors. We've all heard of the will of officers getting the "Blue Flu" and walking off the job, all because the spirit of their department was negatively affected beyond a workable point. As law enforcement officers, we do not back down from a challenge, a threat, or a fight—our spirit is not timid and it is not easily broken. The heart and soul of every man and woman behind the badge is to serve and protect, which means facing the fiercest of enemies at times. There is no place for a timid spirit in this profession.

We gain power over fear and timidity when we accept Jesus Christ into our lives and receive the Holy Spirit, as the Spirit does not give us fear or timidity. He gives us power, love, and a sound mind or self-discipline. So while others struggle with the power to defeat negative thoughts, fear, worry, or lack of self-discipline, as a believer, you have the Spirit within you to face it all.

> *Heavenly Father, thank you for equipping me with your Spirit, a Spirit of victory, a Spirit to face and overcome adversity, a Spirit to face fear, hate, and to operate in love and self-discipline. Amen.*

For the Spirit God gave us does not make us timid,
but gives us power, love and self-discipline.

2 TIMOTHY 1:7

The Cycle of Peace

M any of your seemingly insignificant duties are necessary for keeping the peace and, in many cases, giving peace in our communities. For some, responding to solve a noise complaint is going to give them tremendous peace, especially if they need the sleep so they can focus on their work the following day. You give more peace than you realize, which is a result of perseverance through the resistance you face from those who are insubordinate to authority.

When we restore order in the lives of citizens, we give peace to them. Jesus gave us His peace, a peace that would give us power over fear. Today, you may encounter someone who has experienced a breach of peace in his or her life, and you were beckoned to restore that peace. As a public servant, do your best to ease their troubles, calm their fears, and soothe their pains. But nothing compares to the peace that God gives. Walk in God-given peace today and become a vessel through which it flows to others. Become a healthy part of the cycle of peace.

> *Heavenly Father, thank you for using me to bring peace to your people. Thank you for strength to stand, courage to fight, and words to speak in difficult moments. Amen.*

Peace I leave with you; my peace I give you.
I do not give to you as the world gives.
Do not let your hearts be troubled and do not be afraid.

JOHN 14:27

Are You a Worrier or Warrior?

When you think of a law enforcement officer who is fit for duty, you probably think of a person who is confident, stable, and consistent. It is a difficult task to balance being a worrier and a law enforcement officer. The truth is that most of the things we worry about will never occur. We often craft in our minds scenarios that cause terrible health issues and distract us from being effective in our duties when we are anxious or worry about problems on the job or at home.

So today, if you are guilty of worrying or being anxious, like most everyone else who has ever breathed air, then resolve to surrender those bad habits to your Master. We are bound by love to serve Him, and it is because of that love He wants us to cast our anxieties and cares on Him. Take regular inventory of your thoughts and check your "warrior/worrier" status often to make sure you are on the right side of the fence. Begin today and every day with the best preparation—a clear mind and a full heart—and give up the worry and anxiety today.

Heavenly Father, thank you that you care for me enough to take my worries, anxieties, and cares. I surrender them to you; I give them to you. I no longer want them in my life. Thank you for peace. Amen.

Cast all your anxiety on him because he cares for you.

1 PETER 5:7

The Thankful Servant

Perspective can change a lot. If we were thankful for all we had, would we have time to constantly desire more? If many of us took this approach, society would see a shift in the right direction. As it is now, however, many issues we deal with are because of self-ishness, greed, ungratefulness, and hate. A thankful attitude shifts our minds off the negative and places our perspective on the good, on what we have, and on our accomplishments.

It is difficult to be a thankful public servant who is fit for duty *and* a person who is battling worry or self-centered anxieties. In many cases, we have turned our focus inward and taken it off the mission, the people we serve and those we serve with. Shifting our focus to a thankful lifestyle forces the inward centeredness to be removed and replaces it with a healthy focus on God, others, and mission. Ask God to help you with shifting your focus and lifestyle to that of thankfulness, and watch the useless worry and weighty anxiety begin to dissipate from your life.

Heavenly Father, you did not design me to carry anxiety or worry. I give it to you. Please give me a heart of thankfulness and show me the true gift and power of having a heart for thankfulness as a law enforcement officer. Amen.

Do not be anxious about anything,
but in every situation, by prayer and petition,
with thanksgiving, present your requests to God.
PHILIPPIANS 4:6

A God of Order and Peace

The scene of a shooting is usually chaotic. The first order of business when arriving on scene is to eliminate the threat if it still exists, then to render aid to the victims, gathering witness information, etc. When you step on the scene, the atmosphere immediately begins to change, and if the threat remains, notice is served that the violence is ending. Your function as a law enforcement officer not only brings order to chaotic situations, but it also brings peace in a moment of violence.

While you cannot go and counsel the victims for the remainder of their lives after a traumatic incident, the initial encounter with you often leaves a lasting impression on them and the direction they take in handling the course of trauma and healing. Your words, demeanor, and calm presence are all measures used by God in moments intended by the enemy to destroy the lives of innocent people. Don't take the work you do for granted. Today, as you serve your community, remember the God you serve is not a God of disorder but a God of peace, and you are His instrument to bring peace to His people.

> *Heavenly Father, thank you for giving me the skills and power to restore order and bring peace in my community. Direct my words and my steps; guide my hands as I serve you. Amen.*

*For God is not a God of disorder but of peace—
as in all the congregations of the Lord's people.*

1 CORINTHIANS 14:33

Never out of the Fight

There may come a day when you engage someone who is stronger than you, someone who refuses to be taken into custody, someone who is determined he or she is never going back to prison. It doesn't take long to find yourself on the wrong side of the fight. If that day comes, remember your training. Fight with total confidence. It may seem like hours waiting on backup in a two-minute, all-out fight for your life, but those two minutes could mean the difference between life and death.

Just because you are in distress and pressed down, your face against the asphalt and the suspect reaching for your gun, doesn't mean you are out of the fight. You are never out of the fight. There's another grunt left. There's another swing, another kick, another move; there's a warrior waiting to rise at the right moment to get up off the ground. This is your moment to rise. Maybe you have been oppressed spiritually, but today is a new day. You are never out of the fight, unless you quit, and that is not an option.

Heavenly Father, give me another flicker of fight. Give me one more arrow with more accuracy. Give me more wisdom and discernment than those who seek to destroy me. Give me strength to face whatever may come today. Amen.

The LORD works righteousness
and justice for all the oppressed.
PSALM 103:6

Your Peacekeeper

There are many hours of ongoing training beyond academy. We are required to stay fresh on weapons training, law, and any other updates that come along. One area of training is in firearms. This training is unique in that, if we do not train often, our skills will deteriorate over time. Practice is required. If you go to the range today and try to talk on your phone, not only is the range master probably going to dropkick you, but you will not be accurate if you fire a round. It is because your mind is not on the target.

When our minds are steadfast, or when we lean on God with our minds, we live in a place of peace. But Isaiah 26:3 doesn't stop with saying we will have "peace." He says we would have "perfect peace" if we keep our minds steadfast on God and trust in Him. This means we are not trusting in our strength alone, worrying about our problems or the issues that may come tomorrow, but we lean on the promises of God. He will not fail. If He promises perfect peace, then He will give it, even in the face of adversity.

> *Heavenly Father, I choose to lean on you. I need you and cannot do life without you. I place my focus on knowing you, loving you, and demonstrating my trust in you. Amen.*

You will keep in perfect peace those whose minds are steadfast, because they trust in you.

ISAIAH 26:3

I've Got Your Back

When you receive a new assignment, the first thing you usually think about is who your partner will be. We often say to our new partner, "I've got your back." We say it to reassure each other that we are not alone and we are on the same team. There are times, however, when it may not seem like anyone else has our backs. Considering the number of dangers we face, it is good to know there are others who look out for our well-being. There's a reason you strap on body armor though. But even the armor of God doesn't mention a cover for our backs.

Thankfully, over two thousand years ago, Jesus provided the spiritual covering for our backs when He bore our sins on the cross. That was the ultimate, "I've got your back." Jesus took "I've got your back" to the max. There's no greater love than the love He demonstrated for us, and it should be an example of how we protect each other on and off duty.

Heavenly Father, thank you for covering my areas of weakness that are exposed for the enemy. Thank you for protecting me and providing an example of covering others. Amen.

"He himself bore our sins" in his body on the cross, so that we might die to sins and live for righteousness; "by his wounds you have been healed."

1 PETER 2:24

Good Medicine for the Heart

If you aren't careful, it won't be long before you develop a cynical attitude toward people because of what you deal with on duty. You see some of the most terrible sides of humanity, which can take a toll on anyone. You can let all the negative emotions layer up over the years before they fester into a mess and leave you wondering what happened, or you can make changes now. One of those changes occurs in your heart. Proverbs 17:22 refers to a "cheerful heart," but what makes a heart cheerful?

For one, it is good to pace yourself; you cannot save the world in a day. Knowing your limits allows you clear borders to operate within. Learning to number your days is a tremendous way to gain a cheerful heart, because you learn the perceived or real problems in life are not as bad as you originally thought and you soon realize they have little to no eternal significance. When our center focus is Christ, our hope is not placed in this world or anything in this world, which significantly changes the status of our heart and should encourage each believer in Jesus.

> *Heavenly Father, I thank you for giving me a cheerful heart! Even in turmoil, adversity, chaos, and pain, thank you that my heart is focused on you and not on this world. Amen.*

A cheerful heart is good medicine,
but a crushed spirit dries up the bones.
Proverbs 17:22

Fully Equipped,
Completely Supplied

There's no such thing as having too much ammunition. There's also no such thing as having too many guns, but all those cost money, and lots of it. It takes more than less-lethal firearms or hand-to-hand techniques to police nowadays, and it takes more than these to survive the streets. You have to be nearly the perfect person, and have some knowledge of almost everything and the memory of an elephant. You are required to be fully equipped at all times and 100 percent supplied with everything you need to get the job done.

In most departments, getting those supplies requires you to make a request. In Philippians 4:19, Paul was speaking a blessing over a church who had recently given sacrificially to help meet an urgent need of his. His blessing was reflective of the nature of God, meaning that "according to the riches of his glory in Christ Jesus" is that He has it all. If you doubt your skills, abilities, or knowledge, or wonder if you will make the next bill payments, remember who you serve. He will not fail you if you will entrust your needs to Him.

Heavenly Father, thank you for equipping me and supplying me with all the needs I had for the mission. Thank you for giving me all I need in life. Amen.

And my God will meet all your needs according to the riches of his glory in Christ Jesus.

PHILIPPIANS 4:19

The Unwise Leader

It is possible for you to encounter some questionable leadership decisions over the span of your career. In fact, it may have already occurred. The challenge with gaining rank and experience is balancing confidence and wisdom, and not crossing the border into arrogance and haughtiness. Those are dangerous places to live and walk in, and the end results rarely end well. When our perceptions of ourselves are unhealthy to any extreme, it alienates us from family, friends, and coworkers. And if we see ourselves as something we may truly not be, then we position ourselves for serious pain, letdown, and potential disaster.

While the daunting task of submitting to poor leadership is less than appealing, as subordinates we are required and commanded to respect those in authority and to make their jobs easier. Today, take inventory of your own perception of yourself. If it is at any extreme and unhealthy, then realize the fear of God is the beginning of making the necessary changes. Don't get caught up in your own accomplishments to the point you cannot effectively serve your community.

Heavenly Father, I would be nothing without you. You have given me so many gifts, but I submit to you and ask you to help me avoid participating in or committing any evil acts, and to fear you in a holy, reverent manner. Amen.

Do not be wise in your own eyes;
fear the Lord and shun evil.
PROVERBS 3:7

Call for Assistance

There's no question who the public calls when they are in trouble—they call 911. Being fit for duty means we are fit not just physically but mentally, emotionally, and in every way possible. So that leaves the question, who do law enforcement officers call on when they are in trouble? Like Jeremiah 17:14, calling on God through prayer is our plea for help. We can call on Him, and He will hear us. When someone from our community calls for a police response, they have confidence that we will respond and solve the issue.

You can call on God today knowing He will hear you, respond, and solve the matter. My challenge to you today is this: be open to the *way* He solves the matter. Often, we have an idea in our mind of how we believe God should handle a situation, but His plans are better than ours, and, as difficult as that is to understand, we must trust His plan. If you call on God for assistance, then He will come, and He will not fail you.

> *Heavenly Father, thank you for being a call, a breath, a whisper away from responding to me. You live in my heart, you are always with me, and you eagerly await my requests for assistance. Thank you for coming to my assistance. Amen.*

Heal me, Lord, and I will be healed; save me
and I will be saved, for you are the one I praise.

JEREMIAH 17:14

Record of Confession

Confessing our wrongdoings to another person is countercultural and will make people think something is wrong with us. In law enforcement, confessions usually come during a criminal investigation, but in this case, a confession is healthy, wholesome, and generally not criminal in nature. Healing comes through our confession. Confession allows us to remove the harbored negative emotions of guilt, remorse, or shame. It is best done with someone with whom you can trust sensitive information.

The record of our confession before the heavenly Father is blotted out by the price paid by Jesus only when we accept His sacrifice in our lives. When we reject Jesus, we reject the power of confession, healing, and the effectiveness of prayer. Today, spend a few moments asking God to reveal any suppressed sin in your life, and ask Him for wisdom regarding confession. If you have an accountability partner at church or in a small group, talk with him or her about it. You will be glad you did when you experience a new level of power and effectiveness in prayer.

Heavenly Father, thank you for a clean conscience, for power to overcome sin, and for courage to confess when I do sin. Thank you for healing and restoration in my life. Amen.

Therefore confess your sins to each other and pray for each other so that you may be healed. The prayer of a righteous person is powerful and effective.
JAMES 5:16

Your Fine Has Been Paid

A wealthy man made his way to the municipal court late one afternoon with a pocket full of money. He walked into the magistrate's office and said, "Good afternoon, I needed to see if I could pay a few fines off please." The magistrate looked up his records only to find he had no fines: "Sir, there are no outstanding fines owed." The generous man went on to pay off several fines for minor traffic violations for random people. Can you imagine as those people came to pay their citations and found out their fines had been paid?

We were born into a sinful nature that was doomed from the start. But because God loved us so much, He sent His Son to live and die for each of us, and He paid our price for all our sins forevermore. If we reject the belief and refuse to accept His gift, then we cause double the trouble for ourselves. The peace we have now and for all eternity is because someone else paid our price, and that someone else is Jesus Christ. Your fines have been paid.

> *Heavenly Father, thank you for loving me so much that you sent your only Son to die for my sins. I love you, I receive and accept the gift of salvation, and I ask you to reign in my life. Amen.*

But he was pierced for our transgressions,
he was crushed for our iniquities; the punishment
that brought us peace was on him.

ISAIAH 53:5

Unbroken

A law enforcement career can span two decades or more, and with that comes a lot of suppressed memories, some of which are good and some are nightmares. There are certain calls that will break the heart and soul of any man or woman behind the badge, no matter how tough they are on the outside. The longer we let these pains go unaddressed, the worse they will be when we finally address them. But there is a better way. Science has shown the power of faith and its integral role in dealing with trauma in our lives.

Psalm 147:3 is one example of how God heals our physical wounds and pains and also our emotional and mental pains. When we allow healing through seeking assistance, reading His Word, prayer, and healthy fellowship, God will take those broken memories, those broken emotions, and bring healing to us. As peacemakers, it would be foolish to assume we never encounter violence or have negative emotions and thoughts along the journey in serving our community. Today, surrender those vulnerabilities to your Creator. He wants to bind up your wounds and heal your broken heart.

Heavenly Father, thank you for the promise of healing. I surrender the negative painful memories I may be harboring from my past and give them to you. I now ask for total healing and peace and discernment and wisdom on how to move forward. Amen.

He heals the brokenhearted and
binds up their wounds.
PSALM 147:3

In Good Hands

S ome people say God doesn't have favorites, but I tend to disagree. If there are two people in a room with God (figuratively speaking, of course), and one of them uses his or her gifts and serves and the other sits and complains about everything, never contributing with his or her gifts, which one do you think God will honor? When we live in alignment with God's Word, our lives are covered with His favor and blessing. That is not to suggest there will never be times of adversity, but we will experience a level of living like no other can offer.

When we live in "God's hand," when we live according to His ways and principles, we are under His umbrella of protection and blessing. We remain living in a fallen world, but we are in good hands with God. He will use what used to bring us down to propel us to blessing, victory, and abundant life. Law enforcement is not always easy, but with faith in God we can be victorious in anything we pursue.

> *Heavenly Father, thank you for holding me in your hands, right where I need to be, safe from the dangers of the enemy. Direct my steps today and every day. Amen.*

I put to death and I bring to life,
I have wounded and I will heal,
and no one can deliver out of my hand.

DEUTERONOMY 32:39

Help Is on the Way

Our response time to calls for service are measured in minutes and seconds, which can mean the difference between life or death. Time is how we, as humans, measure life, progress, and many other things along our journey. However, it is measured significantly different on God's watch. When we are in a place of need, we often expect a response immediately. When we base our faith on the speed of God's response to our needs, we are foolishly using two separate standards of measurement. God's time is not our time and will often not align with our clocks.

When we call on God for help, He will come. He will address our needs according to His Word, and He will not fail us. However, when we place worry and anxiety ahead of our faith in what His Word says He will do for us, and allow the timing to discourage us, we can further delay the victory prepared for our lives. Know that, if you are in need, help is on the way the moment you call for it. It will arrive, not a moment too late.

Heavenly Father, thank you for confidence in your timing. Thank you for a heart that leans on your clock and your timing, and has total faith that you will come to my aid. Amen.

Lord *my God, I called to you for help,*
and you healed me.

PSALM 30:2

Keys to the City

There are no magic formulas for eradicating crime from our communities. It can come only through good, solid police work, consistency, and good relationships with the people in your area. If every leader were to seek the will of God, what would our country look like? It wouldn't take long before we experienced a nationwide movement of healing. If we are going to be completely fit for duty as believers in Jesus Christ, we need to have our hearts aligned with the mission of God.

We've been given access to the heart of God through Jesus Christ. He desires for our hometowns to experience healing from ravaged, crime-stricken rampages, and to be restored to a time of peace and order. Believe it or not, He is using you to accomplish His mission today. Don't take your eyes off the prize and don't be discouraged; instead, call on God, humble yourself, and pray, and He will come to your aid. Give God the keys to your city.

> *Heavenly Father, thank you for giving me a right heart to pursue you, to turn from my sin, to humble myself before you, and to call out to you. I know you will hear me, forgive me, and heal my community. Amen.*

If my people, who are called by my name,
will humble themselves and pray and seek my face and turn
from their wicked ways, then I will hear from heaven,
and I will forgive their sin and will heal their land.

2 CHRONICLES 7:14

Defense
Strategy

JULY

Armed with Wisdom

Maybe you have heard veteran law enforcement officers talk about careless courage. You know someone like that too, I bet—no fear, no strategy, just lay it all on the line and go in, guns blazing. I'm not suggesting there are never times we must go into harm's way without hesitation, but we need to have the proper training and mind-set if we do. After initial training, a person's mind-set is such an overlooked and rarely discussed tool. The best thing you could ever do is learn to think, know when to speak, and know when to do work.

King Solomon remains heralded as one of the wisest men to have ever lived. He is famous for his wealth and possessions, but few know of his mistakes. Why? King Solomon sought God for His wisdom instead of asking for stuff. Solomon knew the importance of wisdom and its value over all other things a person could attain. It's not a matter of *if* you will encounter danger, but *when* you will encounter it. When you do, having supernatural wisdom gained only from God can guide you to victory or help you know when to retreat.

> *Heavenly Father, grant me your wisdom above all else. I understand the fear of you is the beginning of true wisdom, and I submit this day to your will. Amen.*

The prudent see danger and take refuge,
but the simple keep going and pay the penalty.

PROVERBS 22:3

Prudent in Pursuit

You are expected to be a proactive yet professional law enforcement officer in all you do. Acting with consideration of innocent civilians means knowing when to back off in pursuit of a suspect. Prudence is wisdom looking forward, not only thinking about the here and now but how your current decisions will affect you and those around you in the future. You have undoubtedly heard the phrase "risk versus reward" in your training. Think about your decisions. Will they honor God, your department, and your badge?

Shunning evil is not something you have the liberty to do. Your job is to confront it, enforce the law, save lives, and protect property. But doing so in an even-tempered manner is critical to your reputation. Don't be known as someone who loses his or her temper quickly over minuscule things. Your calm demeanor can escalate or de-escalate a situation and have a permanent impact on the lives of other people. Live as a person who fears God, seeks His wisdom, and makes decisions with the future in mind, not only the here and now.

> *Heavenly Father, give me discernment today in all the decisions I will be asked to make. Help me make the best decisions for the people I serve. Amen.*

The wise fear the LORD and shun evil,
but a fool is hotheaded and yet feels secure.
PROVERBS 14:16

Unwavering Faith

At some point in your career, you have probably been affected by someone who was unethical in his or her duties or even committed crimes as a public servant. This type of negative behavior brings a great deal of criticism to the law enforcement profession, even though those who are responsible make up a small percentage of the entire profession. When we condone or commit crimes or unethical behavior, we give way to those we confront as law enforcement officers. Each of us are held to a higher standard because of the authority we have been given.

Maybe it didn't begin as a big deal. Maybe it was just an innocent lie or some other seemingly innocent action, but before you knew it, you needed legal representation and were looking for another job. That is how fast it all can deteriorate. Hold yourself accountable, but don't forget you are also responsible for your fellow officer if you have knowledge of improper behavior or activity. Don't muddy the waters; don't give way to the evil you confront.

> *Heavenly Father, give me strength in the face of temptation, strength to stand, and wisdom in difficult circumstances. Amen.*

Like a muddied spring or a polluted well are the righteous who give way to the wicked.
PROVERBS 25:26

Wound Care

Today is a national day of celebration of our independence as a country, but many times remembering the sacrifice required to enjoy freedom is lost amidst the celebrations, cookouts, fireworks, and family gatherings. Today, you may be celebrating independence from a past hurt, a bad memory, or a terrible addiction. Maybe you are not celebrating like everyone else and instead are answering domestic-violence calls and investigating traffic collisions. One day, we will *all* be free from pain and hurt.

This is the hope we have in salvation through Jesus Christ. His promises are always *yes* and *amen*. It is critical that we embrace the promises of God's Word, especially while we deal with the pain and hurt in our world. You can enjoy freedom, knowing there is a promise of peace, healing, and total victory. Your presence represents this hope to many people you may encounter today. Not only are you a guaranteed recipient of God's promises, but you are also a messenger of His promises. Walk in confidence today, knowing not only that God's promises are for you but also that you are part of His plan to bring healing to your community.

Heavenly Father, help me remember the importance of walking in your power, expressing your love, and being compassionate to hurting people. Amen.

"He will wipe every tear from their eyes.
There will be no more death" or mourning or crying or pain,
for the old order of things has passed away.
REVELATION 21:4

Pain Management

On occasion, you may find yourself wondering if God has forgotten you. When you are consistently serving others, it is easy to forget about taking care of your needs. Years of responding to and witnessing traumatic pain takes a toll on any human. Through all the training we have experienced, seldom do we address pain management from an internal perspective. After all, we aren't supposed to talk about those things. But past pain is a weapon the enemy can use to bring us defeat and thwart our God-given purpose if not properly addressed.

Every single moment of pain you have ever experienced or witnessed is recorded by God. He sees all and knows all. We have all wondered why God "allows" terrible things to happen. The answer is simple: We live in a fallen world and sin has consequences. Our hope of healing spans beyond this life, and our impact goes far beyond our career in law enforcement. If you need pain management, God's eyes are not passing you by. In fact, He is the solution to your pain. Much like you have to document everything you do on duty, so God has a record of your life.

Heavenly Father, help me to find healing from the things that bring me pain and misery. Help me to realize I am a human being and will have more positive impact when I operate in total healing. Amen.

Record my misery; list my tears on your scroll—
are they not in your record?

PSALM 56:8

A Partner
through the Darkest Hours

Whether you are responding to a violent crime in progress or a shoplifting call, or are on foot patrol, you are never alone. It can seem as though you are on the streets by yourself at times, but having the promise of an eternal partner will give you the confidence you need to be successful and safe on duty. Take, for instance, responding to a residential burglary in progress. Your training has completely prepared you for the steps you should take to safely, successfully, and securely conduct your job functions.

At the end of the day, you need to know you will never be alone. There are men and women who are completely willing to serve and are fully equipped to do so. However, there may be times when you are alone for what seems to be an eternity. There is a strength within you that, when called upon, will not fail. You must do your part, and part of that is to properly train and prepare, which includes engaging in regular prayer. God will not fail you.

Heavenly Father, gently remind me that you walk with me, even when I feel like I am alone. I acknowledge you are the sole source of my strength. Amen.

Even though I walk through the darkest valley,
I will fear no evil, for you are with me;
your rod and your staff, they comfort me.

PSALM 23:4

The Hands of Justice

For everything with a beginning, there is also an end. The end may not be in sight to you or anyone else at this point, but the end is already established. However, now may not be the "proper" time for the end for something or someone. Proverbs 16:4 is a great reminder that even the wicked have an established end to their plans and actions. You, without a doubt, will be the end of someone's criminal activity today. Your courage, wisdom, experience, and professionalism will take a career criminal off the streets and bring total disaster to his or her plans of chaos.

To this end, you are marked as the hands of justice, enforcing the law and removing wicked and evil people from society. If you have been discouraged by the outcomes of trials in the past, remember your job is not to prosecute or judge but to enforce and apprehend criminals. Your role is part of a complex and often imperfect criminal justice process. Focus on doing your job with excellence and bringing an end to the plans of those who bring pain, frustration, and disaster to the lives of innocent and helpless people.

Heavenly Father, reinforce my training and your promises, and surround me with your protection. Position me to be the "proper end" to the wicked plans of evil people today. Amen.

*The LORD works out everything to its proper end—
even the wicked for a day of disaster.*

PROVERBS 16:4

Opportunity for the Miraculous

There are opportunities for us to be a miracle to someone today, if we look for the opportunities. When we are on duty, we can deliver comfort and peace, restore order, and give back life to those who have lived through what could be described as hell. Through your service, you can take what the enemy intended for harm against a victim and help bring comfort and healing. Your interaction with individuals can be life-altering for the good.

What is the value of adversity? It is whatever we allow to come from it. If we choose to complain, we dig deeper in negative, poisonous living. If we choose to believe God can take whatever comes against us and use it for good, then that is where we will find ourselves. Life isn't a magic fairy tale; it's the result of faith, consistency in relationship with Christ, treating others right, forgiveness, and remaining strong through adversity. God will take the difficult times and use them to elevate us to a place of empowered living. Look for the opportunities for the miraculous.

Heavenly Father, help me see the opportunities where I can be used by you in the lives of other people to demonstrate your love and kindness. Thank you, Father, for turning what was meant to harm me into good. Amen.

You intended to harm me, but God intended it all for good.
He brought me to this position so I could
save the lives of many people.
GENESIS 50:20 NLT

Dealing with Evil

As you exit your patrol car, the suspect you were on the lookout for takes off on foot. He's running as fast as humanly possible, jumping fences and turning corners, attempting to elude you. As you give chase, you call out your location, the suspect's description, and soon you hear the cavalry coming. The suspect probably didn't tell you he was going to run, at least verbally. His body language and eyes gave it away, but his feet had to move. Your duty is to apprehend the suspect, remain safe, protect the innocent, and prepare a solid case.

The difference between good and evil is the fact that evil people want to move quickly without considering others. Evil is not logical or rational. Those who pursue evil schemes, whether violent or nonviolent, will face the consequences. They will eventually have to pay for their wrongdoing if their schemes were criminal. When that day comes, you may be the wall of reckoning. When you are faced with dealing with evil, deal firmly, fairly, swiftly, and justly; do not succumb to the demands to surrender of evil. Evil may attempt to elude you, but you are prepared for this day.

> *Heavenly Father, make my feet swift, give me the strength and endurance needed to pursue the evil in my community, and protect me every step of the way. Amen.*

Their feet rush into sin;
they are swift to shed innocent blood.
They pursue evil schemes;
acts of violence mark their ways.

ISAIAH 59:7

Defending the Righteous

Part of your duty is protecting those who cannot defend themselves. It is an honor to be tasked with standing between their well-being and the evil that lurks beside them. It is reassuring to know God will rescue those who are His, but He is also a just God who will give protection to those who have no way of knowing right from wrong. Life is full of difficult questions, many to which no human, regardless of scientific, philosophical, or theological degrees, can answer.

We can rest in knowing that God will rescue the godly in their time of need. Those who seem to go unpunished for their sins will pay for their evil deeds. Stand up for what is right, moral, true, and good. Most of this world has surrendered their convictions in the name of political correctness, and the least we can do is hold the line of righteousness and justice. God will not turn a blind eye to good or evil.

Heavenly Father, thank you for the task of defending the innocent, helpless, defenseless, weak, and oppressed. Thank you for the opportunity to reflect who you are to my community today. Amen.

For if God did not spare angels when they sinned, but sent them to hell, putting them in chains of darkness to be held for judgment; ... if this is so, then the Lord knows how to rescue the godly from trials and to hold the unrighteous for punishment on the day of judgment.

2 PETER 2:4, 9

The Reason for Lawlessness

The criminal justice system is in place according to the Constitution of our land, but, in the name of freedom and liberty, we have used technicalities to bend and break rules, justify sin, and remove the chains from evil. We've set free some of the most violent people in the world in the name of due process or because of technicalities. The fact that they broke the law in a violent manner had no bearing in the matter. The reason for lawlessness in so many parts of our country, however, isn't the lack of laws, the lack of law enforcement, or the lack of good government. The reason for lawlessness is sin.

We cannot continue to justify sin and expect lawlessness to dissipate at any point in our lifetime. As long as sin exists, we will have job security. Some, however, thrive on the existence and thought of anarchy in America. But anarchy is a weapon against order and government, and you are the line to hold the peace and keep order. Never allow the political propaganda to detract you from the mission you have been given as a peacemaker.

> *Heavenly Father, thank you for the freedom to worship you in America, and thank you for the laws, authority, and leaders we have. I ask you for strength as I hold the line between anarchy and order in a world of lawlessness. Amen.*

Everyone who sins breaks the law;
in fact, sin is lawlessness.

1 JOHN 3:4

Death Is Not
the End of the Story

The pain we feel when we lose someone we love is unexplainable. It's like a part of our life dies with them. Death is a painful and sorrowful experience for the loved ones who remain, but should it be? We know sin entered the world through Adam in the garden of Eden, and because of such we were all exposed to death. But because of Jesus, we have been given an opportunity for eternal life. While we will all face physical death, we can live eternally with Christ.

When we approach life and law enforcement through this angle, no weapon can harm us. This is no excuse to be careless, reckless, or foolish, but it should give us relief in knowing there is nothing any person can do to harm our eternal souls. The threats and dangers in this world are real, but death is not the end of the story. Be encouraged in knowing that you are more than a victor, more than a conqueror, and more than a peacemaker. You were created to have an eternal impact on humanity for the kingdom of God.

Heavenly Father, thank you for the gift of eternal life through your Son, Jesus. Thank you that death has lost its sting, and I can rejoice in life eternally with you. Amen.

Therefore, just as sin entered the world through one man, and death through sin, and in this way death came to all people, because all sinned.

ROMANS 5:12

Good Policing Improves Society

It's no secret how quickly a nation can destroy itself due to immorality, unethical behavior, sin, and crime. But what is your role in preserving the way of American society? Enforcing the law means upholding the foundations and pillars of our society, the very things that sustain peace, law, and order. From city ordinances to county and state laws, each has a role in keeping peace and maintaining a good society. The next time you are sent to a shoplifting call, don't discount the impact you are having on your community.

Think about the impact shoplifting has on the economy. If theft alone was reduced by two-thirds, cost of products and goods would be substantially less. Good policing improves society, regardless of what some may say about the profession. Today, do your part to give life to your community and collectively restore righteousness as the work of God, giving life back to our great nation. All hope is not lost as long as our nation's military is strong and as long as we have people like you here on the front lines.

Heavenly Father, thank you for the responsibility of policing the streets of my community, for being a part of the work of your hands to restore righteousness in the world, and for keeping America safe and strong. Amen.

Righteousness exalts a nation,
but sin condemns any people.
PROVERBS 14:34

Inside the Enemy's Playbook

There are people who want to end your life simply because of the authority you represent. It doesn't matter what your name is or your skin color, family status, social status, or financial situation—what matters to them is the fact you have committed to ending their freedom to commit crime. The enemy that exists wants to eliminate law enforcement because free rein and anarchy could then rule, and there would be nothing else to stop it from taking over.

John 10:10 tells us that the enemy comes to steal, kill, and destroy. We have seen the living proof of this in ravaged families and individual lives across our nation. But as ambassadors for Christ, we are to interrupt those plans and stop those attacks when possible. When we know the plans of the enemy in our profession, it makes our jobs easier in strategizing to counter the attacks. The enemy is the same, regardless of jurisdiction, the nation of origin, gang affiliation, or motives. Today, be wise, and know and understand the plans of the enemy. Give life to those you encounter, and relentlessly pursue and eliminate criminal activity.

> *Heavenly Father, thank you that your Son came to give me life and life to the full, and that you have fully equipped me to overcome the world and the schemes of the enemy. Amen.*

The thief comes only to steal and kill and destroy;
I have come that they may have life,
and have it to the full.

JOHN 10:10

Supernatural Protection

Many of you have experienced or know someone who has experienced something unexplainable. Whether it was divine intervention, wild coincidence, or some other form of fate or destiny, a moment when any other person would have been seriously injured or killed, you survived unscathed. While it is certainly not doctrinally sound, I believe God uses everyday people to provide divine intervention in times of dire need. Some call it being in the "right place at the right time"; I call it supernatural intervention.

Today, you may be the angel that someone has been praying for—an elderly person or the victim of a vicious domestic-violence case or maybe even a child who has been neglected. You could be the answer to their prayer. God's Word tells us that He has heavenly messengers encamped around those who fear Him, but He also uses people to meet the needs of those who call on Him too. When we are aligned with God's plan, we become part of the answer to prayer. When we realize that, we realize the power of supernatural protection. It's all around us.

> *Heavenly Father, I ask for you to use me as you will, as your messenger, to deliver those who are oppressed and victims of crime. As I fear you, encamp your heavenly angels around me and those who serve with me. Amen.*

The angel of the LORD encamps around those who fear him, and he delivers them.

PSALM 34:7

Armor for the Enemy's Schemes

The firearms instructor stood before the group of new candidates and demonstrated the proper standing position for firing a service weapon. One young officer couldn't seem to grasp the concept. "No, son, place your foot here. Good, now place your right hand here." This went on for a few minutes before he began to talk about taking cover and the importance of body armor. The necessity of body armor isn't for times of peace; it's for when things go bad. We don't wear it to look cool, but when things get nasty, it can save our lives.

The armor we wear is to protect us from the attacks of the suspects who would try to end our lives. In the same manner, the armor of God is to protect our spirit man so we are fully equipped to stand against the attacks of the enemy. Just like when we are on the range, however, we ought not be careless with our armor, our weapons, or our skills; rather, we should take care of them, stay prepared and trained, and be ready to do battle against the schemes of the enemy.

Heavenly Father, thank you for equipping me with the full armor of protection spiritually and for the wisdom and common sense to wear my armor every day. Amen.

Finally, be strong in the Lord and in his mighty power. Put on the full armor of God, so that you can take your stand against the devil's schemes.

EPHESIANS 6:10–11

Sustaining Power

When a natural disaster or major crime occurs, it often calls for all sworn officers to help, and that means long hours and several days without a break. This may not happen often in your area, but when it does, it is exhausting. Law enforcement work alone is not only physically exhausting but also mentally exhausting as well. There's a lot of thinking required and an exorbitant amount of stress. Through all the difficult times, stress, long hours, and exhaustion, there's good news: difficult times don't last. You are equipped to sustain and are surrounded by people who will support you and lift you up through the tough times.

Second Thessalonians 3:3 starts off with a wonderful reminder, "But the Lord is faithful." Even when we feel like we have reached an empty tank, we have nothing left to give, and our faith is on empty and we cannot go on, He promises to sustain, strengthen, and empower us. When we choose to lean on His promises, we find strength and hope that the world cannot offer. It is our faith in Christ that sustains us, protects us, and propels us to the finish line every time.

> *Heavenly Father, thank you for the power to finish well. Thank you for strength to endure difficult times and adversity, and to be more than a conqueror. Amen.*

But the Lord is faithful, and he will strengthen you and protect you from the evil one.

2 THESSALONIANS 3:3

The Devil's Playground

We live in a world under the control of evil, and the only thing holding evil back from having total rule is the mercy of God. We live and operate in the devil's playground; people are not the enemy. In Ephesians, Paul had a way of showing us who the real enemy was: "For our struggle is not against flesh and blood, but against the rulers, against the authorities, against the powers of this dark world and against the spiritual forces of evil in the heavenly realms" (Ephesians 6:12).

If we are not clear about who we are at war against, then we will not be effective in battle. It is essential to know your location, and this is all the more true in these times in which we live. It would behoove you to equip yourself with high-quality training, equipment, and a proper mind-set, but also daily prayer and fellowship with God. With these steps, you will be prepared to face the plans and dangers in a world that is laced with danger, and you will be equipped to give peace to a world that seeks answers only God can give.

Heavenly Father, thank you for victory, protection, and a prosperous career. Place a shield of protection around me and those who serve with me. Grant me favor in your sight and in the sight of those I serve with. Amen.

We know that we are children of God, and that the whole world is under the control of the evil one.

1 JOHN 5:19

Long Arm of the Law

What happens when the day comes and one of our own loses his or her life in the line of duty? We stop at nothing short of exhausting all resources and manpower, and calling in assistance until those responsible are apprehended and held responsible for their actions. Sadly, it's happened all too often. And with the decline in society, it will happen again.

At the end of the day, even the strongest believers in Christ may have questions after a line-of-duty death, but knowing we can rest in the peace found in Jesus gives us hope and strength to continue. It takes a different breed of people to place themselves in harm's way for a society who often doesn't recognize them. But to those who violate the laws, those who take the lives of our brothers and sisters or any other human being, we are all committed to bringing them to justice. Today, think of how God can use you to bring peace to someone in a troubling situation, or how apprehending a violent criminal can give a victim or victim's family closure.

Heavenly Father, thank you for this life of law enforcement. Preserve my life as I walk in the midst of trouble and danger. Guide my feet and give me discernment as I serve. Amen.

Though I walk in the midst of trouble, you preserve my life.
You stretch out your hand against the anger of my foes;
with your right hand you save me.

PSALM 138:7

Cream of the Crop

Not everyone who applied to your department was hired. In fact, you were likely selected from a pool of hundreds of applicants—but they only selected the best of the best. You endured rigorous testing and training and eventually made the cut. In the end, it was worth it. The citizens of your community are thankful that they do not have the bottom of the stack responding when they need them the most; they get the best when they get men and women from your department.

In the same way, Father God did not send a cheap substitute to rescue us from this present evil age, a world dominated by evil. No, He loved us so much that He sent His only Son, Jesus, to rescue us from our own destructive living. There's nothing wrong with striving to be excellent in all we do—after all, the Father set that example a long time ago. We should do our best in all we do. And at the end of the day, He gets the glory for the work we do, for the lives we impact, and for the evil we apprehend.

> *Heavenly Father, thank you for sending your Son to rescue me from my own destruction. Thank you for empowering me to overcome and conquer this world. Amen.*

The Lord Jesus Christ ... gave himself for our sins to rescue us from the present evil age, according to the will of our God and Father.

GALATIANS 1:3–4

Specialty Rescue Team

Our faith is often challenged in difficult times. It's easy to be strong in our faith when everything is going good, but how we respond when things don't go well is a true testament to our character in Christ. Law enforcement officers will lose their lives in the line of duty, and many will be faithful Christians. These bodies we live in will not last forever, and at the appointed time we will leave for eternity. Our life as believers does not end when this physical body ceases to function; life only begins at that moment.

Second Timothy 4:18 says we will be rescued from this life. We will be rescued from a life where we intimately know pain, hurt, sorrow, and disappointment. Our perspective has always been that all the chips are on the table when we go on duty. But that is far from the truth. When we shift our thinking and living to the eternal instead of the things of the earth, we begin to think with the mind of Christ, and our service as law enforcement officers becomes exponentially more effective.

> *Heavenly Father, thank you for giving me abundant life. Give me a long and prosperous life, and give me favor. When my time comes to leave, may I leave having fulfilled the purpose and mission you set before me. Amen.*

The Lord will rescue me from every evil attack
and will bring me safely to his heavenly kingdom.
To him be glory for ever and ever. Amen.

2 TIMOTHY 4:18

Our Shield and Protector

This life is temporary; it is like a blip of time on the radar of existence. It's over before we know it. Our lives are part of a significantly bigger plan, so our job is to make sure we are doing our part being involved in the plan, reaching others with the message of the love of Jesus Christ.

When we are afflicted with pain or injury, know that God did not send those to punish you. He is not waiting for you to mess up so He can punish you, but He loves you with an everlasting love. In all things, whether we are serving or resting, He will watch over us so that we are not taken before our appointed time. As His servants, He will protect us as we trust Him, follow His guidance, use wisdom, and obey His commands. His mercy will keep us, even in our errors and foolishness, but only for a season; therefore, follow the leading of the Holy Spirit as He guides you.

Heavenly Father, thank you for peace, even in the face of death. Thank you that I have eternal life because of your Son. Grant me wisdom and discernment, and keep me from foolish decisions that would cost me. I trust you, Father, and give you my life. Amen.

The LORD will keep you from all harm—
he will watch over your life; the LORD will watch over
your coming and going both now and forevermore.
PSALM 121:7–8

The Difference between Cover and Concealment

If we pulled up to a house and someone began firing shots at us, as trained law enforcement officers, we know what would provide adequate cover and what would not. It is important to quickly find a place that will protect you and keep you from being struck. *Take cover* is a phrase that is used a lot in movies, but we know the real-life application of cover and the proper time for concealment.

When we say, "God is our hiding place," it does not mean we are cowards; rather, it means we have enough wisdom and common sense to know when to take cover from attack. Concealment is the life we used to live, going through the motions—maybe going to church and maybe reading the Bible. We were inconsistent, with no passion and no enthusiasm. But when our focus in life shifts from the problems of this world to our eternal significance, we realize the power of refuge found in Christ. He will truly protect us from the attacks of the enemy. Lean on Him, and He will come to you.

Heavenly Father, I am placing myself under your protection, at your mercy, and I ask for your direction and leading. I cannot do this without you. Thank you for your divine power to accomplish what you have placed me here to do. Amen.

You are my hiding place; you will protect me from trouble and surround me with songs of deliverance.

PSALM 32:7

Know Your Limits

We all have a breaking point—we're human beings. It's basic biology. At some point, if we don't recognize our limits and operate within them, then our limits will let us know where they are and will issue warnings. But what will you do when you encounter your giants? Will you cower down and flee? Will you abandon your fellow officers to fight alone?

We must be excellent ambassadors for God as representatives of His great name, and as such, never run as cowards. He will give us strength to fight, and He will deliver us from those who are our enemies. Most of you don't have a problem with fear. In fact, most of you have zero issues with fear; the issue is with knowing your limits. Yes, we serve a faithful God who will be with us through every battle. But at the same time, we must not bring reproach to His name through our actions.

Today, work within your limits, but serve in such a way that those who serve alongside you want to know more about this Jesus you proclaim. After all, what more powerful testimony is there than the transformed life?

> *Heavenly Father, thank you for giving me the eyes to see, the mind to know, and the heart to understand my physical limitations. Give me the will to work within them and the power to overcome them when absolutely necessary. Amen.*

I called to the LORD, who is worthy of praise,
and have been saved from my enemies.

2 SAMUEL 22:4

Ambushed and Attacked

One Sunday morning, I stopped a vehicle for speeding. The gentleman was not happy with me and commenced to use obscene language to express his dissatisfaction with my services. The difference was that this man had a name tag on his shirt that said *deacon* with his church name across the top. As I handed him his citation, I asked him to please travel safely, to which he replied with a wish for me to take an eternal trip south. My reply was, "I am sure your pastor would be proud of your behavior."

On that particular Sunday morning, both the deacon and I were probably snarky and, in a sense, both in the wrong. As ambassadors for Christ, it is important to remember that everyone will see our mistakes and that when we do sin, it will be highlighted for many to see. No matter the circumstances, we should always strive to be professional, but also kind, patient, and understanding, knowing everyone we meet is enduring different circumstances. How will you represent Christ to your community today?

Heavenly Father, help me be a living example of what your Word does when it transforms a person. May those who know me see the change you have made in me through your mighty Word. Amen.

In purity, understanding, patience and kindness;
in the Holy Spirit and in sincere love.

2 CORINTHIANS 6:6 NIV

A Mighty Defender

The views we have of God as children often change drastically as we age based on our life experiences. As children, we may have seen God as a mighty warrior and a great defender of people, but as we aged, life happened, bad things occurred, and our faith was shaken. We began to doubt, and because of this, we began to see God as one who punishes us for our mistakes or as someone or something that doesn't exist at all. The truth is that He does exist, for He has never changed.

The same God we saw as a mighty defender and shield in our lives and the same God we used to believe could and would do the impossible still exists and still can do those things. The things you face may cause your faith to be shaken to the core, but hold firmly to the promises in His Word. As you do, the love of God will wrap around you as a reminder that He exists. He will prove Himself mightily in your life again, if not today then very soon.

Heavenly Father, if there is any unbelief in me, please help my unbelief. If there is any doubt in me, please help my doubt and take it from me. I give it to you. Heal my perspective of you as God, as my heavenly Father and as my Mighty Defender. Amen.

But you, LORD, are a shield around me, my glory,
the One who lifts my head high.

PSALM 3:3

Skilled Warrior

earning the skills, the craft, and the necessary arts of being a warrior requires more than mere physical training. It requires us to be totally in tune with our bodies, knowing our physical limitations and having the mental power and strength to crush them when needed. When David wrote Psalm 144:1, it was a declaration of confidence in the skills God had given him. Once you've defeated giants, you know it's beyond your own human strength. You know it was not totally up to you—you are only the vessel—and if you are willing, God will provide all you need for battle.

The difference is in where we are today and where David was with his confidence in God. As Americans, we complain at the slightest of discomforts, but he slayed bears and giants. You are a skilled warrior, but are you where you could be if God sharpened you to become a precision instrument? Today, know you can place your confidence in His Word. We can learn much through our instructors, mentors, and leaders, but the lessons God gives us are even more valuable, even invaluable.

> *Heavenly Father, thank you for training my hands, for giving me the necessary skills for battle on the streets and on my knees in prayer, and for total victory wherever I may go. Amen.*

Praise be to the LORD my Rock,
who trains my hands for war, my fingers for battle.

PSALM 144:1

Spirit and Truth: The Way to Victory

Working different shifts can make attending worship services difficult. But the place of worship isn't as important as your heart and the nature in which you worship. If shift work prevents you from attending worship services regularly, then you need to be more intentional with those times. It gives you more reason to have time to study the Bible and pray individually or with your family at home.

Make a commitment to worship God in all you do, from the time your eyes open to the time you lie down for bed. This is not a call to live a life of rigorous legalism, by which we base our relationship with Christ solely on our performance; rather, it is a call to diligently pursue fellowship with Him through His Word and prayer and the way we treat others. Our lives have tremendous potential to reach others for His kingdom. With the right heart, we can demonstrate the love of God to those who may have never experienced His love before, giving us the opportunity to lead others to victory. Worship is a powerful weapon in our arsenal. If we are consistent in worship of the Father, it can be life-altering.

Heavenly Father, cleanse me of all sin and of all wrong-doing, and accept my worship. May my thoughts, words, and deeds bring you glory in all I do today. Amen.

God is spirit, and his worshipers must worship in the Spirit and in truth.

JOHN 4:24

Shelter from the Elements

July in America brings with it soaring temperatures and scorching heat. It's always nice to find a cool place to finish some paperwork, but we always should be mindful of our surroundings. After standing in an intersection for an extended period directing traffic, or investigating a traffic accident or working a crime scene, getting somewhere out of the elements brings refreshment to your body, which is important if you have a long shift ahead of you.

Psalm 91:4 has a portion of Scripture that applies here: "and under his wings you will find refuge." This is a Hebrew metaphor referring to the protection God gives from oppressive desert heat. If you have ever experienced heat exhaustion, you know heat can wear you down. With the knowledge you have regarding hydrating your body, taking breaks as you are able, and finding shelter when it is feasible, you will be more than prepared to not only survive the battle against those on the streets but also the elements of weather as well.

> *Heavenly Father, thank you for providing relief in the elements of our climate. Thank you for protecting me in dangerous weather situations and for guiding my vehicle and my feet as I travel. Thank you for safety all around me. Amen.*

He will cover you with his feathers,
and under his wings you will find refuge;
his faithfulness will be your shield and rampart.

PSALM 91:4

Instruments of Justice

Upright law enforcement officers don't begin their shifts wanting to use force. They may not have a problem using force to protect themselves or others, but they don't go looking for people to "rough up." The existence of every peace officer is for the benefit of their community and our nation. No innocent people should ever fear your presence, but they should know if they do wrong, they have reason to be afraid.

Many criminals on the street have no fear, no conscience, and no moral compass, so they have nothing to lose. Serve your community in a way that everyone who abides by the law knows they can approach you, but those who do wrong should be fearful because they know you will not cut them a deal, you will enforce the law, and you will not let them go without a fight. You have been given the authority to keep the peace and restore order, but to do so in a way that is fair and just. What you do for your community is for the good of everyone.

Heavenly Father, thank you for the calling on my life to serve as a law enforcement officer. I ask for wisdom, discernment, guidance, and an even temperament. Amen.

For the one in authority is God's servant for your good. But if you do wrong, be afraid, for rulers do not bear the sword for no reason. They are God's servants, agents of wrath to bring punishment on the wrongdoer.

ROMANS 13:4

Unchanging Power

Our physical appearance may change, but our values, morals, and character should remain unwavering. There's no doubt that from the day you first took your oath to serve, you have outwardly changed. But have you allowed your morals, values, or your character to be affected? What a testament of faith it would be to stand at retirement and have others say that we were always a person of the highest integrity and that no one could find anyone who said anything bad about us.

We are made in the likeness of God, and while our physical bodies change, our spirits do not. We may gain weight or lose it, but we should never lose our morals and character. Thankfully, Jesus is never changing—He is the same yesterday, today, and forever. The same Jesus who walked this earth nearly two thousand years ago, who spoke life to Lazarus, who healed the blind man, the lame man, and rose from the dead, has never changed. Our relationship with Jesus Christ should be empowering as law enforcement officers. Today, commit to walking in His unchanging power and being consistent in your walk with the Father. Today is a new day with new opportunities.

Heavenly Father, thank you for the unchanging power of your Son, Jesus. Thank you for the access to the power through the Holy Spirit. I ask you to fill me with your Holy Spirit today. Amen.

Jesus Christ is the same yesterday and today and forever.
HEBREWS 13:8

Heart
of a Hero

———

AUGUST

No More Time for Talking

There is no doubt you have a high degree of intellect or you wouldn't be able to perform the number of complex tasks required of you. Take, for example, your ability to de-escalate a situation by talking to the suspect and/or victim. You possess the skills and ability to not only think about what to say but to act on those thoughts. Your faith and action make you a powerful force for good. If you were to do nothing when you arrived on a scene, the results could be disastrous.

In our spiritual walk, when we hold faith dear to our heart but never exercise it in action, we lack power. Much like our spiritual walk, there is a time to move from talking to "exercising" our faith as a law enforcement officer. It is always great when we can solve a situation with words, but if we must handle business, then do it with excellence, and do it swiftly. Our lives as believers are empowered when we take the faith we have in God and use it in action for His glory. What marvelous results we see when we do.

> *Heavenly Father, thank you for the heart to serve your people. Thank you for faith and the guts to take action on that faith. Show me the line in the sand when it is time to act and quit talking. Amen.*

You see that a person is considered righteous by what they do and not by faith alone.

JAMES 2:24

An Inseparable Pair

The heart of every law enforcement officer is to serve his or her community, to make it a safer place to live, and to protect those who are defenseless against the violent and evil people who exist. The challenges we face in our world are growing, and this requires a strong faith, strong family, and a resilient commitment to our work as peacemakers. There are those who would suggest crime will disappear with faith alone, but we know that is not possible. We know it requires the good work of men and women.

Faith and works cannot exist separate of each other. As law enforcement officers, we cannot expect to be effective without having both faith and works in our life, for they are truly an inseparable pair. Today, are you matching your faith with the actions and work you do? Will you accept the challenge to pair your faith with your work and see the power of the inseparable pair working together in your life as a believer in Jesus Christ?

Heavenly Father, thank you for the power of both faith and deeds in my life; as I strive to serve you with excellence, you will receive the glory in all I do. Amen.

But someone will say, "You have faith; I have deeds."
Show me your faith without deeds,
and I will show you my faith by my deeds.
JAMES 2:18

Lift the Weaker Ones

There are some who are not as strong as others and some who may lack the aggressiveness that the other "alpha dogs" would like them to have. But, my brothers and sisters, I encourage you to not look down on those who may seem weaker than you. You don't have to *earn* the title *hero*; you *are* a hero in the eyes of most of the people you serve. Those officers who are weaker—physically, mentally, and possibly spiritually—should not be demeaned by you or treated as less than you are.

There are certain situations where it is necessary for a fellow officer to find another line of work (for example, if he or she is a coward). We should not merely tolerate weaker officers; instead, we should mentor them, strengthen them, challenge them, and help them reach their goals. Who are we to judge the potential of someone who hasn't been given a fair shot at serving with us? Through proper mentorship, they can be built up and strengthened to excellence. That is how we keep the thin blue line strong for years to come.

> *Heavenly Father, help me to encourage younger officers today, and help me to diplomatically handle those who, for their own safety, need to find another career. Amen.*

We who are strong ought to bear with the failings of the weak and not to please ourselves. Each of us should please our neighbors for their good, to build them up.

ROMANS 15:1–2

Serving the Persecutor

If you have ever had a complaint filed against you, the frustration associated with that can be detrimental to your progress and success on duty. It lingers in your mind while you await a decision. It has been said that those who are proactive on the streets will generate more complaints than those who are not proactive. You will, over the course of your law enforcement career, find yourself having to answer to unfounded complaints. Does that affect your approach on duty? It can, but do not allow it.

Loving our friends and family is easy—it comes naturally in most cases. But loving those who hate and persecute us … that is what love exists for. It is perfectly normal to find loving our enemy a difficult task, especially within our own strength. But through the new life found in Jesus Christ, we are not only empowered to love those who persecute us but also expected to love them. Jesus commands us to love our enemies and pray for those who persecute us. Complaining does no good, but praying will change the circumstances.

> *Heavenly Father, thank you for empowering me to love not only those who love me but also those who hate me and persecute me. Remind me of the power of praying for those who seek to harm me. Amen.*

You have heard that it was said, "Love your neighbor and hate your enemy." But I tell you, love your enemies and pray for those who persecute you.

MATTHEW 5:43–44

Selfless Service Never Dies

W e've all heard the stories of law enforcement officers who went above and beyond the call of duty. From the officer who buys groceries for an individual who has no means to do so, or the officer who helps a parent purchase a child safety seat—these are examples of absolute selfless service. Maybe your opportunity looked a little different. Maybe the results of that one call still linger with you, and you second-guess your actions. Your selfless service is the epitome of what a law enforcement officer is, and you should be commended.

You can be an "average" street cop, but your one moment of selfless service could cement you as a hero in the eyes of a citizen you serve. After all, service is the backbone of your duty, today and every day. In traffic stops, accident investigations, domestic complaints, or shoplifting calls, you have the opportunity to have a permanent, positive impact on someone's life. It's your choice. The true joy of law enforcement is when you give to someone who will never repay you.

Heavenly Father, strengthen me in moments of terror and peace to provide humanity with selfless service, following the examples you have provided. Amen.

And if you spend yourselves in behalf of the hungry
and satisfy the needs of the oppressed,
then your light will rise in the darkness,
and your night will become like the noonday.

ISAIAH 58:10

A Proper Response to Insults

It is easy to respond to verbal insults in a negative way, especially for young or inexperienced officers. While it may seem to offer a degree of temporary reprieve, it is often the opposite that happens. Thinking back to much of your training, you may recall academy instructors in your face, yelling and trying to provoke you to some negative reaction. Most of the time, your response would either further escalate the situation or de-escalate the situation. You have the power to overlook insults that can pay tremendous dividends for you in the future.

How often were you tempted to respond with some sarcastic response, or, even worse, a sharper, more negative response to an insult? Most of the time, that situation would have a negative ending without your prudent response to those insults and harassment.

What is the proper response to an insult? In most cases, it is silence. Ignore it. In fact, if the world would give less attention to stupidity, we would see less crime. When we show a hot temper and respond in an immature manner to the provocation of someone, it shows our areas of weakness, which we all have. Today, be challenged to give no credence to the insults hurled your way by those who bear no value in your life; rather, respond with prudence.

> *Heavenly Father, thank you for the wisdom to respond to insults properly and with prudence. Amen.*

Fools show their annoyance at once,
but the prudent overlook an insult.
PROVERBS 12:16

Where Were the Protesters?

There's a lot of talk today about fairness, equality, and civil rights. As law enforcement officers, we work to protect each of these precious pillars of our country. We've seen the mess caused by riots and violence when people react based on false information—it has cost the lives of many innocent people. One thing we never see, however, is a protest for the lives of a fallen law enforcement officer.

It may be tempting to get discouraged by those who take to social media to spread misinformation or use the mistakes of some to claim the entire law enforcement profession is out of line. It may be discouraging to see the same people you serve protesting on behalf of a violent criminal but never raising their voice to defend the name of a brother or sister who made the ultimate sacrifice. This is part of the heart of a hero. We do not need the protests, but with each other and God, we can do our work and do it well.

Heavenly Father, if I become discouraged in the midst of a confused society, help me to remember my purpose and goal. Help me to keep my focus on you and on serving my community as I serve you. Amen.

By oppression and judgment he was taken away.
Yet who of his generation protested?
For he was cut off from the land of the living;
for the transgression of my people he was punished.

ISAIAH 53:8

Servants Are
the Greatest Heroes

The chain of command in any department exists for a reason—to keep order, to establish a hierarchy, and to maintain a flow of information throughout the organization. However, some of the greatest supervisors I ever had the pleasure of serving with were "in the trenches" with the rest of the officers on patrol. They weren't abandoning their post as supervisors, and they weren't trying to fraternize with the squad; rather, they were serving.

There was a robbery in our city where two supervisors were responsible for apprehending the suspects. They did not call out the information and instruct lower-ranking officers to do the work—they did it. They set the example and deepened the respect they had with other sworn personnel. Today, regardless of rank, remember the call. The call is to serve and protect. I have seen officers of every rank do the "dirty work" necessary to get the job done. None of us are beyond serving, and the day we believe we are is the day we need to retire and head home.

Heavenly Father, thank you for giving me the heart to serve your people. Remind me that the level of serving I do determines the level of greatness I achieve. Amen.

*Sitting down, Jesus called the Twelve and said,
"Anyone who wants to be first must be the very last,
and the servant of all."*

MARK 9:35

One Unit. One Team. One Mission.

Nothing can destroy a department like low morale, but we have to work through it and overcome it. There are many factors that affect the morale of a law enforcement agency, but one we can do is ensure that we focus on being unified at the micro level, from the zone or unit level to the squad or shift level to the division level, all the way up. If we will focus on unity and being of one mission, then the issue of low morale will have less effectiveness on our overall performance.

This mission begins with one person—you. It begins with the decision to be of like mind with others, to work in peace, to compromise with your fellow officers as best you can, and to work toward one common goal, blocking out the negative influences. When we focus on the same love mentioned in Philippians 2:2, we will see a different atmosphere in our departments. This all begins on our shift and in our squad, with a decision to stop the excuses and make the change.

> Heavenly Father, I resolve to work in unity with my fellow officers, for one common purpose and one common goal, and remove the dissension and bickering, to eliminate crime and to bring peace and order to my community. Amen.

Then make my joy complete by being like-minded,
having the same love, being one in spirit and of one mind.
PHILIPPIANS 2:2

Lives above Reproach

There is an expectation of perfection for every person who wears a badge, no matter the rank, experience level, department, or jurisdiction in which they serve. This has come with the dehumanization of law enforcement through various media outlets, such as movies, video games, and songs. We are all going to make mistakes, and, yes, we are all going to commit what is called, according to the Bible, sin. But we are made blameless before God by the blood shed by His Son, Jesus. When we live a life in pursuit of Him, it causes every other area of our lives to line up in righteousness.

To experience success in law enforcement, we must have proper motivation in our hearts before each shift. Our character must be impeccable and our walk must be blameless. Living above reproach means no other person can point to us and say we violated the law or that we even tested the waters in violating any laws because we were people of the utmost integrity during our careers. Know you can trust the path God has for you, and while you lean on His promises, He will release success in your life and shield you all your days.

> *Heavenly Father, help my life be above reproach for those who see it, and may those who see me, see you, and recognize the change you have made in me. Amen.*

He holds success in store for the upright,
he is a shield to those whose walk is blameless.

PROVERBS 2:7

Granting Mercy, Giving Grace

A quick temper can cause more trouble for you than just about any other issue. It can lead to use-of-force complaints, federal lawsuits, and civil rights complaints. There's a time to move swiftly, but it should not be based on our temper. When we live with understanding and wisdom, knowing thoroughly who we are dealing with on the streets and who we are, and having confidence in our training and faith in our eternal God, we display great patience instead of foolish behavior.

On the firing range, you've likely heard the phrase, "Slow is smooth, smooth is fast." If you are quick to respond to a situation with a poorly thought-out plan, chances are you will have to deal with more issues as a result of your temper and the way you handled the situation. There are times when we have to let go of the words and actions of others and times when addressing those in the moment would cause more trouble than they are worth. Be someone who is constantly seeking the wisdom only God can give; be generous with granting mercy when possible; give grace often, because there will be times you will need it as well.

Heavenly Father, thank you for wisdom, patience, new mercies, and grace. Help me in my response to provocation, and guide my words in moments when my emotions could get the best of me. Amen.

A person's wisdom yields patience;
it is to one's glory to overlook an offense.
PROVERBS 19:11

Clear Identity

You wear a uniform so you can clearly be identified as a law enforcement officer. While there are times you need to blend in and not be identified, there is also a good reason for wearing a uniform. But our identity is not rooted in our work or our service in law enforcement; our identity is in Christ. When we lose our identity in the mix of what we do when we wear the badge, we risk losing our families, friends, and eventually our careers, not to mention our relationship with the Father.

We cannot expect to experience change in our lives if we never spend time reading the Bible or praying, for this is where we find and establish our identity in Christ. Then we can walk in the perfect will of God and experience resounding success throughout our careers. Today, commit yourself to a time each day for reading the Bible, praying, and finding your identity in Christ, who *He* says you are in His Word. He will reveal to you His perfect and pleasing will.

> *Heavenly Father, in a world of corruption and evil, allow my identity to separate me from the crowd. Renew my mind and transform my thinking as I commit to studying your Word and spending time in prayer. Amen.*

*Do not conform to the pattern of this world,
but be transformed by the renewing of your mind.
Then you will be able to test and approve what God's will is—
his good, pleasing and perfect will.*

ROMANS 12:2

The Blessing of a Lasting Work

There's a great deal of self-gratification when you can help someone get off the streets, stop committing crime, and become a productive member of society. It takes a special person to care about others this much, especially people who cannot repay you. But it is proof that the work you do has the potential to be enduring and meaningful. When we have the favor of God on our lives and on the work we do, the lives we interact with will be changed for the better.

There is no doubt you are equipped to do a great job in whatever capacity you serve in your department, and the citizens of your community are grateful for your service. But when we live our lives independent of the faith and power of God, we lack the necessary fuel to have a lasting impact. Today, commit your pursuit to God, in your personal life, family, career, future goals and dreams, and as you live in reverent fear of Him, His wisdom and favor will rest on you. Then your work will be lasting and meaningful.

Heavenly Father, thank you for your favor on my life, the favor that establishes the work I do and causes the services I provide to have lasting results. Amen.

May the favor of the Lord our God rest on us;
establish the work of our hands for us—
yes, establish the work of our hands.

PSALM 90:17

Their Only Hope May Be You

Will you answer the call when your number is dispatched? No matter how dangerous the situation, no matter how risky the circumstances, you are the hope of a hopeless and helpless people. It may be a wife who has been beaten to the point of near death or a child who has been severely abused or a man who has been critically wounded—whoever it is, you are the hope for those who have no one else to help them. Your responsibility is to simply go when you are called.

Your power is one that not only can apprehend and arrest criminal suspects, but you can provide relief to victims and connect them with powerful resources to help them get their lives back on track. Never take your role in law enforcement for granted, and don't become so hardened that you don't believe the voice of the hurting person who needs assistance. Listen for the cries for help. Maybe those cries are audible, maybe they are not, and maybe the issues are emotional and run deep. Active listening skills can provide you with another powerful resource to make you an asset to those who are hopeless. Today, you may be the answer to their prayer.

> *Heavenly Father, use me, my service, and my commitment to my community to help your people in need. I am here. Send me. Amen.*

For he will deliver the needy who cry out,
the afflicted who have no one to help.

PSALM 72:12

A Powerful Advocate in Times of Need

Most medium- to larger-sized agencies have juvenile investigators who work together with their local child advocacy centers. These organizations are instrumental in working cases where children are victims of crimes or witnesses to a crime. Specific procedures for interviews must be followed. To continuously advocate for the children of our communities is a testament to the heart of law enforcement and their passion for the innocent and helpless. The number of homes with one or both parents gone is staggering, and even if one parent is home, he or she is not always truly present, which creates issues with the children. These parents often rely on uniformed patrol officers to help "parent" their children.

There should never be a time when helpless or elderly people cannot come to you for help and receive it. If you cannot help them, find someone who can. When we advocate for those who cannot speak for themselves, we are reflecting the nature of our heavenly Father, who has always been a refuge for the oppressed. Today, commit your service to advocating for those who cannot speak for themselves, whether they are children, the handicapped, or the elderly. In doing so, you will be demonstrating to them the nature and love of God.

Heavenly Father, help my service reflect who you are, and help those I encounter see your love in my actions. Amen.

The LORD is a refuge for the oppressed,
a stronghold in times of trouble.

PSALM 9:9

August 16

Officer Needs Assistance

The alert tones go off. Your heart rate increases, your ears perk up, you reach down and turn the knob on the radio up. "Be advised, officer needs assistance …" If you are on break, it's over. If you are doing paperwork, it can wait. If you were on a traffic stop issuing a citation, today is that person's lucky day. When an officer calls for assistance, everyone drops what they are doing and immediately responds. Until another officer arrives on scene and clears the call, you go with prudence and care, but you go quickly.

It is no secret that when we call for help, there are many who will come to our aid. There will be times we find ourselves in situations that are overwhelming, but even in those moments we have access to the peace that nobody else in this world can possibly fathom. Today, know you can call for help—on the radio, in your prayers, and on the phone. If you are battling something privately, there is help. It is not a sign of weakness to seek assistance. You will be better for it in the long run.

> Heavenly Father, I know through all I do for you, there will be times I am overwhelmed. In those moments, remind me that you have taken the burden and given me peace and you are my help in my time of need. Amen.

Do not be far from me,
for trouble is near and there is no one to help.

PSALM 22:11

A Hero's Honor

We could sit around and complain about all that is wrong in life, in our department, or in our country, but at the end of the day, the only thing that matters is action. Complaining resolves nothing. When we match our faith in God with action and are determined to finish well, we will not be disgraced. Instead, we will receive a hero's honor. We may receive many rewards during our career in law enforcement—medals and letters of commendation—but nothing compares to the rewards we have waiting for us in eternity.

Ignore the discouragement that surrounds you. If you have complaining voices around you, block them out and set your mind and heart to be determined to finish each call, each day, and each shift with excellence for the glory of God. The heart of a hero is not to just serve but to serve well—not to just serve well but to be determined to finish well. Today, I challenge you to dig deep and overcome the negative influences in the world, as they could certainly distract you. Set your sights on the goal, and finish strong.

Heavenly Father, thank you for helping me in all I do and for helping me finish strong. Thank you for the determination and willpower to be excellent in service for your glory. Amen.

Because the Sovereign LORD helps me,
I will not be disgraced.
Therefore, have I set my face like flint,
and I know I will not be put to shame.

ISAIAH 50:7

You Were Just in Time

I f we are not totally dependent on God, we will falter because we lean on our own understanding. Israel experienced God's divine deliverance on numerous occasions in the Old Testament. While these stories are dated, we can rest knowing that the same God who rescued the Israelites then has not changed, and He is able and willing to rescue us in our time of distress. When we attempt to live with our own power, strength, and understanding, we find ourselves in difficult situations that often require us to call for the help of almighty God.

Even good people are faced with adversity; we should be prepared to respond to their needs when called upon. Most people do not have the training and experience in dealing with stressful, violent situations. But you do. You know how to address these circumstances and remain in peace while doing it. Fight off the temptation to do it all in your own strength. It is not possible. Lean on the supernatural power of the Holy Spirit and God's Word, and watch what He does through your life as you serve your community.

> *Heavenly Father, thank you for placing me in the right place at the right time, for putting me in position to serve those in need and in distress. Strengthen me to serve as a law enforcement officer. Amen.*

Then they cried out to the LORD in their trouble,
and he delivered them from their distress.

PSALM 107:6

The Hope of a Nation

It may seem that righteousness and justice no longer have a place in America. From within, we are destroying ourselves. There is division over every issue at every corner. We cannot seem to agree on anything.

Habakkuk is a prophet who makes a complaint to the Lord, and in response the Lord gives him a clear vision of what is to come. Sometimes, it seems like we have lost all hope and there is no way to be saved. But there is always salvation and hope.

Your service is part of a greater role in protecting the life of this great nation. Through diligent police work, you keep the enemies at bay and flush out criminal activity from the homes and neighborhoods of innocent civilians. You play a role in the hope of our nation. What God is doing in America is not over. Righteousness and justice will be restored. Peace and order will be reestablished in our communities. Continue to shine as a lighthouse of hope to those who may have no hope.

Heavenly Father, thank you for the hope we have in you, and in you alone. I ask for your mercy on my life and on my country. Move in my heart and life and across this great nation in a mighty way once again! Amen.

Look at the nations and watch—
and be utterly amazed.
For I am going to do something in your days
that you would not believe,
even if you were told.

HABAKKUK 1:5

A Time to Celebrate

There is an appropriate time to enjoy the fruits of your labor, to celebrate your victories, and to rest. David knew the meaning of celebrating, especially when God delivered him from the hand of so many enemies and repeatedly gave him victory. Likewise, it is necessary for each of us to take time to reflect on the success we experience, the victories we have, and being saved in the face of danger. David was a singer and a dancer—he was demonstrative in his worship and celebration.

Doing life alone is not the way it was meant to be, and when we have people to celebrate with, people to go through difficult times with, it makes the journey a little bit sweeter. Today, take time to celebrate your victories. Celebrate with your family and with your squad; take time to bond with those with whom you serve, because there is nothing that can replace the power of unity, and a good celebration can help kick-start the process.

Heavenly Father, thank you for victory. Even though I may not have the victory at this moment, I know I am victorious because of you. Because of that, I celebrate! Amen.

David sang to the LORD the words of this song when the LORD delivered him from the hand of all his enemies and from the hand of Saul.

2 SAMUEL 22:1

Peace in the Raging Storm

While we know God is with us in all we do, He expects us to use our faith. You use your faith every day—to do a job with such great risk is a great demonstration of faith. But what happens when we find ourselves in the middle of a hopeless situation? Just like the disciples, we are empowered and expected to use faith to speak to the storm and tell it to be still.

After Jesus rebuked the wind and the waves, He asked His disciples, "Where is your faith?" We have all been given a measure of faith. Use your faith, exercise it, stretch it, and grow it; it's like a muscle or your firearms skills—the more you use it, the stronger it gets. Put it to the test. Match your faith in God with your biblically based actions and watch your life change. Know that Jesus is no longer sleeping, but He expects us to use the faith we have been given.

Heavenly Father, forgive me for not using my faith and demonstrating it as I should. Today, I will be a good steward of the gift of faith you gave me. I will honor you, both in the times of peace and in the storm. Amen.

The disciples went and woke him, saying,
"Master, Master, we're going to drown!"
He got up and rebuked the wind and the raging waters; the
storm subsided, and all was calm. "Where is your faith?"
he asked his disciples.

LUKE 8:24–25

Often Outnumbered, Never Outsmarted

Responding to riots, free-for-alls, or major events where large fights are possible can leave you highly outnumbered. You never want to put yourself in a situation where you are in a physical fight with two hundred people by yourself. It's not brave; it's stupid. After all, it would probably be over a minor ordinance or misdemeanor. But there's a time to use wisdom and common sense. But if you must fight, do not be afraid. Do not stand and let them see your fear, and do not let those who are against you see you if you bleed.

The prophet in 2 Kings 6:16 recognized he was not alone. He knew his help came from a host of heavenly armies, which is why he said, "Don't be afraid." He knew there were more on his side than there were on the other side fighting against him. There may come a day when you are in dire need of help, when you are highly outnumbered and help is a long way away. If that day comes, know that God will and does intervene to help His own. We may be often outnumbered, but we are never outsmarted.

> *Heavenly Father, thank you for the power of common sense, faith, and wisdom. Thank you for divine protection over me, wherever I go, and no matter how many are against me. Amen.*

"Don't be afraid," the prophet answered.
"Those who are with us are more than
those who are with them."

2 KINGS 6:16

It'll All Be Worth It

I t may be difficult to see how a believer in Jesus Christ who is persecuted for his or her righteousness could be blessed, but God's Word will never return to Him void. Many of you who serve your communities live in a way that honors God and glorifies His name, and because of that, you face various persecutions. You were once required to prove yourself on the streets to those you serve with, and, as such, you must remain strong and steadfast through persecutions that may come to you because of your love for God.

Those persecutions will not decrease in this present age; they will only become more intense, and we should remain faithful to the Father to demonstrate our love and heart for His kingdom. We remain strong and steadfast by keeping our focus on the love God has for us and on the eternal reward, not on this present life. We must remember this life, while it may seem permanent, is but a vapor, and we must prepare for eternity. In doing so, our hearts will be aligned with the Father's heart, and we will focus on loving others in a way that reflects His nature.

> *Heavenly Father, grant me the strength and firmness to stand strong through persecution, to honor and glorify your name, whether I am on or off duty, until my last breath. Amen.*

Blessed are those who are persecuted because of righteousness, for theirs is the kingdom of heaven.

MATTHEW 5:10

Never Bow to Sin

There are only two paths in life: the path of evil and the path of good. You answered the call to hold the line between evil and good so evil doesn't overtake righteousness, so those who are enslaved by their own sin do not enslave others. When you place someone under arrest, you are essentially seizing them and taking their immediate freedoms because of their criminal behavior. They became a slave to sin and had to pay consequences for it.

You can choose to bow to sin, succumb to the pressures of life, give in, and become like those who wear the chains around them. You can be a slave to sin. But this way leads to death. Or if you become a slave to love, bound because you were first loved, then you have a desire to be obedient to the words of Jesus and to love others, which leads to righteousness and life. This is the way of His kingdom, and thus you serve to restore righteousness in your community.

> *Heavenly Father, thank you for empowering me to address the lives of those who break the laws of my community. May all I do glorify your name. Amen.*

Don't you know that when you offer yourselves to someone as obedient slaves, you are slaves of the one you obey—whether you are slaves to sin, which leads to death, or to obedience, which leads to righteousness?

ROMANS 6:16

Poisoned by Pride

One of the most common complaints a citizen makes against an officer is that he or she was cocky or arrogant. While sometimes these complaints are simply because the officer issued them a traffic citation, there are times when many of us are guilty of exemplifying these qualities. When we allow pride to poison the heart with which we serve, it can taint the fruit of our labor and the entire harvest can be ruined. Pride and arrogance often lead to evil behavior and perverse speech, a cycle that will usually show itself over time. If not, pride will ruin a person and cause him or her to face terrible embarrassment.

It may be difficult to work with someone who is arrogant or prideful or who cannot talk without cursing. But we should not hate the person. It is almost impossible to tolerate someone who has been poisoned by pride. Today, ask God to search your heart, to root out any seed of pride so that you may honor Him in your work. You have come too far and done too much for His kingdom in your community to have it ruined by pride.

> *Heavenly Father, search my heart, search me, reveal any existence of evil pride in me and show me. If it be, remove it so I can become closer to you and bring glory and honor to your name. Amen.*

To fear the LORD is to hate evil; I hate pride and arrogance,
evil behavior and perverse speech.

PROVERBS 8:13

A Time to Walk Away

If you have been working in law enforcement for long, you know there are people who try to lure you into useless arguments that will simply drain your energy, waste your time, and generate a complaint. There are times when a healthy debate is called for, but in general we should avoid arguing with people who cannot do so in a logical, rational manner. We should not delve into senseless controversies that bear little to no benefit either, for these things often bring no glory to the kingdom of God.

Think about these things from the aspect of profit and loss. What profit does a senseless debate have, or investing your time and energy into a foolish controversy? It may generate some, but in the long run it will bankrupt your personal stock. Your personal reputation will be little to nothing if all you want to do is argue with everyone. It is necessary to walk away from certain conversations, and sometimes this is hard to do. In all we do, we should seek to live in a way that is useful and profitable to the kingdom of heaven.

Heavenly Father, give me wisdom and the wherewithal to walk away from those conversations I may be lured into that will not bring you glory. Help me stay focused on the task at hand. Amen.

But avoid foolish controversies and genealogies and arguments and quarrels about the law, because these are unprofitable and useless.

TITUS 3:9

A Hero to Those
Who Need You Most

When you have seen the works of God with your eyes, when you have witnessed His mighty hand move in your life, it is extremely difficult to contain your praise for Him. It is natural to have a feeling that wants to exclaim His praises and share the news with others. Your assignment may be lacking in glamour, but it may be right where you need to be to rescue the poor and connect them to the resources they need to receive life-changing help.

It is important to understand the power of *where* you are always, not necessarily because of the threats but because of the opportunities that are presented. Today may be the time when you get to invest in the life of someone who is ready to change. Never give up hope. Pursue and apprehend those who rob the working, innocent, and needy. Relentlessly pursue those who would burglarize homes and businesses, for this is the calling on your life, the reason for which you were born. When you do this with excellence, you provide rescue and reprieve to the victims, and cause them to say, "Who is like our Lord?"

> *Heavenly Father, may my actions today cause others to rejoice in your great name. May my service be done in excellence to bring you glory! Amen.*

My whole being will exclaim, "Who is like you, Lord?
You rescue the poor from those too strong for them,
the poor and needy from those who rob them."

PSALM 35:10

Cherry-Picking the Law

When we try to use God's Word like a vending machine, picking and choosing what we want to apply to our lives, we put ourselves in positions of defeat. It's like working on duty all day writing tickets for speeding, not wearing a seatbelt, and having no insurance, and then driving home while violating all those laws. We cannot, in good conscience, enforce a law we cannot abide by.

Jesus was not commanding us to observe all the laws, live in perfection, or die in sin. He was telling us that we should not cherry-pick from the commandments—we couldn't teach the laws in public one way and violate them in private and expect to receive a blessing from God. That is the epitome of hypocrisy. May your life be a living example of God's Word and commandments. Be careful not to do like the Pharisees. Strive for excellence in all you do, not in the name of legalism, but in the name of holiness.

> *Heavenly Father, thank you for the words of your Son, Jesus. Give me knowledge and understanding of your Word as I read and study, and help me to carry it with me as I go about my day. Amen.*

Therefore anyone who sets aside one of the least of these commands and teaches others accordingly will be called least in the kingdom of heaven, but whoever practices and teaches these commands will be called great in the kingdom of heaven.

MATTHEW 5:19

Acts of Valor

One of the first things we learn through the Law Enforcement Code of Ethics is to not use our authority for our own advantage. While it may sound like this is something we would never do, one decision can lead to a series of consequences that unravel quickly. We should always be mindful, especially with current technology, that we are always being monitored, and we should always be serving with the utmost integrity and character.

Our service should never be tarnished with selfishness or arrogance, but should be decorated with valor, selflessness, and honor. Regardless of how powerful or skilled we are, we should never fall into the trap of taking advantage of the position we hold. Today, remain humble, with quiet confidence, always seeking to improve and help those around you to become better at what they do. When we focus on being the best at what God has called us to be, through practical measures, He will bless us with greater responsibility along our journey. Pursue acts of valor and righteousness, honor and selflessness, and avoid tarnishing the badge you so proudly wear.

> *Heavenly Father, may my service as a law enforcement officer bring you honor, and may it never be about bringing me personal advantage or gain, but benefit those I serve. Amen.*

In your relationships with one another, have the same mindset as Christ Jesus: Who, being in very nature God, did not consider equality with God something to be used to his own advantage.

PHILIPPIANS 2:5–6

Life by the Spirit

We can treat our career in law enforcement with the mindset that it is a career that we can enjoy, serve and help others, and make a difference, or we can see it as a curse. Either way, our perspective will set the tone for our attitude toward our work. But I am telling you, we were called to be free, not to indulge in the flesh or in sin, but to serve.

When we grasp the power behind this Galatians 5:13, it will change our view of law enforcement. We will see our position as a life led by the Spirit, where we can serve humankind humbly in love, because we are free. What other profession allows us to begin and end each day with the chance to be someone's hero? It may not be flashy, and you may not even realize it when it happens, but years from now, when someone comes up to you and thanks you for what you did, you will realize that your service was not in vain. That, my friends, is the power of a life being led by the Spirit.

> *Heavenly Father, lead my life by your Holy Spirit. May I not take this freedom for granted and indulge in the things of this world, but instead serve your purpose. Amen.*

You, my brothers and sisters, were called to be free.
But do not use your freedom to indulge the flesh;
rather, serve one another humbly in love.

GALATIANS 5:13

Ministers of His Good News

God uses us to reveal His mysteries to others—He uses everyday common men and women, doing everyday work, which turns into extraordinary results. We are servants, first of Christ and then to our community, who are entrusted with the mysteries of His Word, to love people, care for others, enforce the law, and pursue evil. This is not a task to be taken lightly. You have the heart of a hero, the potential to leave a legacy in your community.

What greater legacy could any person ask to leave than a legacy of service to God and others? When we as peacemakers commit our lives, first personally and individually, then professionally, to the purpose God has given us, we will see His direction. Through training, mentorship, discipleship, and experience, we will become excellent in service, bringing honor to our leadership and to Christ. Remember that you are on the road to leaving a legacy to rise and serve with excellence and integrity for younger officers, for your children, and for other people who know you.

Heavenly Father, thank you for giving me a heart to serve and the attributes of a hero. Thank you for searching my heart continually, for leading me by your Spirit, and directing my steps today and every day. Amen.

This, then, is how you ought to regard us:
as servants of Christ and as those entrusted
with the mysteries God has revealed.

1 CORINTHIANS 4:1

Standoff

SEPTEMBER

September 1

Courage to Face
the Greatest Fears

With one echoing boom after another, the volley of a twenty-one-gun salute rang through the air on a cloudy winter day. Dressed in their finest attire, his brothers and sisters held their salute with tears running down their faces. Later, when I returned home from attending the out-of-town funeral, I hugged my wife and kids a little firmer than usual. It took all I had to emotionally hold it together that day, but inside I was a wreck.

We are trained to control our emotions in even the most volatile situations, and suppressing our emotions often bleeds over into other areas of our lives. The reality of law enforcement is danger, fear, and the potential for injury or death. There is also the reality that we can be affected in numerous ways, including PTSD, anxiety, alcohol abuse, and relationship issues. Thankfully, that is not the end of the story. As you face the realities of your duties today, including fear, know that you are fully empowered, fully prepared, and fully equipped to carry out the duties of your calling.

> *Heavenly Father, give me the courage to face the fears I will encounter, guide my steps, and place a shield of protection around me and those serving with me. Amen.*

Have I not commanded you? Be strong and courageous.
Do not be afraid; do not be discouraged,
for the LORD your God will be with you wherever you go.

JOSHUA 1:9

Truth Creates Conflict

At some point in life, we face painful truths. Often, the confrontation with truth creates conflict that leads to calls you answer daily. It's not always easy to be the messenger of truth, or the recipient. If all the law enforcement officers in America were asked why they served, many of the answers would sound different but come down to the same root reason: commitment to truth. Our relationship with Jesus is based on our consistent commitment to Him.

Our duties are carried out because of our commitment to truth and community. When the commitment fades, the motivation to serve will fade too. The reason why any of us serve boils down to our commitment to the cause; it is a high calling to serve as part of the thin blue line. While everyone you encounter will not want to adhere to truth, they will be held accountable for their response to it. Whatever your assignment, be a good steward of the truth today.

Heavenly Father, help me keep my focus not only on the reason why I began my career as a law enforcement officer but also on you. Protect me from the attacks of the enemy, both spiritually and physically. Amen.

Jesus answered, "You say that I am a king. In fact, the reason I was born and came into the world is to testify to the truth. Everyone on the side of truth listens to me."

JOHN 18:37

A Righteous Risk

Every shift you strap on a gun belt and body armor, you accept the unknown risks. While others tell you how hard your job is and how they could never do it, you carry out your duties without hesitation. One distinguishing difference between what some call a job and what others refer to as a calling is the amount of risk they take to accomplish their duties. I cannot think of another profession where you can carry out the acts of faith so true as a law enforcement officer. Risk requires faith, and we strengthen our faith by addressing risk.

During today's duty, allow the voice of God's promises to ring true in your heart. Just as you make instant decisions based on extensive training and experience, so you can listen closely to His works for discernment and direction. Today may bring previously unconquered challenges and leave you asking questions. But know this: you have been appointed to face these risks as an authority under God's command. You are well trained and conditioned to respond to and address each issue you face. As you cling close to the leading of His Word, you will find protection and wisdom to face every risk you encounter.

> *Heavenly Father, guard me against unseen risks. You alone are the one giving me the courage to face this day, and I thank you in advance for courage, freedom, and protection. Amen.*

You will not fear the terror of night,
nor the arrow that flies by day.

PSALM 91:5

September 4

The Audacity of Obedience

It's natural to have apprehensions when faced with certain situations. When we are facing great danger, fear, pain, or sorrow, our instinct is often to attempt to elude those and find a place of comfort. One of the biggest differences between you, those with whom you serve, and the rest of society is the moment before a response to danger. Obedience to your call is your priority, and it takes audacity to face the things you deal with.

Think about the emotions Peter felt when Jesus stood *on the water* and commanded Peter to get out of the boat and walk to Him on the water. Most of our responses would be to call for assistance. It is easy to get distracted, lose our focus, and begin to falter in life when we focus on what is around us: the storms, circumstances, criticisms, and finances. When we keep our eyes on Jesus—when we keep our focus on His Word, on His commands, and have the audacity to live in a way that honors Him—we will make it to Him every time.

Heavenly Father, thank you for the faith to step out of the boat. Thank you for the audacity to obey, to overcome fear, and to serve my family and my community. Amen.

"Come," he said.
Then Peter got down out of the boat, walked on the water and came toward Jesus. But when he saw the wind, he was afraid and, beginning to sink, cried out, "Lord, save me!"
MATTHEW 14:29–30

A Perfected Love

It seems like at every corner, you face criticism. There is no doubt that our society has drastically changed over the past decade. One thing that remains unchanging, however, is God's love and the power He gives us to deal with a hateful world. We could easily fall into the trap of being negative and cynical and fall into the trap of living in fear, but those are not the fruits of love.

While 1 John 4:18 refers to the genuine love a believer possesses in Jesus Christ, which is a sign of salvation, we can also see a figurative parallel of the power of serving in love and the freedom we have from fear. When we know the love of God and are saved by His power, then we no longer fear His judgment; therefore, there is no fear in love. May love be used to drive out fear in practical ways, and may love cause you to be the tool God uses to drive out fear in the lives of others. Watch His Word come alive as you study it.

Heavenly Father, thank you for the life-changing love you have shown me. Fill me with your love and empower me to live in a way that casts out all fear and exudes love in all I do. Amen.

There is no fear in love. But perfect love drives out fear, because fear has to do with punishment. The one who fears is not made perfect in love.

1 JOHN 4:18

Destined for Victory

If we're not careful, especially considering our chosen profession, then we will develop a cynical, pessimistic attitude toward the world. It is strange that we work so diligently to give peace and order to so many, but in return we often find ourselves in a state of internal distress. This occurs when we allow the world to overcome us instead of us overcoming the world. To put it simply, we were created and equipped by God, through His Son, to overcome the world, not be defeated by life.

You are more than a conqueror, and nothing can pin you down for long. Not sicknesses, relationship problems, financial issues, career issues, depression, or anxiety. Nothing can keep you from the victory God has set for you if you will accept the path to peace laid out by Jesus. In this world, we will have trouble, but in Jesus we will have peace, and thankfully He intercedes on our behalf. Today, ask God to reveal your identity as one who is "more than a conqueror" in Christ. When you see yourself as God intends, the troubles of life won't stand a chance.

Heavenly Father, thank you for giving me the power to overcome this world, for power to overcome my own emotions and to be victorious in life. Amen.

I have told you these things, so that in me you may have peace.
In this world you will have trouble. But take heart!
I have overcome the world.

JOHN 16:33

The Power of One

There are always going to be negative things said about the work you do as law enforcement officers—from activists, politicians, or the media. It is an absolute certainty that there will always be someone to complain about your professional work. At the end of the day, however, their complaints are indicative of the positive impact you are having in your community. But if you remain united in solidarity, unwavering as one body, then you will not be shaken.

Romans 8 tells of the sufferings of God's people. Many of us do not know *true* suffering because of our faith. We may face economic and social consequences, but many of us have never witnessed someone losing their life because of their Christian faith. If we can remember in times of trouble the power of one, the power of unity, and that if we have God with us then we have all we need, then we will come out on the other side victorious. Make your own personal resolution to ignore what is being said about you or your professional work. Focus on the goal and do not let foolish things bring division in your department.

Heavenly Father, thank you for unity, at home and on duty. Thank you for the power you have in my life and for giving me the fuel to get through the trials. Amen.

What, then, shall we say in response to these things?
If God is for us, who can be against us?
ROMANS 8:31

September 8

Inseparable Bond

You may feel like your life has been too messed up for God to love you or for you to have a relationship with Him. In fact, you may even feel like the difficult times are God's way of punishing you for the bad things you have done. But there is nothing you have done or can do that can change the love God has for you. After all, He loved us so much that He sent His only Son for us. How cheap would it make that love look if it were to change based on our performance?

There is nothing in this life, neither seen nor unseen, that can separate us from the love of God. The love He has for us is unchanging and unaffected by anything we could possibly do. Today, know that while you may mess up, sin, or make a mistake, He still loves you—nothing can change that. What a marvelous reminder of the true power of an authentic holy love.

Heavenly Father, thank you for the inseparable, unchanging love you have for me. Remind me of your unchanging love when I mess up, and rebuke condemnation and guilt when it rises up in me. Amen.

For I am convinced that neither death nor life, neither angels nor demons, neither the present nor the future, nor any powers, neither height nor depth, nor anything else in all creation, will be able to separate us from the love of God that is in Christ Jesus our Lord.

ROMANS 8:38–39

The Burden of Self-Pity

We should never buy into the thought that any life is less valuable to God. At the end of the day, you represent the single hope that Jesus Christ stands for—you are a living reminder of the hope that all people are created equal. If we will work, commit ourselves, and never quit, then we become the greatest—if we will only serve.

The issue is that few are willing to serve. Many are willing to receive, but few want to actually give. The Creator of all that exists knows *you* and loves *you,* and your life matters to Him—*every* life matters to Him. When we are tempted to buy into the fear this world is trying to sell, remember He knows all and sees all. If God does not allow the sparrow to starve, then He will not allow you to suffer for long. You were created to love, to be loved, and to change the world around you.

Heavenly Father, if I am ever tempted to believe my life doesn't matter because of my past or what someone else says, remind me of how you feel about me. Help me to show those I encounter the love you've shown me. Amen.

Are not two sparrows sold for a penny? Yet not one of them will fall to the ground outside your Father's care. And even the very hairs of your head are all numbered. So don't be afraid; you are worth more than many sparrows.

MATTHEW 10:29–31

The Chains of Anger

Someone on your shift will see the result of a person who cannot control anger almost every time they work. Whether it is during an assault call or disorderly conduct, there are many who cannot control anger because it has them enslaved. Anger is another poison that ruins the blessings in our lives by placing us in bondage. As men and women who are empowered and given authority to apprehend and arrest those who break the law, many of us walk around in bondage to our own emotions. While others are set free, we remain imprisoned inside our own selves.

The consequences of our anger can be far reaching, expensive, and extremely painful. It can cost us everything we have. When we respond in anger, it is not possible to respond in love, because love and anger do not mix. Anger does not produce the righteousness God wants from us. Ask God to root out any existence of anger in you today, which can be the result of unforgiveness, bitterness, or other unresolved issues. Let God handle the problems, vindicate you, and be at peace.

> *Heavenly Father, I surrender any negative emotions, including anger, to you. I want you to be pleased and glorified with my life and the work I do as a law enforcement officer. Help me in my weaknesses. Amen.*

Human anger does not produce the righteousness that God desires.

JAMES 1:20

267

United We Stand

September 11, 2001, will forever be remembered by Americans. For a moment, our nation became one. People united across political, cultural, racial, and religious divides. We were truly the United States of America. But somewhere along the way, we faltered and forgot. Maybe apathy took over. I'm not sure if we just forgot how it felt that day—how our guts sank in our stomachs when we saw those planes fly into the Twin Towers—but if we are to survive, we must come back together again.

We've lost confidence in each other. Dare we ever lose confidence in the one who is to our left, our right, in front, or to our rear in battle. We're being brought to our knees by division, and the only way to destroy the heart of America is to rip her apart from the inside out. But there's hope. Can we keep our emotions in check in the face of total devastation? If total war breaks out, will we remain confident, not in our abilities but in God's sovereignty and power? Do not be shaken by the roars of the enemy. You are not alone in this battle.

> *Heavenly Father, thank you for unity, for victory, and for helping me to serve in a way that not only honors you but also honors the sacrifices made by so many who have given their lives. Amen.*

Though an army besiege me, my heart will not fear;
though war break out against me,
even then I will be confident.

PSALM 27:3

Mere Mortals

You wouldn't be in law enforcement long if you allowed fear to control your decision-making. This is not to suggest that there are not times we should not have legitimate fear; it is a natural human emotion, but we must control it. As we place our trust and hope in God, we know our life in Him is eternal and our purpose here is to lead others into a relationship with Christ.

Jesus tells us that He came to give us abundant life. We cannot have that kind of life when we live in constant fear. We are mere mortals. Negative emotions left unaddressed can lead to physical sickness and other ailments. Don't stop with conquering fear in your life, but help those who are serving with you. Help them to find the strength to get over the mountain and find freedom. We are mere mortals, but in Christ we are given eternal life. Prepare now for what will last forever.

> *Heavenly Father, there is nothing anyone can do to my soul to take away my relationship with you. The only power fear has in my life is the power I give it, so today, I take that power away from fear. I trust you and place my faith in you alone. Amen.*

When I am afraid, I put my trust in you.
In God, whose word I praise—in God I trust
and am not afraid. What can mere mortals do to me?

PSALM 56:3–4

September 13

Trade It All for Peace

I met an officer with over three decades of experience who worked numerous homicides, including the murders of children. Over the years, it had taken a toll on his mind. He began to share with me how he knew of officers who had worked several murders and were taking numerous medications just to get through the day. If they asked for help, their department would leave them high and dry and they would be without a job. This is the effective and practical purpose of the transcending peace of God.

When we try to bottle up all the garbage we deal with over the years, it will eventually show. Having the peace of God is not merely a state of mind, but an inner tranquility in the midst of the storm. It's better than any drug we could take. If you are dealing with the pain of past calls or scenes, then I encourage you to find practical help—talk to your pastor or a chaplain, or find a counselor you can talk with. There is help available. You do not have to carry this burden alone. God's peace is real and is available to all who will accept and receive it.

> *Heavenly Father, I open my mind and heart and thank you for the comforting, healing, and renewing peace of your Holy Spirit given to me. Guard my heart and mind. Amen.*

And the peace of God, which transcends all understanding, will guard your hearts and your minds in Christ Jesus.

PHILIPPIANS 4:7

It's a Dead-End Street

When you find yourself on a dead-end street, you can either turn around or you can stop when you reach the end of the street and stay there. With the latter, you will eventually starve and die. While that may not sound like a future you find promising, it is exactly how many of us live—letting negative emotions weigh us down, carrying senseless burdens, and worrying about things we have no business worrying about—when we should be focused on living, our family, and our assignments when we are on duty.

We find a lot of references to the "fear of the Lord" in the Bible; we also find a lot of commands from Jesus to not fear. These are not contradictory statements. The fear of God will cause us to obey His commands, while the fear of this world will cause us to sin and lead to death. The fear of this world leads to a dead-end street, but the fear of God is the opportunity for us to turn around and head in the right direction. Commit to living from the fountain of life found in the fear of God. Leave the dead-end street and never return.

> *Heavenly Father, reveal to me the benefit and understanding of having a fear of you. I know my fear of this world has skewed my perspective of fear, but I ask you to change it. Amen.*

The fear of the LORD is a fountain of life,
turning a person from the snares of death.

PROVERBS 14:27

Honor God with Your Authority

Living like we are defeated does not honor God. This is because we were created in His likeness and empowered to overcome this world by His Son, Jesus. Even as law enforcement officers, we should live each day victoriously, honoring those we serve and those who are responsible for our lives as supervisors and leaders. The problem is that people only respect those they can benefit from. But in the end, we are supposed to respect everyone.

That sounds like it may cause us to be viewed by others as weak or vulnerable, but actually it strengthens us. Respect is something that seems to have died with the greatest generation that has ever lived, and a generation who demands entitlement took its place. It's difficult to enforce the law in a society of people who have no respect for authority and feel they are owed everything. But when we honor God with our actions, respect others even when we disagree, and love people regardless, He will bless our lives like we cannot imagine, and we will have great peace as a result.

> *Heavenly Father, thank you for the unity and peace that comes from respecting others; thank you for the blessing I receive when I respect others when they don't respect me. Help my actions to reflect your love to a society who may not love me in return. Amen.*

Show proper respect to everyone, love the family of believers, fear God, honor the emperor.

1 PETER 2:17

September 16

Don't Shoot the Messenger

A mind properly conditioned for traumatic situations before they arise will be adequately prepared for the battles that come. If you trust in God, have a heart that is steadfast in His Word, and do not lean on your own understanding, then you will not be shaken at the sound of bad news. The faithfulness of God is reliable, His Word is true, and His promises are always good. How we respond in the moment of adversity will determine the level of our peace and blessing.

If we panic, don't trust God, and fail to lean on Him, then we will find ourselves trying to fix the problems with our own solutions, which only leads to more severe issues. We must be even-tempered, have control of our emotions, and have faith that what God says is true and that He will guide our steps. There will be tough days, there will be bad news, and yes, we will see terrible things, but at the end of the day, we will not be shaken because we are founded on the Word and filled with the peace of God.

Heavenly Father, thank you for the foundation I have in your Word, the peace and strength to sustain me through difficult times, and the wisdom to guide me through life's storms. Amen.

*They will have no fear of bad news;
their hearts are steadfast, trusting in the LORD.*

PSALM 112:7

Take Care of Your Heart

The beginning of our careers is a time when we start out with slick hair, crisp uniforms, polished boots, and a fitness level that is unmatched. As the years roll on, however, the stress piles up; we begin to neglect our bodies, our minds, and our spirits; and soon we are staring down the gauntlet of medical issues, depression, anxiety, sleep apnea, obesity, and joint problems. If we aren't intentional from the beginning, then our health will snowball before we have a chance to take control of it.

Maybe your emotions have gotten the best of you and you have allowed stress to dominate your lifestyle, causing heart disease, high blood pressure, anxiety, and other related problems. Do yourself and those who love you a favor: go visit your doctor. Have a thorough physical done, have your heart checked, and then work on changing your diet. Start making changes by walking, exercising, and weightlifting. Not only will this help your body become healthier, but it will also help you address the stressors of the job more adequately.

Heavenly Father, give me the drive and self-discipline to begin taking care of my physical body. Help me to remove pride and take the necessary steps to get healthy again. Amen.

Do you not know that your bodies are temples of the Holy Spirit, who is in you, whom you have received from God? You are not your own; you were bought at a price. Therefore honor God with your bodies.

1 CORINTHIANS 6:19–20

Enemies Subdued

What joy it is when God takes pleasure in the way we live. This is not a fantasy available only to a few, but it is possible for each of us through a relationship with Christ. For some, their lives have been tumultuous from the beginning, and to no fault of their own. But through the power of total desperation and surrender to the will and purpose of God, we can find peace, joy, and fullness of life through His plan. And as Proverbs 16:7 says, even our enemies will make peace with us.

What kind of life does the Lord take pleasure in? He takes pleasure in the life of a person who is obedient to the commands He has given, especially the greatest command to love God and love others. When we live and operate based on the foundation of that single commandment, the rest fall into place, because it is a godly and holy love, one that is selfless and pure. Know that as you pursue your relationship with the Father, He takes joy in you. He loves you! And as you remain consistent in obedience, He will cause your enemies to make peace with you.

> *Heavenly Father, thank you for showing me the path to a life that is pleasing to you. Thank you for causing my enemies to make peace with me as a result. Amen.*

When the Lord takes pleasure in anyone's way,
he causes their enemies to make peace with them.

PROVERBS 16:7

Secret Paths and Alleyways

If you have any experience on patrol, then you know the secret paths and alleys, the shortcuts, the places where crime hides and a foot patrol is needed. New officers don't know these secret paths, and, in the event of a foot pursuit or responding to an officer in need of assistance, they will need to know these hidden places. When you patrol these areas day and night, you can help prevent criminal activity or interrupt it in progress, but if it is left neglected, then victims are taken advantage of or other laws are broken.

We are given many options in life, but too often our perspective is narrowed to one or two options. We get tunnel vision. It's human nature. Ask God to teach you His secret paths, His ways, and the most efficient direction for your life. These passageways may cause you to avoid danger or they may bring you to a place where you interrupt an attack on someone else, a place where you can intercede or pray for someone else. Seek God's direction for your life, because when you are on His path, your emotions are easier to manage and life is better.

Heavenly Father, thank you for giving me the ways and paths you have for my life. Reveal them to me so I can walk in them. Amen.

Show me your ways, LORD, teach me your paths.

PSALM 25:4

September 20

Complete Power

Taking an oath, swearing to uphold the Constitution, and abiding by the Law Enforcement Code of Ethics were all requirements before you were given arrest powers in your state. If all you did was take an oath but never received authority, what good would your service be? Maybe you would have been better suited in a nonprofit or civic organization. Complete power and authority is required to survive the streets as a law enforcement officer. It takes a special person to be able to handle that type of power.

When Jesus walked this earth, He not only saw humankind in the physical form, but He saw their eternal being as well. He knew them from the beginning to the end. He knew everything about everyone. So when Jesus said that "nothing will harm you," He did not mean that if you are bit by a rattlesnake, it would not harm you—that is foolish. If you are bit by a rattlesnake, you need to seek medical attention. Rather, the words of Jesus are directed to our spirit man, the part of us no person can touch as long as we are in relationship with the Father.

Heavenly Father, thank you for the total power for complete victory in life—over every foe, over every enemy—and complete protection in this physical body, and in my mind and spirit. Amen.

I have given you authority to trample on snakes and scorpions and to overcome all the power of the enemy; nothing will harm you.

LUKE 10:19

Seize the Day

We have limited time and limited energy on this earth. Most of us have limited resources to sustain us, but the intangibles we have inside of who we are—like love, faith, hope, and passion—are not limited. When we focus on making the most out of every opportunity, we will get the most out of life. Depending on our own natural strengths, resources, and abilities will only get us so far, but when we adhere to the wisdom we get from God's Word and use what we learn from experience, we can make the most of every opportunity.

There is nothing wrong with planning, whether it be short term or long term. This is wisdom in practice. Having a plan, being flexible, and relying on the power of the Holy Spirit enables us to take a potentially negative situation and turn it into a positive one. Today, even in the midst of evil, make the most of every opportunity, using the wisdom, knowledge, skills, and abilities you possess. God has equipped you and empowered you to make this day great.

> *Heavenly Father, help me make the most of every opportunity I am given today. Even during great evil and in the face of great danger, help me to reflect your love and mercy. Amen.*

[Make] the most of every opportunity,
because the days are evil.

EPHESIANS 5:16

The Foiled Plot of Terrorists

Removing the opportunity for someone to commit a crime is one of the greatest strategies in law enforcement, while interrupting a plan to commit an act of terror is another. When you are proactive in pursuing evil, you have no time to focus on fear or the effects of terror. Your focus is on protecting those you serve, and yet you know you are not alone in your endeavors. Eliminating the acts of violence and terror require you to focus on the task at hand, not wring your hands in worry and fear.

When you are tempted to take the bait of fear, remember whose team you are on. You are on the winning team, on the team with the victory already written in the books. There's nothing to fear—your God is great and mighty. He is using you to foil the evil, violent, and deadly attacks that hateful people are trying to carry out against innocent everyday hardworking Americans. Do not be terrified by those who would seek to destroy you; strap up, be courageous, trust God, and do your job well.

> *Heavenly Father, open my spiritual eyes to see the true power you have given me, and open my physical eyes so I can see past the surface and identify the plans of the enemy in my community. Use me to save your people from harm. Amen.*

Do not be terrified by them, for the LORD your God, who is among you, is a great and awesome God.

DEUTERONOMY 7:21

Not My Jurisdiction

If you've ever responded to a call outside your jurisdiction and had to call for the appropriate agency, you know the reason why. There may be a certain lack of joy associated with this if it is five minutes before your shift is over and you are sent to a traffic collision that is outside of your jurisdiction, but you respond until you are either told to stand down or until you get on scene and the responsible agency arrives.

Isn't it good to know our God isn't like some of the gods in the Old Testament who provided protection only in their local territories? He says He will go with us wherever we go. God promises that He will never abandon us in difficult places or in places where others may not go. He will be by our side, regardless of where we are. Not only that, but as we trust His commands and lean on His wisdom, He will direct our steps and take us into the fulfillment of the promises He has for us. All His plans for us will come to pass as we follow His path.

> *Heavenly Father, thank you for never leaving my side, no matter how dark, how dangerous, how treacherous, or how stressful life may be. I know you are always by my side. Amen.*

I am with you and will watch over you wherever you go, and I will bring you back to this land. I will not leave you until I have done what I have promised you.

GENESIS 28:15

A Plan for Achievable Victories

Throughout your career, you will face situations that seem impossible through your own abilities and strengths. Maybe it is a personal battle or a call you have trained for your whole life, but when it comes you know in your own strength you cannot make it through. We can walk around and repeat senseless affirmations and phrases, but until we learn to pair our strength with the power of God, we will never reach our peak in life and we will never see our full potential.

Moses knew Israel would fail if it depended on its own strength to face its enemies in battle. He took the message found in Deuteronomy 3:22 to them to encourage their faith and resolve to lean on the power of God through all battles, that God would give them the victory. Today, no matter what battles you may be facing in your life or career, know that God sees right where you are. Do not lean on your own power and ability to survive, because your heavenly Father wants you to do more than *just* survive—He wants you to be victorious.

> *Heavenly Father, thank you for courage, for victory, and for unmatched strength for life's battles. I submit to you my strengths and weaknesses and ask you to give me your power to face life's challenges. Amen.*

Do not be afraid of them; the LORD your God himself will fight for you.

DEUTERONOMY 3:22

Born to Win

"You're just an average man, nothing special. In fact, why don't you go kill yourself?" I will never forget hearing those words enter my mind, but the moment they hit my ears, something else happened inside of me. I had walked around with my head down, looking and living defeated, but inside those words triggered an alarm that awakened a sleeping giant. The challenges we face can seem overwhelming at times, but with the proper mindset, knowing we have the power through Christ to overcome, and He has created us as a victor, we are more than able to succeed.

As you progress through your career, remember the power you have as a child of God through the regular reading of His Word, prayer, and worship. You have not only been given the power to overcome this world and your enemies, but 1 John 4:4 says you *have* overcome the world. Don't dwell on what you perceive as your weakness; instead, focus on the power and strength you have through Christ. Remember that you were born to win, which means those negative emotions have to come under control today.

Heavenly Father, thank you for total victory in my life. Thank you for your Son, Jesus, who has given me power to not only be victorious but to overcome this world. Amen.

You, dear children, are from God and have overcome them, because the one who is in you is greater than the one who is in the world.

1 JOHN 4:4

Tent Dwellers

As we age, our bodies begin to break down, ache, and weaken, and we eventually die. Our body is only temporary; the Bible refers to it as an "earthly tent." Tents are flimsy. We use tents for various uses as law enforcement officers, especially working a crime scene or as a temporary command post. Anytime a gust of wind blows, if we don't have the tent secure, it will fly off and be easily damaged.

While replacing tents can get expensive and chasing them down in a windstorm can be frustrating, the "earthly tent" we live in cannot be replaced, but our eternal body cannot be touched or affected by human hands. For now, we are merely tent dwellers, and we should stay in touch with the Father as much as possible to ensure our total victory until we receive our eternal reward. Do not worry what others may say or do to you; it may affect your feelings, and you can conquer that, but it cannot touch your eternal reward.

Heavenly Father, thank you for the rewards you have prepared for those who love you. Help this temporary body of mine to last as long as possible, for me to have the strength, stamina, and endurance to serve, until my mission for your kingdom is completely accomplished. Amen.

For we know that if the earthly tent we live in is destroyed, we have a building from God, an eternal house in heaven, not built by human hands.

2 CORINTHIANS 5:1

A Time to Go Hands-On

There comes a time when verbal attempts of de-escalation are no longer effective. There comes a time when you have to go hands-on to put an end to the situation and make sure everyone is safe. That is just the way it is. You can only talk so much, cajole so much, and make so many deals before you have to put someone in handcuffs. Do your job as a professional and do not use excess force, but do not allow the implied burden of guilt placed on you by society to cost you your life either.

Hesitation for a second can cost you a fight. Many times, God's power is given to us through the wisdom gleaned through our experience, training, and mentorship, but He still does intervene supernaturally. We are expected to use what we have, paired with the power of God, and not make stupid decisions. When the time comes and you have to go hands-on, be swift, fair, just, firm, decisive, and professional. They will not overcome you, for God is with you—you are well trained, and you are prepared for the moment.

Heavenly Father, in the moment I am faced with the decision to do battle, do not allow my emotions to make the decision. Help me to have godly wisdom and discernment to make the right call. Amen.

"They will fight against you but will not overcome you, for I am with you and will rescue you," declares the Lord.

JEREMIAH 1:19

To Those Who Are Listening

The truth is that losers are not held to high standards; champions are. As champions in Christ, we must adhere to and obey His commands. Luke 6:27–28 gives us strong commands, some of the most difficult words Jesus spoke in the New Testament. When He told us to love our enemies, He was telling us to step outside our comfort zones, because, after all, how cheap is a love if we only love those who love us in return?

As law enforcement officers, if we only protected those who loved us, our service would be in vain. We must do good for those who hate us too. Overlook the hate, the cursing, and the way others mistreat you today, and bless them, pray for them, and love them. Living up to a high standard may seem impossible, but with the grace of God, new mercies every morning, and the power to sustain us, we have what we need to make it.

> *Heavenly Father, thank you for the power to love those who hate me, for the heart to serve those who mistreat me and those who curse me. Thank you for giving me the heart to serve my community in a way that reflects you to those I encounter. Amen.*

But to you who are listening I say: Love your enemies, do good to those who hate you, bless those who curse you, pray for those who mistreat you.

LUKE 6:27–28

Remember the Good Times

I f the day ever comes when you find yourself feeling hopeless, take the time to remember the days when God sustained you. Remember the days He delivered you and all the miracles, breakthroughs, and divine interventions—all the things for which you should be thankful. So many people can share stories of how God has played an intricate role in their lives, and those testimonies will bolster your faith. Remember the days of old; these times may be treacherous, but the battle is not unfamiliar to the seasoned sheepdogs. They have been here before.

There have been many generations of law enforcement who went before you and saw extraordinary miracles. If they could speak to you now, they would tell of His faithfulness. In your time of need, remember the promises He has given you. His Word is never failing, and He will always come through for you, just in time. Take time to reflect on where you have come from, and be thankful for those who paved the way for your freedom, faith, and profession. How can you live in a way that leaves a legacy for future generations?

> *Heavenly Father, help me to always remember your goodness, even in times of despair, and to come before you with a thankful heart all my days. Amen.*

Remember the days of old; consider the generations long past. Ask your father and he will tell you, your elders, and they will explain to you.

DEUTERONOMY 32:7

Overcoming the Pain of Betrayal

Selfishness and greed can cause human beings to behave in terribly evil ways, including betraying their own family and friends. You may have experienced this same deep pain in your life. Maybe you have had to arrest your own family members or friends, and they claim you betrayed them. When you are betrayed, when someone expresses true hate toward you, it can cause a lasting pain in your heart. Hate can create the roots where other issues can arise. We shouldn't allow the actions of others to affect our attitudes, lives, or emotions; rather, we should love them as Christ has loved us.

You may be tempted to get revenge, argue, fight, or gossip to overcome the pain of betrayal. But in the end, this does nothing productive and drives you deeper into a pit of despair. When we take power over our emotions and learn to express love to those who need it most (in other words, those who hate us), then we are truly demonstrating the love of Christ. This is the way we overcome the pain of betrayal.

> *Heavenly Father, no matter what others may say or do to me, may my life, actions, words, and thoughts reflect the love and nature of you and the love you've shown me. Amen.*

At that time many will turn away from the faith and will betray and hate each other.

MATTHEW 24:10

Specialty Operations

OCTOBER

Get Distracted, Get Defeated

The hysteria people dive into anytime a major storm is approaching usually causes more harm than good. Their focus is on the storm, on the negative, and on the destruction, usually due to a lack of preparedness. If our focus is on the right fog line of the roadway, guess where we will end up? The same principle applies in life with our thoughts. You may be facing difficult circumstances, but do not let those distract you from your ultimate purpose.

Most of the time, the things that go wrong are nothing more than a small part of your life. Storms are not sent by God, sickness is part of life, and we live in a fallen world. It's all part of the package. But because of Jesus, we are more than overcomers. The relationship problems, difficult coworkers, citizen complaints, and financial issues are not the enemy. The enemy is not of this world. You cannot fight spiritual battles with the weapons you wear on your duty belt. But tunnel vision can still cause you to be defeated. Focus on Christ today.

> *Heavenly Father, keep my focus on you. Keep my eyes on you. Help keep my focus off the problem and remind me of the weapons of warfare to use against the enemy. Amen.*

For the weapons of our warfare are not carnal
but mighty in God for pulling down strongholds.
2 CORINTHIANS 10:4 NKJV

No Roadside Court

Enforcing the traffic laws of your jurisdiction helps keep motorists safe. As you encounter the angry driver, sarcastic driver, hateful driver, or the suggestive driver, remember to focus on your purpose. But don't forget about the driver who has been self-educated through social media and Internet videos, demanding their trial on the side of the road. You know this is a trap, a strategy to intentionally provoke you so they can hopefully get the citation dismissed, at the least.

If you fall captive to the deceptions of drivers, a traffic stop can go from dangerous to volatile to all-out war in a matter of seconds. Keeping your focus and not being distracted will help you to not only remain safe but to locate other potential hazards or violations as well. Do not fall captive to the allure of the temptation to argue or debate or the deceptive philosophies of some people. You know the truth of God's Word—keep your focus and you will be fine.

Heavenly Father, thank you for giving me a clear lens to see through and perfect vision with immaculate focus. Amen.

See to it that no one takes you captive through hollow and deceptive philosophy, which depends on human tradition and the elemental spiritual forces of this world rather than on Christ.

COLOSSIANS 2:8

What's on Your Mind?

When you are constantly surrounded by negative people, negative words, and negative influence, you need to have a strong mind-set to battle those so you do not begin to display the same attributes. The natural draw is toward the negative, toward the poison, but we should dwell on God's Word and of what is established in heaven, not on all that is wrong here on earth. If our entire mind-set is on the earthly, we lack the appropriate power to be fully equipped as overcomers and more than conquerors. Focusing on the wrong thing allows the enemy an opportunity for a blindside attack.

As you begin your day, think about *what you are thinking about*. This is not to suggest you become weird or alienated from your relationships, but do not become so entangled in the things of this life that you forget about the reward that awaits you in eternity. Jesus taught us to pray "on earth as it is in heaven." That is what we should be living. We should have our focus on how God intended this world to be in the beginning and live in the reality that He has called us to be fully empowered men and women who are focused on Him, watching for the miraculous to occur.

> *Heavenly Father, thank you for the power to focus on the solution, which is the reality you have given me. Amen.*

*Set your minds on things above,
not on earthly things.*

COLOSSIANS 3:2

Prepare Your Shields

Flaming arrows used to be a thing of the past until Molotov cocktails became popular. Now they are used in riots and protests where confrontations with law enforcement are present. When you are sent to address these situations, you are given the proper gear and equipment to protect yourself. When you are given the proper equipment, and have the proper mind-set and focus, a solid team on your side, and strong faith and support from family, then there's nothing you cannot face on the streets without being totally victorious.

Having your shields ready at the right time is essential to stopping the enemy's attacks. If you have a shield by your side but not where it can stop the incoming projectile, it is useless. Likewise, if you hold the shield in front of your face for five hours and exhaust yourself five minutes before the attack, it was for nothing. Patience, strategy, and preparation are all keys to defeating the enemy's attacks, both on the street and in our lives spiritually. Today, take up your shield of faith. Prepare yourself and be guarded against the attacks the enemy will launch your way. We will not be defeated, because we are prepared and focused.

Heavenly Father, show me the power of taking up my shield of faith and the importance of it, and give me understanding of this Scripture. Amen.

Above all, [take] the shield of faith with which you will be able to quench all the fiery darts of the wicked one.
EPHESIANS 6:16 NKJV

Keep Your Feet Moving

I once had a pastor who told his philosophy of traveling in inclement weather: "It doesn't matter how bad it gets, just keep your vehicle moving." The same is true when running: no matter how slow my pace, as long as my feet kept moving, I would reach the finish line. As a competitor, that hurt my pride, and it may affect you in the same way. But I would rather finish than fail.

This is what enduring to the end is all about. It means you stay in the race and don't throw in the towel when things get tough. It means, sometimes, that you may have to carry a brother or sister to the finish line. Whatever you do, keep your feet moving. Don't stop where you are and focus on the problems of today because things get tough—this is not the end. If things haven't gone your way or if life has been difficult, know that if you keep digging in, trusting God, and keep your focus on the finish line, you will reach the end and you will receive your reward. Enjoy the race.

Heavenly Father, help me to endure through difficult times and not always place my focus on the negative. Show me the good in life so I can celebrate and be thankful and get an extra breath to finish my race. Amen.

But he who endures to the end shall be saved.

MATTHEW 24:13 NKJV

First One in the Door

There's always been someone to blaze the trail, a person who had the guts to stand up and be the first to go in. Maybe that's you. When making an entry into a building, whether serving a warrant or clearing a building, there is usually one person who leads the way; that officer is usually referred to as the point man or shield man. That person has a dual responsibility of both eliminating threats and carrying a shield. Many times, we are leading the way in the lives of our children, families, and communities and don't even realize it.

The first in our faith was Jesus, who was the author and finisher of our faith. He went in eliminating the threats and providing a shield for us as we follow, so we no longer had to fear what was to come. Today, as you go about your life, even if you are handling business on duty, think about how those who have gone before you led the way, how you can lead the way for others coming behind you, and how a legacy of faith can change the world in which you live.

> *Heavenly Father, thank you for faith that leads me, guides me, and sustains me. Amen.*

Looking unto Jesus, the author and finisher of our faith,
who for the joy that was set before Him endured the cross,
despising the shame, and has sat down at the
right hand of the throne of God.

HEBREWS 12:2 NKJV

You've Only Got One Shot

Whatever you do, do it with excellence and do it with all your might; don't do it halfway. Only a lazy person would expect to put in half the effort and get the full reward. Life only comes around for us here on earth once—we get one shot at this, that's it, so why should we waste our time worrying, winging our way through our days and halfway completing what we're put here to do? Think about how our world would look if everyone got a hold of the vision behind Ecclesiastes 9:10.

If we go through life with apathy, we will never experience the best God has for us as a person, or as law enforcement officers. After all, once we enter eternity, there's no coming back for second chances, do overs or retakes. Most of the time, you only get one chance in law enforcement to make a good impression, to have a good career, and have a positive impact. Start well, keep your mind in the right place, and stay focused. Do whatever you do with excellence, no matter how minor or insignificant it may seem at the time.

> *Heavenly Father, thank you for this life. I ask you to give me wisdom to navigate it and the passion to do all I put my hands to with excellence for your glory. Amen.*

Whatever you do, do well. For when you go to the grave, there will be no work or planning or knowledge or wisdom.

ECCLESIASTES 9:10 NLT

It's Not in the Budget

You are highly valued, not just in the eyes of God but in the eyes of those who decided to hire you, train you, equip you, and put you on the streets. After all, He gave everything so we could have eternal life. But for your law enforcement career, have you considered the cost of hiring an officer? While the starting pay, benefits, and other variables differ by department, it is safe to say it is a tremendous investment to hire an untrained, inexperienced person. That's a statement from people who are placing tremendous value on your life when they hired you!

We cannot put a price tag on a life; it is invaluable. We were bought at a high price, the price of the life of Christ, which no person can number; it was the price of His blood shed for our sins. If our focus is not on who He has called us to be, who God said we are in His Word, then we begin to lose sight of this and fail to glorify God. Take care of your body and your spirit by taking time to rest, exercise, and honor God in all you do.

> *Heavenly Father, let all I do with my body and in my spirit honor and glorify you. Amen.*

For you were bought at a price; therefore glorify God in your body and in your spirit, which are God's.

1 CORINTHIANS 6:20 NKJV

Officer's Medal of Honor

Between 2007 and 2016, roughly 1,577 law enforcement officers lost their lives in the line of duty.* These valiant heroes who have given their lives for another person, whether it was a stranger or their brother or sister in blue, remain the greatest demonstration of love on earth. We are all going to be called home one day, and we have a choice to make right here and right now. We can choose to focus on the mess this world is in and all the negative things, or we can focus on the promises God has given us, like we see in Philippians 3:14.

Many of your fellow officers are fighting silent battles because of losing a partner or close friend in a line-of-duty death. Do not let these fellow warriors fight this battle alone; help them in their own race, because it is not a race we run alone. We know the medals we earn here will never compare to the rewards God has for us in heaven. We should not focus on rewards and accolades here, but knowing that those who paid the ultimate sacrifice are honored for their heroism should encourage us all in our pursuit.

> *Heavenly Father, help me to be mindful of those around me who may be silently battling. Amen.*

I press on to reach the end of the race and receive the heavenly prize for which God, through Christ Jesus, is calling us.

PHILIPPIANS 3:14 NLT

---

* See ODMP.org for more statistics.

Unbridled Anger Is Reckless

Even the animals in the wild know the power behind bridling anger. Take, for example, the lion. Soon enough, everyone will know it is present, and the power of *who* the lion is will be felt. It would make a fool of itself if it made a scene, scaring the prey off before apprehending it. Much in the same way, if we were to unleash our anger or rage in an undue fashion, what profit would there be? Surely there is a season for when righteous anger is justified, but unbridled anger is reckless and foolish.

For some, the approach like an unbridled wild animal is all they know. They scare off everyone in their path—family, friends, and anyone with whom they could develop a relationship. Today, whatever the root of your anger is, don't allow yourself to become prey. Bridle those emotions, use them as fuel, flip the tables, and do not give the enemy any margin in your life to take authority over you. A bridled passion and a controlled anger properly managed and used can have a positive impact on the world.

Heavenly Father, thank you for the power to overcome my emotions—even anger. Thank you for teaching me to control my emotions. Amen.

"Be angry, and do not sin":
do not let the sun go down on your wrath,
nor give place to the devil.
EPHESIANS 4:26–27 NKJV

Called to Speak Life

From giving courtroom testimony to policing the streets or interrogating a suspect, we know weapons are not always physical. And sometimes we create weapons against ourselves with negative emotions or thoughts without even knowing it. In fact, psychological attacks of the enemy are common, as are spiritual attacks. No weapon formed from the enemy to attack you in those areas will prevail either, if you stand on Isaiah 54:17.

When you read this verse, the first thing to come to mind about the line "you will refute every tongue that accuses you" is the false accusations of others. However, what we speak over our own lives, situations, and circumstances are sometimes things that oppose the faith we claim to possess and the words God has for us. When we live in opposition to what He has for us, then we experience undue friction and resistance, when all we must do is realize that sometimes we are our greatest weapon, fighting against ourselves—it is often our mind and our tongue. Remain cool under pressure, and stop self-sabotaging yourself with your thoughts and words. Speak life, walk in faith, and live victoriously.

Heavenly Father, forgive me of opposing the words and plans you have for my life through my negative thoughts, words, and actions. Amen.

No weapon forged against you will prevail,
and you will refute every tongue that accuses you.

ISAIAH 54:17

Sometimes "Rights" Aren't Enough

Society has drastically changed over the past twenty years. Americans have always been passionate about their rights, but for some reason, it seems that with the presence of social media, some folks don't even take time to educate themselves on what their rights are before they take a stand. You can drive 155 miles per hour in a vehicle pursuit to apprehend a suspect—you probably shouldn't, but you can. Why can you? Because it's your right. Why shouldn't you? Because everything is not beneficial.

I could list examples of things we have rights to do, but just because we have rights doesn't make them constructive or beneficial. There are times we should step aside from the platform of our "rights" and look through the lens of what is beneficial and constructive for everyone impacted by our decisions, not just ourselves or a few. When our focus is limited or narrow-minded, it results in negative circumstances. Consider the weight your decisions have on those around you and if they are profitable to all involved.

Heavenly Father, grant me the capacity to see through the lens of not just my rights but the impact my decisions have on those around me. Amen.

"I have the right to do anything," you say—
but not everything is beneficial. "I have the right
to do anything"—but not everything is constructive.

1 CORINTHIANS 10:23

Favor on the Firing Line

Any moment of any given day can bring unique challenges, distress, and life-altering battles. Most people do not begin their day with the thought of getting into a gunfight or having to fight for their life. Think about how different your mind-set must be from the rest of the world and how that affects your interaction with others. It's not uncommon for us to focus on the thing or person attacking us and completely forget about our heavenly help or others around us. It is nearly impossible to focus on two things at once.

If we take the time to cry out to God in our time of need, He will hear us and grant us favor and protection. Pursue a relationship with Christ, combined with your excellent skill set and continued training, so when the day comes, you can call on Him. If there are two people opposing each other who are equally skilled in battle, the only thing that separates them is willpower and the favor of God. May God answer you in *your* time of distress and protect you in all you do.

> *Heavenly Father, thank you for favor, even on the firing line. I ask for your divine intervention in distress, protection on and off duty, and protection for my family and those who serve with me. Amen.*

May the LORD answer you when you are in distress;
may the name of the God of Jacob protect you.

PSALM 20:1

Don't Focus on Worthless Things

Where your eyes focus, your feet will follow. If you are always looking to the right or left, your feet will take you where your eyes are focused. The same applies with driving a vehicle. This is not to suggest that we should compromise our situational awareness, but in our spiritual walk, it is different. As law enforcement officers, our eyes are always moving and we are always on guard against complacency and tunnel vision, but in our pursuit of Christ, we should neither look to the left or the right, but look straight ahead.

Think about standing at attention. You know there is someone in charge, and you are generally surrounded by others who are watching you. There's no need to look to the left or right; you know the orders are to look straight ahead. This is so that you will not focus on worthless things and listen clearly to what the commander has to say. Fix your heart's focus on pursuing a relationship with the Creator, and do not veer to either side. Keep your eyes fixed on what He has called you to do, thus fulfilling your purpose in life, living as more than a conqueror.

Heavenly Father, help me to keep my heart fixed on you, to keep my eyes set on the goal of having a relationship with you. Keep me from being distracted by worthless things. Amen.

Let your eyes look straight ahead;
fix your gaze directly before you.
PROVERBS 4:25

Power to Pass the Test

Tests are a part of life and part of receiving your certification to become a sworn law enforcement officer. The problem is when we are taking a test we are unaware of. Most of the time, before we take at test, we have time to prepare, rest, and study. But life isn't always like a classroom. Sometimes the test is laid in front of us before we think we're ready. One resource shows the Greek meaning for the work *temptation* in 1 Corinthians 10:13 also means *tested* or *test*.

Think about some of the moments in your life when you could have been tested without being notified first. Maybe it was a compromising situation with a member of the opposite sex, or a potentially compromising situation with a large sum of money. When we are in these situations and pass these tests, we ultimately find great rewards on the other side. Be aware of these tests in life and live in a way that, at any time you are presented, you will pass and be promoted.

Heavenly Father, thank you for your faithfulness to me through tests in life. Amen.

No temptation has overtaken you except such as is common to man; but God is faithful, who will not allow you to be tempted beyond what you are able, but with the temptation will also make the way of escape, that you may be able to bear it.

1 CORINTHIANS 10:13 NKJV

Heavy Duty

Anytime we think of the word *drunk*, we often relate it to excessive alcohol consumption. If you have served any time on patrol or traffic enforcement, then you know the effects impaired drivers can have on the lives of innocent people. But there are many other things that can cause us to become impaired. For example, lack of sleep is a dangerous silent monster that will sneak up on us if we are not careful. It is in our moment of weakness that the enemy will strike the hardest and do so relentlessly.

Will you remain sober in your heart, spirit, and flesh? It is impossible to keep our focus on the promises of God's Word when we are burdened with our own anxieties, which is one of the enemy's greatest strategies. He knows if we can remain distracted, beat down, and exhausted, we won't be able to prepare. Pull up your armor, gather your might, and call out for the assistance of the Holy Spirit. The duty and burdens in life are indeed heavy, but the power of Christ in our lives empowers us all the way.

> *Heavenly Father, help me remain sober in mind, heart, body, and spirit, not only in vigilance against the attacks of the enemy, but in watching for the return of your Son, Jesus. Amen.*

But take heed to yourselves, lest your hearts be weighed down with carousing, drunkenness, and cares of this life, and that Day come on you unexpectedly.

LUKE 21:34 NKJV

Right to Search

A thorough search is critical to officer safety. If you are justified in doing either a frisk or search, do it thoroughly and methodically. As an experienced officer, you know this. The things discovered while searching a person can vary from a set of keys to a firearm, an edged weapon to illegal narcotics. If you do not have the right to frisk or search an individual, then you will not be policing for long or you will find yourself in federal court soon enough.

The right to search and the right to protection from unlawful search and seizure doesn't apply to what is inside our hearts and God's power to search them. David often asked God to search his heart, which is a bold request. If we're honest, there have been times when we wouldn't want God searching our hearts, minds, or anything about us. Since He's God and He knows all about us anyway, that's not going to be something we can control. While others may be focused on temporary things today, focus on what pleases God. Ask Him to search your heart. When we set our focus on Him, we find favor in His sight.

Heavenly Father, I ask you to give me a clean heart, to wash me, forgive me, and purify me. Search my heart, Lord, for any offensive thing, any hidden sin in me. Make me clean before you. Amen.

You have searched me, LORD,
and you know me.

PSALM 139:1

October 18

Live in Peace with Others

There are some folks in this world who won't settle until they've created havoc and chaos; an offer for peace won't do. In those situations, you've been trained on what to do. But when at all possible, leave the ball in the other person's court. Make all efforts to live at peace with others, as much as others will allow. You cannot force people to adhere to this, which is why we have laws, as well as people like you wearing a uniform with arrest powers and people working in jails and prisons. When it is possible, navigate relationships and situations in a way that peace is dependent on the other person—you've done all you can do, so now it is up to them.

When our relationships are in turmoil, whether professional relationships or personal ones, it can be difficult to focus on what we are supposed to focus on, such as our duties, assignments, spiritual walk, family, and the safety of those around us. Today, focus on mending relationships and keeping peace, and maybe it is time to remove the "weeds" of bad relationships of people who just won't allow peace to be.

Heavenly Father, thank you for the power to make peace in relationships, for restored relationships, and for the will to move on from those which will never heal. Thank you for wisdom and discernment. Amen.

If it is possible, as much as depends on you,
live peaceably with all men.
ROMANS 12:18 NKJV

All Hat, No Cattle

It is usually easy to tell when you are going to have a fight with a suspect. It is not always the one who is quick to talk or speak disrespectfully, but it may be the one with the long, hollow stare. There are times you have been met by someone who is loud and boisterous, cursing, making a big scene, and those are usually met with resistance as well. You have been trained to give verbal commands, but that is part of your *training,* not some random act based on emotion.

The difference between you arriving on scene giving verbal commands and taking control and the suspect's irrational behavior is the thought given to his or her behavior. When we take time to focus on the situation, having confidence in our training and our faith in God, we will be prepared for any situation we may face. There are times, however, when the behavior is not due to the individual being "wicked" but to his or her mental condition, be it a mental disorder or caused by a substance. Either way, when we take time to *think,* we take time to *focus.* And when we focus, we gain clarity and power over the situation.

> *Heavenly Father, thank you for the power to think, for clarity of thought, for wisdom, for discernment in dangerous situations, and for the ability to make split-second judgments. Amen.*

The wicked put up a bold front,
but the upright give thought to their ways.
PROVERBS 21:29

"R" Is for Retreat

Many battles have been won not on the assault but in the retreat. At times, it is best to pull back from the line of attack and allow the enemy to come closer. There is no dishonor is using the superpower better known as common sense to regroup and reattack with more manpower and a better strategy. This is a better plan than going in with anger, a lack of preparedness, and being ill-equipped.

We have all seen the nasty fruits that come from those who allow their own personal wrath to get in the way of their professional duties, especially as it pertains to the use of force. My brothers and sisters, when you feel this emotion in you arising, no matter the situation, it is not worth the consequences and embarrassment to you, your family, or your department to go forward. This is not an excuse for cowardly behavior; rather, it is a way out of situations if you allow your own temper to get out of hand. Focus on taking control of your emotions and do not allow others to have power over you.

Heavenly Father, if I am faced with a situation where my anger is taking over, help me to move past personal pride and remove myself from the situation if possible, so I can honor you, my calling, and those I serve with. Amen.

Refrain from anger and turn from wrath;
do not fret—it leads only to evil.

PSALM 37:8

Yes, I Hear You

The ability to communicate with another person is hindered by a lack of listening. Just because words are being heard audibly does not mean there is understanding. This can be detrimental at a professional level or on a personal level. Often, a conflict can be resolved swiftly by our ability to actively listen to the other person communicate his or her concern, no matter how upset or emotional he or she may be. However, if we are quick to speak or respond in anger, it removes the opportunity to make peace or deliver a resolution to the situation.

For some, actively listening requires intentional effort and hard work. This may mean we have to put our smartphones down, look the other person in the eye, and verbally respond to his or her words. Our words and tone of voice have tremendous power, and it takes focus to keep them in line. However, when we make this a common practice in our everyday life, it becomes part of our behavior. Focus on actively listening to those you interact with today and respond with intentionality.

> *Heavenly Father, may my ears be open, not only to hear but to listen to those who speak and communicate with me. May my words be covered with love and grace. Amen.*

So then, my beloved brethren,
let every man be swift to hear, slow to speak,
slow to wrath.
JAMES 1:19 NKJV

October 22

Shift Change

Whether it is the early morning or evening shift change, the need to have continuous coverage patrolling your area is essential to public safety and mission success. As you are already aware, there are times when you are required to remain on duty after your regular shift has ended until an officer from the oncoming shift arrives on scene to relieve you of your duty. This is part of the commitment you and your department keep to your community.

I liken this comparison to the old law in the Bible and the atonement we received through Jesus Christ. In a similar fashion, the laws of God found in the Old Testament acted as a guardian until Christ came, providing us with the coverage of our sins until His perfect atonement. When we needed it most, we received relief for our souls, but not just for our souls but for our bodies and minds too, for the abundance of life on earth. There's never been a moment when you've not been covered. Place your focus on the power of a God who is ever present, always on time, and knows just what we need and when we need it.

Heavenly Father, thank you for sending your Son to fill the gap between you and me permanently. Amen.

So the law was our guardian until Christ came that we might be justified by faith.

GALATIANS 3:24

For the Honor of the Badge

There was a generation before ours who knew the meaning of honor, loyalty, courage, and commitment. They knew what it meant to live in way that brought honor to those responsible for them, God, and their country. Today, it often seems like many have thrown these principles to the side and instead focused on less important things like entertainment, social media, and other selfish endeavors. Sometimes, even when we may be justified in venting our feelings, it would dishonor our superiors, pastors, family, God, and fellow officers if we did so; therefore, it is not worth venting.

While there may be temporary reprieve in venting about something today, think about who would be honored through your actions if you chose to hold back on those words. As law enforcement officers, we know the importance of honor, and we should always strive to bring honor to our profession, to those who are in leadership, to those who have gone before us, to God, and to our families. A culture that focuses on honor will be a culture that knows great peace.

> *Heavenly Father, help me today to see the value and path of honor in all I do, especially when I feel like venting my feelings. Amen.*

A fool vents all his feelings,
but a wise man holds them back.

PROVERBS 29:11 NKJV

Moments of Impatience

I f our lives were free of responsibility, then the issue of patience would not be as critical as it is in law enforcement. Whether we are driving to a high-priority call and other motorists will not move, or the traffic signal is taking too long to change on our way to lunch, having patience can be a powerful weapon we use to our advantage or one that works against our favor. Typically, the issues that trigger our tempers are related to impatience, but they are rooted in goals, deadlines, schedules, or in our idea of how long a specific event or service was supposed to take.

Throughout life, we are often faced with choices, and we often have the choice to take control of our emotions when it relates to patience. As Proverbs 15:18 states, we have the power as a patient person to calm a quarrel with our temperament, words, presence, and attitude. But when we are quick to argue or hot-tempered, we will escalate a situation that could be solved with peace.

Heavenly Father, help me in my moments of impatience, and let my words bring peace to chaotic situations. Amen.

A hot-tempered person stirs up conflict,
but the one who is patient calms a quarrel.

PROVERBS 15:18

Dropping Empty Magazines

We've all been hurt by someone, and we all have handled it in different ways. Some internalize the emotions until they are so buried inside that the pain is numb, while others express the pain they experienced at the hands of someone else to everyone else they encounter. This is often the result of unforgiveness, which I like to compare with carrying around empty magazines on our duty belt in a gunfight. They. Are. Useless.

Unforgiveness is hurting only *you*. It is holding no one back but *you* alone. In fact, even if you weren't wrong and the other person was, when they don't make the first step to forgive, then your expression of forgiveness is a major extension of peace and can do great things to maintain, heal, or restore relationships. Today, I am challenging you to get rid of the empty magazines you are carrying around with you. Until you have reloaded with the grace and mercy of God, His forgiveness, and forgiving others, you will always be stuck and burdened with those pains.

Heavenly Father, help me to take the first step, even when it is not my place to forgive, in order to live in peace. Amen.

Bear with each other and forgive one another
if any of you has a grievance against someone.
Forgive as the Lord forgave you.
COLOSSIANS 3:13

God-Approved Plans Succeed

Anytime a special operation is to be executed, generally a senior officer or supervisor is required to approve the plans or strategy, or at least to be aware of them. This is not so those carrying out the plans are being micromanaged, but to ensure there is nothing overlooked or simply to have another set of more-experienced eyes review the strategy. There are several reasons this is beneficial, both tactically and legally, for you, those involved, and your department.

When we try to go our own way and create our own plans, we often find ourselves in difficult situations. However, as we seek God's wisdom, it is easier and more beneficial to commit our work to Him from the beginning, and then our plans will succeed. Another way to put it is that your God-approved plans will lead you to reach your goals, causing you to experience fulfillment and joy in life. Today, stop trying to do it all on your own and surrender to God's plans. Give it a try, and watch what He does with your life.

> *Heavenly Father, I commit to you my work, my family, and my life. I ask you to take it all and establish the plans in my life, making them yours. Amen.*

Commit to the LORD whatever you do,
and he will establish your plans.

PROVERBS 16:3

Knowing the Law Isn't Enough

Ignorance is no excuse for violating the law. Take, for example, someone who does not know the speed limit but blatantly and recklessly speeds down the highway. For them to say, "I did not know the speed limit" does not justify unsafe driving. In the same sense, many *know* the law but continuously violate it. We can study the law our entire lives and remain immoral, criminal, and useless to society if we fail to adhere to that law. The same applies to the precepts of God's Word.

Think about how many church services people sit through, collectively, throughout America in a year's time. All too often, we associate performance or attendance with right standing with God, when His commands tell us that obedience is the only satisfactory requirement. Do not conform to the rest of the world. Do not settle for merely hearing or knowing to do good or God's Word, but obey His Word. Actually, put good works to action. When we shift our focus from learning, knowing, and acquiring to doing and serving, we become world changers.

Heavenly Father, thank you for equipping me with the knowledge and understanding of your Word. Give me the will and strength to obey and live your Word. Amen.

For it is not those who hear the law who are righteous in God's sight, but it is those who obey the law who will be declared righteous.

ROMANS 2:13

The Duty of the Sheepdog

Our culture often associates the term "ministry" with a vocational full-time pastor whose full responsibility lies within the church and its people. While this is partially true, the work you do as a law enforcement officer is "ministry," especially considering your role as a sheepdog. You are responsible for keeping people within the confines of the law, which requires you to be held to a certain standard, above reproach and blameless. If you think about the characteristics of the breed of dog known as a "sheepdog," it is similar.

The temperament of the wolf is violent, but you are not quick-tempered, nor do you pursue dishonest gain. While Titus 1:7 was written for the elders or overseers of the church, it can apply to the positions you hold in authority. You are required to live above reproach, both professionally and personally. Take time today to focus on the calling God has on your life. Be thankful for what you do. And take good care of your flock.

Heavenly Father, thank you for entrusting me with the care of your people. I ask you to keep me in good standing in your eyes and in the sight of others. Amen.

Since an overseer manages God's household,
he must be blameless—not overbearing, not quick-tempered,
not given to drunkenness, not violent,
not pursuing dishonest gain.

TITUS 1:7

A Time to Rest

There is a time for everything under the sun. While it may be tempting to worry when you lay down in bed to sleep, let your heart rest assured in knowing God is in total control. For some, the only time their minds can think is when they lay down in their beds to sleep. This is one of the biggest reasons for the difficulty of getting adequate sleep each night. Taking a few moments before going to bed will allow you time to clear your mind (you can write your thoughts down if that helps).

There is a time and necessity for rest. You are not invincible, as much as you and everyone else wishes you were. Take time today to take care of your body and mind. If you do not have good habits before bed, ask your doctor if he or she has any suggestions for you to create new healthy habits to ensure better, healthier sleep patterns. Before you go to sleep tonight, focus on the things you should be thankful for, for the good in your life, and for the blessings you have.

Heavenly Father, I ask you, in my time of rest, to relax my mind and body. Allow me to recharge and reset to prepare for the next day. Amen.

Tremble and do not sin; when you are on your beds, search your hearts and be silent.

PSALM 4:4

The Champion's Salute

While everyone around you is bickering and in an upheaval of chaos, you can either choose to participate in it or remain focused on your work. Champions do not allow the little things to throw them off course but remain disciplined to their path, pressing forward toward the prize before them. You have a choice as a law enforcement officer: you can go in every shift and do just enough to get by, get your check, and go home, or you can focus on finishing strong while looking at the bigger picture.

If you allow the actions of others to affect your performance on duty in a negative way, then you have allowed them to take a little bit of your reward—a reward they did not earn. Whether you ever verbally share the good news of God's love, mercy, and grace to anyone, or if your life reflects it, live in a way that others see the handiwork of God in your life. Stay focused on finishing well. Follow through, be consistent, and live with passion.

> *Heavenly Father, my life is nothing to me unless it glorifies you. Strengthen me to serve you, to serve others, and to live in a way that shares your message. Amen.*

However, I consider my life worth nothing to me;
my only aim is to finish the race and complete the task
the Lord Jesus has given me—the task of testifying to
the good news of God's grace.

ACTS 20:24

Watch Their Hands, Listen to Their Words

There's nothing quite like interviewing a suspect and *knowing* without a doubt that they are lying to you. It's like parenting, really. I've always told my kids that if they were honest with me, the consequences (if there were any) would be significantly less than if they lied to me. Throughout your training, you have been taught numerous ways to detect indicators of potential deception in either verbal or written statements. Empty words are powerless and meaningless; they waste time, manpower, and other resources.

Let's call them what they are: empty words are lies. We can say they are "little white lies" or "half-truths" or whatever else makes us feel good at the time, but at the end of the day, these things do nothing to help us in the moment.

Today and every day, focus on the suspect's hands. They can lie to you, but their words cannot kill you. Watch their hands, listen to their words, and do not be deceived.

> *Heavenly Father, may all I think, say, and do be done in honesty and truthfulness. Help me to detect dishonesty in those I interview. Amen.*

Let no one deceive you with empty words, for because of such things God's wrath comes on those who are disobedient.

EPHESIANS 5:6

Blessings
for Law
Enforcement

NOVEMBER

Called for Redemption

We often hear of adolescents who grow up without a father. As well, a father may be physically present but is not interested in the details of the child's life. Studies have shown that fatherless children are at a higher risk of alcohol abuse, drug abuse, sexual abuse, and other issues.[*] When children grow up in father-absent homes, other men must step up to the plate. We often view God as a heavy-handed authoritarian waiting for us to mess up so He can destroy us. But He is a loving, kind, and merciful Father.

As the father of the prodigal son welcomed him home with a great feast, so God is prepared and ready to accept anyone who will seek Him. Maybe you have saved the life of another during your duties. Your day began like any other, then the opportunity arose. You weren't seeking it, but you were on the lookout and prepared to respond. So God was proactive in His approach. He is searching. When you join the family of God, much like the family of blue, you come under an umbrella of protection and provision.

> *Heavenly Father, I ask you to reveal your unfailing love to me in a way I have never experienced. Allow me to radiate that love to others so they may see you through my life. Amen.*

Do not fear, for I have redeemed you;
I have summoned you by name; you are mine.

ISAIAH 43:1

---

[*] National Fatherhood Initiative, "The Father Absence Crisis in American [Infographic]," November 12, 2013, http://www.fatherhood.org/the-father-absence-crisis-in-america, accessed November 1, 2017.

Love Exemplified

When we try to determine someone's worthiness of love based on actions, it becomes a game of performance whereby we keep tally of wrongs and rights. Love isn't measured by wrongs and rights; rather, it is given regardless of whether it is ever reciprocated. The single greatest example of love demonstrated in history is the birth, life, death, and resurrection of Jesus Christ. While we were undeserving and still sinners, and many did not love Him, He came to give His life for each of us.

Each day we live and serve is a day where we can exude the same love Jesus has for us, because, as believers in His Word, we have His love in our hearts. From patrol to parenting and everything in between, there are numerous opportunities to show our love today and every day to people, even people we may deem undeserving. Through these opportunities, we can demonstrate the true love of Christ to a hurting world, through our words, actions, and service, which are all done in love.

Heavenly Father, thank you for the example of love being demonstrated and for giving me a heart to love and serve others. Amen.

But God demonstrates his own love for us in this:
While we were still sinners, Christ died for us.

ROMANS 5:8

In Spite of Terror

The number-one goal of most of America's enemies, both domestic and abroad, is to create fear in the hearts and lives of the American people. These evil monsters not only wish to physically harm and murder innocent human beings, but they also want those who survive to live in fear every day. When you prepare for duty, preparing your heart and mind for the day to come, you are preparing to confront the darkest fears of humanity.

Your service is not in vain. Stopping the attacks of mad people, regardless of their method of attack, means you save countless lives. Serving as a law enforcement officer *in spite of fear* means you provide your community with the hope of peace. When the opportunity arises and justice is issued to those who destroy the lives of innocent people, you were part of restoring joy to many righteous and good citizens and ruining the lives of those who seek to harm your community.

> *Heavenly Father, thank you for courage to stand and face the darkest terror, the darkest fear, and the vilest of enemies, and for granting me victory over them. Amen.*

When justice is done, it brings joy to the righteous but terror to evildoers.

PROVERBS 21:15

Security Clearance Required

One of the most debated and argued topics in society is Jesus being the only way to heaven. In a time when our rights and freedoms are justification for every sin under the sun, we should strive to hold true to the roots of our faith and God's Word. Just as the law you enforce, there is only power in the Word when the Word is read, understood, and applied. This doesn't mean our lives will always be easy or everything will always go our way, and it doesn't mean we have to like everything we endure.

What it means is that we submit to the lordship of Jesus Christ, to His leading and promises, and when we do, we abide in His abundant life. As law enforcement officers know the chain of command in their departments, so having access to God the Father through Jesus means accepting His sacrifice, believing in Him, and developing a lifelong relationship with Him. This is one of the most profound, life-changing, and empowering decisions anyone can ever make.

Heavenly Father, thank you that I have access to you through your Son, Jesus, who lives in my heart as my Lord and my Savior. Reveal to me your nature, as my Father, as God, as my commander and leader. Amen.

Jesus answered, "I am the way and the truth and the life. No one comes to the Father except through me."

JOHN 14:6

The Empowered Officer

On a dark highway in south Alabama, a rookie patrol officer initiated a traffic stop on a speeding vehicle. As the officer engaged his lights and sirens, the suspect vehicle proceeded to increase its speed. After a brief pursuit, with assistance of other officers and nearby agencies, the suspect vehicle came to a stop. But that wouldn't be the end of the call. After the vehicle came to a halt, the driver began firing rounds at the responding officers.

Without proper authority, these law enforcement officers would be no different than the average person responding to such a wild encounter. But because of the training, authority, and lawful power afforded to each of them by the Constitution of the United States, they can enforce the traffic and criminal laws of our country. Because of the authority and power endowed upon each officer, a dangerous criminal was apprehended without incident. When we have the power, we can overcome any challenge. I challenge you to seek the infilling of the precious Holy Spirit today. You will be better equipped to face the challenges of this world.

> *Heavenly Father, I ask you to fill me with your Holy Spirit. Direct my steps, order my path, and empower me for victorious living. Amen.*

But you will receive power when the Holy Spirit comes on you; and you will be my witnesses in Jerusalem, and in all Judea and Samaria, and to the ends of the earth.

ACTS 1:8

First Is Last, Last Is First

Most newly sworn officers are ambitious and have a strong desire to achieve promotions and experience various details in law enforcement. Others are perfectly content serving as a patrol (or beat) officer for the entirety of their careers. There is nothing wrong with either ambition. However, the person who seeks the seat of leadership is often not the best candidate for the job. In some cases, the best candidate for the job is seen doing the everyday, mundane, simple tasks seemingly below his or her pay grade.

The misconception that "we arrive" when we achieve some specific rank or position is misleading, at best. To be a true leader, regardless of the division you serve in, you must seek to serve. This is the most accurate and telling sign of a true leader, even if he or she is not yet fully qualified to do so. To protect and serve? Absolutely. Be an excellent servant and you will reap the rewards beyond anything you could imagine.

Heavenly Father, please keep my eyes attentive to opportunities to serve your people today and to lead our teams by example through following you. Amen.

But seek first his kingdom and his righteousness, and all these things will be given to you as well.

MATTHEW 6:33

Wise Men Seek Godly Counsel

Joint operations between local, county, state, and federal agencies are critical in the success of many missions where all these resources are required. For example, in a major hostage situation, you will likely see these agencies pull together. What separates the great from the average?

I recall a case where a certain federal agency was on scene to assist our department with an investigation. It seemed like all they did was plan, and when they were not planning, they were planning to plan. When called upon, this agency's team carried out their assignment like it was an art. With the precision of a surgeon, they eliminated the threat and brought the innocent to safety with no innocent lives lost and minimal injuries. This tells me that with good counsel and planning, we can accomplish anything. It is my prayer for you that you would take time to seek good, godly counsel in your next crisis instead of reacting based on emotion.

> *Heavenly Father, I ask you to give me wisdom and discernment and the common sense to know when to seek good help. Amen.*

Plans fail for lack of counsel,
but with many advisers they succeed.

PROVERBS 15:22

Stolen Valor

We've all seen stories of people who dress in military attire and claim certain achievements and awards, when, in fact, they never served or never earned the awards they claim to have received. Who are we to pretend we are the reason for our own successes? Who are we to pretend we are the sole reason for our own salvation, breakthrough, or miracle? We could not save ourselves! It was by grace, through faith, and not from ourselves. God has equipped us to accomplish every mission He has given us.

In this world, if a king lays down his life for others, he is immortalized as a hero and legend; if a police officer gives his or her life in the line of duty for others, that officer is a hero forever. We dare not take credit or participate in the victory for which they paid the price. In God's kingdom, we are the beneficiaries of the sacrifice made by God in sending His Son, Jesus Christ. It is because of His sacrifice that we can experience freedom and abundant life today.

Heavenly Father, if ever I should forget, remind me that in all my doing, I am not my own hero, but you, my Savior, have always been my shield, my protector, and my rescue. Amen.

*For it is by grace you have been saved, through faith—
and this is not from yourselves, it is the gift of God—
not by works, so that no one can boast.*

EPHESIANS 2:8–9

Committed to Doing Good Work

Paperwork is seldom an exciting task, but if it is not completed correctly, thoroughly, and with accuracy, it can have serious repercussions if the case goes to trial. Complacency and laziness will always be the leading cause for poor quality work in law enforcement, and both can get you or your coworkers injured or killed. Being someone who pays attention to detail, even the smallest of details, and leaves nothing uncovered, will lead you to a prosperous career.

Going the extra mile means putting in extra work, doing your work with excellence, and doing this with a consistent commitment over a long period of time. You are the handiwork, the custom-crafted work of God, created in Christ Jesus to do good work, which He made you to do from the beginning. So when people say, "You must have been born for this!" know that you were born for this career, this life. But don't do it halfway; do it with excellence.

> Heavenly Father, thank you for creating me and calling me to serve in law enforcement. May all my work glorify and honor you, and may it all be done in excellence. Amen.

For we are God's handiwork,
created in Christ Jesus to do good works,
which God prepared in advance for us to do.
EPHESIANS 2:10

True Identity

L ife has a way of causing people to change over time. Whether it is due to success, failure, pain, or great loss, our minds, hearts, and outlook change as we mature and age. Another part of our life that changes is our outward appearance. Most people do not look the way they did when they graduated high school. If you encounter someone you used to spend a lot of time with and your appearance has changed drastically, one of the first things you will hear is, "I could hardly recognize you!"

Seeing someone you have not been around in over twenty years and not being recognized is one thing, but what if you went into your own home and your family did not recognize you? As believers, our true identity is found in Christ, and those who do not know Him, do not recognize Him as such. They do not recognize Him as Savior or Healer; they do not recognize His existence. Today, think about the traits you display to others. Will others recognize Christ in you, or will they see the world in your actions?

Heavenly Father, thank you for giving me a true identity found in you. May all I do cause others to recognize you and your nature through my actions, my words, and my service. Amen.

He was in the world, and though the world was made through him, the world did not recognize him.

JOHN 1:10

Recognizing the Source of Everything

Resisting the urge to fix life's problems is a difficult proposition. As a child, my father would let me "help" him work on different projects. I wasn't doing anything, but I thought my work was contributing to the progress. In the same way, I often wonder if God lets us go through life from time to time, letting us think we are doing the work so we will feel like "big kids," all the while He is orchestrating it all. He knows how we are wired—He did it.

But I would suggest there is great power when we recognize the source of everything. When we can identify the source, we can be thankful, and when we are thankful and express that thanks to the appropriate source, we find favor. The apostle Paul ended Romans 11, letting us know in a subtle way that all things, seen and unseen, were made by, for, and through God. Recognize the source of everything you have or will ever need today, thanking God in advance, and watch a major change begin to occur in your life.

> *Heavenly Father, thank you for being my source, my only portion, the only cup I need. Thank you, Father, for meeting all of my needs, both now and always. Amen.*

For from him and through him and for him are all things.
To him be the glory forever! Amen.

ROMANS 11:36

Failure Is Not an Option

There are going to be bad days, days where you want to curl up in a hole and hide. You're going to make mistakes. That's a part of life. If you aren't making mistakes, then you probably aren't trying, progressing, or taking risks. Anyone can soar through life unscathed. A fighter can get in a boxing match, throw all the punches, and bounce around like a champ for nine rounds, but until he gets punched in the mouth, nobody knows what he's made of. We will all fall, but those who keep getting up succeed.

During your career, there will be some embarrassing moments. You can either keep going or just quit—it's your call. But if you want to be excellent, if you want to glorify God in all you do, if you want to leave a legacy of greatness, then you have to get back up *when* you fall. Every single time. Today, wipe the nasty memories of past mistakes from your mind. Just because you did it in the past doesn't mean you are going to do it again. You will succeed, and you will not fail, because you will not quit.

> *Heavenly Father, thank you for gifting me with the tenacity, resiliency, grit, and courage to keep getting back up after I fall. Amen.*

When people fall down, do they not get up?
When someone turns away, do they not return?
JEREMIAH 8:4

Time Is Ticking

Time never stops. Even when our life ends, time is still continuous. Many of us are guilty of procrastinating so much good in our lives in the name of the "right time." But when we think about it, when will that be? The average life expectancy of a male in America is 76.4 years of age, which is roughly 27,886 days. It's essential to move in the right season and in the right time.

All people have different goals and desires they want to achieve. What is yours? If you can honestly say that you have accomplished everything you want in life, then good for you. If you have a lot of loose ends undone, the good news for you is that the hand on the clock is still moving. As long as time is moving, you are winning. Getting in sync with God's plan for our lives can seem like an impossible task, but it is possible when we seek His plan and direction first. Ask God what time it is in your life, on His watch. As He begins to reveal your season, align yourself with Him and watch His promises fulfill in your life.

> *Heavenly Father, thank you for the gift of life and time here on earth. Help me to get the most out of my time so that I can accomplish my tasks and the purpose for which you created me. Amen.*

There is a time for everything,
and a season for every activity under the heavens.
ECCLESIASTES 3:1

Giving Honor Where It Is Due

While many voice their opinions of dislike, hate, and political agendas against law enforcement, the majority of Americans support you. There are still children who want their pictures taken with officers in uniform, and there are still media outlets who give honor to law enforcement officers for their heroic actions. If we're honest, the decline in our society began when we devalued honor. Whether it was for parents, elders, teachers, or for some other deserving person or cause, somewhere along the way, we justified the reasoning for it.

Our society cannot be repaired overnight. Restoring honor will take generations of intentional leadership and parenting and people taking responsibility for their actions, even as parents, for instilling the meaning of honor in their children. Today, think of ways you can honor those in leadership. It may seem foolish and it may seem like a waste of time, but if you will give honor, then in your season, honor will return to you.

Heavenly Father, thank you for revealing to me the true power of honor in our world. Help me to first honor you and to honor the deserving people in my life, all for your glory. Amen.

So whether you eat or drink or whatever you do,
do it all for the glory of God.

1 CORINTHIANS 10:31

The Ties That Bind

There is no greater power for an organization than unity. When a group of people come together with no divisiveness among them, for one mission and one goal, they will achieve what they set out to do. When you talk to veteran officers, many will tell you the bonds of law enforcement are in shambles and not as strong as they used to be. Whether that is true or not, let's address it.

With over seven hundred thousand law enforcement officers in the United States from every walk of life, every faith background, every race, and every sexual orientation, we are bound to have disagreements. When we step foot in the briefing room, those disagreements, valid or not, stay off duty and outside. We are brothers and sisters. We are family. When one suffers, we all suffer; when one hurts, we all hurt. Let us not allow the bonds of our unity to be weakened, but let us come together across every jurisdiction to unify for one common good.

> *Heavenly Father, thank you for the power of unity. Let me never be a reason for division in my family or my department, but help me to bring peace and unity. Amen.*

I appeal to you, brothers and sisters, in the name of our Lord Jesus Christ, that all of you agree with one another in what you say and that there be no divisions among you, but that you be perfectly united in mind and thought.

1 CORINTHIANS 1:10

Nerves of Steel

Shortly after breakfast on a quiet Sunday morning, your number is called over dispatch. As you respond to your assigned call, you are going through the different scenarios in your mind. And as you arrive on scene, you are met at the door of the property by an armed male and immediately you have a decision to make. Do you run, do you take cover, or do you close the gap between you and the suspect, disarm him, and end the threat?

Maybe you don't recognize it because it is your nature. The nerves it takes to make those instant decisions are not common in everyday people; it is like the words of God are being brought to life through your actions when you do things like that. Throughout your career, you will do heroic deeds, some of which no one will ever know about. Even so, you are His witnesses through your courageous actions, working through the fear, serving with excellence and honor, and never quitting.

> Heavenly Father, thank you for courage, for nerves of steel, and for reminding me that you have told me not to be afraid or not to tremble. I know you are in control and will guide me. Amen.

Do not tremble, do not be afraid.
Did I not proclaim this and foretell it long ago?
You are my witnesses. Is there any God besides me?
No, there is no other Rock; I know not one.

ISAIAH 44:8

Perfect Judgment

Learning from each other is something we should do on a regular basis. As uniformed law enforcement officers, we often represent the authority of the jurisdiction we are sworn to serve, under county, state, or federal laws. Aside from those powers, our uniforms, badges, gear, and training mean nothing. Think about what Jesus said in John 5:30. The only person to walk this earth in perfection knew that His purpose was to please the Father, not Himself.

Throughout our lives, we see a pattern of Christ in our world, even in places where He is rejected. From the order of our society, family, government, law, and even interpersonal decision-making, the patterns and examples of Jesus are evident. We are to please the Father in all we do, to be fair in our judgment, and to honor Him, but we are also to be pleasing and honorable to those who are in leadership over us, which is the order God's Word has established. As we seek to please the Father, we will become better subordinates, leaders, spouses, and parents.

Heavenly Father, thank you for showing me the pattern of pleasing you through your Son, Jesus. Help me to please you by hearing your Word, obeying your Word, and being fair in all I do. Amen.

By myself I can do nothing; I judge only as I hear, and my judgment is just, for I seek not to please myself but him who sent me.

JOHN 5:30

A Timeless Gift

Our family has a tradition of playing "Dirty Santa" every year during our Christmas gatherings. It's where everyone brings cheap gifts, then we all draw numbers and try to steal the best gift—in an orderly fashion, of course. It's only appropriate at Christmastime. Many of those gifts are stored away to be reused the next Christmas—it's truly a vicious cycle. This often lightens the mood and, to be honest, makes us thankful for what we receive.

Timeless gifts are often things that are not purchased with money but are handmade or required a great deal of thought put into the idea. From before the beginning of time, grace was given to us in Christ Jesus for all we need. His mercy, grace, and perfect sacrifice are the eternal and timeless gifts that no other gifts can compare to. Today, think about the perfect and timeless gift God has given you and how it has empowered you to be victorious in every area of your life.

> *Heavenly Father, thank you for the perfect and timeless gifts you have given me. May I always live in a way that reflects a thankful heart to you, in my thoughts, words, and actions. Amen.*

He has saved us and called us to a holy life—
not because of anything we have done but because
of his own purpose and grace. This grace was given us
in Christ Jesus before the beginning of time.

2 TIMOTHY 1:9

Misaligned Intentions

There are always people who are doing good deeds, but recently I noticed someone who was upset because there was no local media covering his efforts of "good deeds." The purpose of doing good is not always to receive something in return, even if those good deeds are done for media attention or exposure for a business or product. At the end of the day, if our heart is out of alignment with God's intentions, then our actions will be out of alignment also. Everyone will eventually see through our actions. One of the secrets of blessing comes as we serve or give in secret, and do so anonymously.

When we read the phrase "your heart" in Matthew 6:21, it is referring to our mind, emotions, and will. Knowing that, if our heart is out of sorts before we speak or act, no matter how good the deed or word is going to be, the seed we were going to plant is poisoned from the beginning. Ask God to check your heart, your mind, your emotions, and your will to ensure they are aligned with His nature, will, and Word.

> *Heavenly Father, thank you for giving me a heart that treasures your ways, your Word, and seeks to honor you. Amen.*

*For where your treasure is,
there your heart will be also.*

MATTHEW 6:21

Raised Up for Greatness

I t is not by accident that you are in the position of authority. You have tremendous power to have a good influence on society, and with that power comes tremendous responsibility. Throughout the Old Testament, there are times when God raised up leaders who honored Him and were rewarded, and there were times when leaders dishonored God and faced harsh consequences. What a joy it would be for you to be a light for your community through the position you hold and for the name of God to be proclaimed through your love and service.

From your first ceremony of being sworn into office to being promoted and climbing the ranks, the authority and position you are entrusted with is to be honorable to the people you serve. Through all you do today, let those you encounter and interact with see the hand of almighty God in your life, guiding you, leading you, and changing you for His good. He has not placed any leader in authority for his or her own benefit but for His own glory, so that others may come to salvation through Christ.

Heavenly Father, thank you for the responsibility and authority I am entrusted with. Today, I ask you to bless my decisions, and may all I do honor your name. Amen.

For Scripture says to Pharaoh: "I raised you up for this very purpose, that I might display my power in you and that my name might be proclaimed in all the earth."

ROMANS 9:17

The Power of Articulation

Poorly written incident and offense reports can mean the difference in someone who is guilty of committing a crime receiving the punishment he or she deserves or being released back into society. Failure to articulate the details of the case, especially if it involved use of force or a violent crime, can lead to severe consequences against you, or the victim not receiving any closure in the case. There is tremendous power in articulation in all your reports. There will be many people who read them over the years.

Our plans in life may seem good in our own eyes, just like our own reports may seem good at times. Yet, without the divine blessing of God, His direction and leading, and His power articulating those plans, we will never reach the fullness He desires for us. Take time today to listen for His voice through His Word for the proper answer for your life. There are many answers, but only He has the *proper* answer for what you need.

Heavenly Father, when I pray, help me to speak clearly and to remember you desire relationship above performance. Open my ears to understand, my eyes to see, and my heart to move when you speak. Amen.

To humans belong the plans of the heart,
but from the Lord comes the proper answer of the tongue.

PROVERBS 16:1

Thorough Investigations

There are many details to investigating a crime scene—gathering evidence, interviewing witnesses, taking photographs, and documenting important notes, not to mention preparing to interview any and all suspects. A thorough investigation means that from the time the first officer arrives on scene to the time of the close of the case, everything is done with excellence. The victims deserve this much from us, and we have been shown the importance of such thorough work through our training.

When we overlook the details, we are not as thorough in our investigation as we should be, and the completion of the case will not be as it should. Think of the work God has begun in your life and how you would be if He overlooked the details of your life. He promises to finish what He started in us until Christ returns. As such, we should strive to mirror His nature of excellence and thoroughness in all we do. We are given the promise that God began a good work in us and He will not stop until it is finished. Don't become stubborn and refuse to allow Him to do what He said He would do.

> Heavenly Father, I invite you to complete the good work you began in me. May my service to my community reflect your nature of excellence, both today and forever. Amen.

Being confident of this, that he who began a good work in you will carry it on to completion until the day of Christ Jesus.

PHILIPPIANS 1:6

Abundance Mind-Set

Rarely do we achieve our full potential in life. It has been said the average person only uses a small portion of his or her brain. What would this world look like if the opposite were true? Fear, doubt, anxiety, worry, and hate were never supposed to be part of our lives. It's *not* natural to have these emotions, which is why they are called negative emotions. When we buy into the lie of negative emotions, we cannot access the power of the mind of Christ.

Yes, God is good and His power is greater than anything, but we must allow Him to work in and through us. When we surrender our negative emotions and thoughts, we surrender what has been serving as barriers between where we are and the fullness of where God has called us to be. This is the abundance mind-set. Cut the ties with what has been holding you back from reaching your full potential in Christ, and watch how much more fruitful your life becomes in Christ.

Heavenly Father, I submit to you all my thoughts and emotions. If there are any that hinder you from moving and having control in my life, I surrender them. I ask you to do immeasurably more than I could ask or think in my life, according to your power. Amen.

Now to him who is able to do immeasurably more than all we ask or imagine, according to his power that is at work within us.
Ephesians 3:20

Blinded by the Light

While many are protected, there are still people in America living in oppression because of a community overrun by criminals. These people are scared to speak out, to ask for help, or to say something about the issues. There is only one solution to their problem—that is people like you. Fear may have these oppressed people thinking law enforcement cannot help them, that you cannot come into their neighborhood and flush out the criminals. But darkness must go when light enters in and dwells.

Are there innocent people in your community living in crime-ridden areas of town? You are placed here on this earth, not only as a believer in Jesus Christ but also as a law enforcement officer, to be the salt and light to this world. Today, provide hope to those who are hurting, afraid, and oppressed, so they regain their lives of peace. How can you help flush out those who torment the innocent and helpless?

Heavenly Father, thank you for using me to be the salt and light of this world and to free those who are oppressed and afraid because of the evil of others. May my work shine your light in the dark places of my community to flush out the evil that lurks. Amen.

The people living in darkness have seen a great light;
on those living in the land of the shadow
of death a light has dawned.
MATTHEW 4:16

The Great Interrogator

The structure of law enforcement agencies across America vary, so it is difficult to assume the culture of any one agency to be the same as the next. But there's one thing for certain: interview and interrogation skills apply across the board, from coast to coast, north to south, and everywhere in between. These skills are like our firearms skills though—if we don't stay current with them, then when we need them the most, we will have nothing to pull from.

Learning to communicate with other people is a powerful and often underutilized skill in our society, especially considering the abundant use of smartphones today. If we take time to actively listen to what other people are saying, we can gain valuable insights without them telling us specifically what we want to know. If you want to determine the motive in a crime, then draw it out. Insight is a powerful tool, according to King Solomon. Think outside the box today. Think about Proverbs 20:5 and how it applies to you in the interrogation box or on the streets. It may just take you down the road to some big leads you need.

> *Heavenly Father, thank you for giving me insight, teaching me the value of insight, and helping me to hear beyond the words a person speaks. Amen.*

The purposes of a person's heart are deep waters,
but one who has insight draws them out.

PROVERBS 20:5

The New You

Everyone around us has something in common: we all have a past. If we are honest, does it matter how bad that past is? Maybe your past has things you don't want to ever think about again. But the joy of God's mercy and grace is that He washes that guilt and condemnation away forever. This world may want to bring it up again, but we know what God's Word says about our sins. Once God forgives them, they have been separated from us as far as the east is from the west. You are a *new* creation; the old is no more.

Getting accustomed to the new you may take some time. The old desires may want to creep up every once in a while, but you have power over those things in Christ. As a law enforcement officer, you know the power of a clean slate and what it can do for a person. Maybe you need a fresh start, a clean slate, a new you. Maybe you just need a spiritual upgrade. Today, you can be made new in Christ, and the old will never be known again.

Heavenly Father, thank you for making me new in you, for new mercy every day, for grace, for forgiveness, and for removing my old ways. May my life glorify you, both now and forevermore. Amen.

Therefore, if anyone is in Christ, the new creation has come: The old has gone, the new is here!

2 CORINTHIANS 5:17

Firmly Established

He's running! That's the last thing to cross your mind as the suspect speeds off on foot. In a series of moves that lasts less than a few seconds, you are in pursuit. One wrong move, however, and you are on the ground telling dispatch the last location you saw the suspect. May your steps be established and firmly planted with each thud of your boots on the ground. Whether on foot patrol or in pursuit, may *no* hazard cause you to stumble.

Never allow the plans you have for your life or your ideas of what the future should be like serve as an inhibitor to the growth and direction God has for you. Our hearts can lead us astray if we are not fully focused on the Father. As we pursue Him, however, our steps will be established and our feet will move swiftly. Let us pursue the Master today. May the plans in our hearts become His plans, and may our steps be established firmly in His order.

> *Heavenly Father, thank you for giving my steps firm establishment with each landing, for keeping me from any hazard or trap. May my plans be yours and yours become mine. Amen.*

In their hearts humans plan their course,
but the Lord *establishes their steps.*

PROVERBS 16:9

Remembering the Reason Why

Life has a way of causing us to forget *who* we are in Christ, a way of trying to keep us depressed and frustrated if we stay focused on the pain, evil, and sadness surrounding us. As believers in Jesus Christ, we were not called out of our old life of darkness to go into the shadows. We were called to be His light to this world. But too often we allow our selfish desires to get in the way of that.

As a child of the King, commit to studying His Word and knowing it like you know the laws of your state. Study and be prepared so you can give an answer. At the end of the day, whether you are wearing your uniform and serving the public, or if you are off with your family or friends, you are called to serve. Above all, remember that you are special to God and unique. You may be the cream of the crop, but you are the apple of His eye.

Heavenly Father, thank you for loving me the way I need to be loved, for using me to be your light in a dark world. May I always remember why you saved me, not only for my own sake but to tell others. Amen.

But you are a chosen people, a royal priesthood, a holy nation, God's special possession, that you may declare the praises of him who called you out of darkness into his wonderful light.

1 PETER 2:9

When We Don't Feel God Near

America has experienced her share of horrific, violent tragedies over the years. One thing about all of these horrible incidents is what happens to us as Americans. For a brief moment, most of us lay down our differences, unite, and come together. Have you ever noticed this? It's almost like the plans of the enemy backfire. Of course, we cannot undo lost lives, and we cannot permanently heal scars and horrible memories. But when we unite as one people, we become the most powerful force on the planet.

There will be more violence in America; that is a given. But in those times, as men and women like you rise up to the challenge, as you set the example for the citizens of this nation in service, they will begin to see how God can and does cause good to come out of horrible situations. He will work for the good of those who love Him. There has never been a better time than now to unite as Americans. What a legacy it would be for generations to come.

Heavenly Father, thank you for working for the good in my life, even through the terrible and devastating. I know you have called me according to your purpose, and I trust you. Amen.

And we know that in all things God works
for the good of those who love him,
who have been called according to his purpose.

ROMANS 8:28

Good Intentions

Over the span of your career, you will meet a lot of people who tell you how much they appreciate you. But you will also meet people who hate you, despise you, and want to bring you harm. When you took your oath of office, you knew the risks, the dangers, and what the world that you would be entering was like. But to know that the God you serve has a plan for your life means that His power, His plan, and His destiny will always outweigh that of this world and the enemy.

If the day comes and the burdens of your calling seem like they have become too heavy to bear and you cannot continue, then remember: "For I know the plans I have for you." If you ever feel worthless, useless, and forgotten in this world, then remember that God "plans to prosper you and not to harm you." You serve a loving, heavenly Father who knows all your needs. He will not abandon you in the middle of battle, and He will never turn His back on you. God has a plan for your life.

Heavenly Father, thank you for giving me a plan for my life—plans to prosper me, to protect me, and to give me a hope and future. Amen.

"For I know the plans I have for you," declares the LORD,
"plans to prosper you and not to harm you,
plans to give you hope and a future."

JEREMIAH 29:11

31
Declarations
over Law
Enforcement

DECEMBER

You Know the Enemy

It's difficult to see when there's a person firing bullets at you, but that person is not the enemy. The enemy is the evil one, the devil. However, our services will be rendered useless if we fail to stop the threat, and we must do so to protect innocent people, the suspect, other officers, and ourselves. Having the proper mind-set *before* you get into a lethal-force confrontation will better prepare you to respond to it after the dust settles.

Just as you can reach for your firearm without looking for the holster, so you need to be familiar with your spiritual weapons as well: the Word, your faith in God, prayer, and a mind focused on winning. Having the mind-set of a winner means you are honest about the opponent you face, have a clear strategy, and are just in all dealings. Take time today to sharpen your skills as a law enforcement officer, to meditate on the Word of God, and to pray, and begin developing the proper mind-set of a champion.

> *Heavenly Father, thank you for giving me a clear mind and bringing to memory every piece of training and every tactic I need in the moment I need it. Amen.*

For our struggle is not against flesh and blood,
but against the rulers, against the authorities,
against the powers of this dark world and against
the spiritual forces of evil in the heavenly realms.

EPHESIANS 6:12

You Have Power Over Your Thoughts

Our minds are filled with thoughts, even beyond our consciousness—more thoughts than we can comprehend or recognize. We identify with thoughts that are tied to our beliefs, which are the thoughts we entertain, and these eventually become the words we speak and the actions we take, leading to life's circumstances and outcomes. Too often we allow negative thoughts to have control over us, causing us to make negative decisions that lead to poor outcomes.

As we fill our minds with the promises of God, and command every thought to come into obedience to Christ, we begin to experience a renewed mind-set. There is simply no way to have a winning mind-set if we are always filling our thoughts with worry, anxiety, doubt, fear, unbelief, or anger. Today, command these thoughts that come against what we *know* is the Word of God to come into obedience to Christ. Begin this process by renewing your mind through daily reading His Word and intentionally monitoring your thoughts. In a short time, you will notice a drastic change in your perspective, your energy level, and your overall disposition.

Heavenly Father, as I submit my thoughts to you, renew my mind with positive, holy, powerful thoughts to change my life. Amen.

We demolish arguments and every pretension that sets itself up against the knowledge of God, and we take captive every thought to make it obedient to Christ.

2 CORINTHIANS 10:5

December 3

You Are Fair and Just

We have been given so much from God, but the power to choose is the essential foundation of our freedoms and liberties in this great nation. Who else gave humanity free will? With such a gift comes responsibility. There are times when it seems best to dispense revenge, but at the end of the day, we leave no room for God's wrath. This usually costs us more in the long run. Being fair and just goes beyond everyday dealings; it means having a solid handle on our emotions.

For some, being fair and just means holding true to their word and treating everyone equally, while for others it means not being a person who uses authority to get revenge. This can be tempting, but it is a dark, hollow, lonely road. There have been people who have walked that path, and it did not end well. When we try to do the work only God is assigned to do, we find ourselves writing checks we don't have the money for. Let God handle the dirty work, be a person of your word, be fair, be just, and treat everyone like your grandma is watching, and you will build great relationships.

Heavenly Father, thank you for reasonable courage, allowing you to take revenge, and giving me the heart to be just and fair. Amen.

Do not take revenge, my dear friends,
but leave room for God's wrath, for it is written:
"It is mine to avenge; I will repay," says the Lord.

ROMANS 12:19

December 4

You Know There Is Help

Acccording to a 2013 study by the United States Department of Justice, approximately half of all law enforcement agencies in America (48 percent) employ fewer than ten officers.[*] Many of these agencies will depend on a larger agency for assistance with major crimes or incidents, but there is still a requirement for twenty-four-hour coverage. This may cause you to have concern with a call for assistance if the need arises, taking into consideration the number of officers on the shift, the number of square miles covered, and the call volume.

It's no secret there are numerous challenges throughout every facet of law enforcement, from the layers of emotion that build over a career caused by the things we deal with to balancing the mindset of a warrior and being a parent. We are empowered by the Holy Spirit to sustain through our career, never alone, never abandoned. Take peace in knowing you will *always* have backup, you will *always* have a Helper, a Comforter, and an Advocate in the Holy Spirit.

> *Heavenly Father, thank you for the power of your Word, for the gift of your Son, Jesus, and for filling me with your Holy Spirit. Make your power known to me today. Amen.*

But the Advocate, the Holy Spirit, whom the Father will send in my name, will teach you all things and will remind you of everything I have said to you.

JOHN 14:26

---

[*] United States Department of Justice, *Bureau of Justice Statistics*, accessed October 31, 2017, https://www.bjs.gov/content/pub/pdf/lpd13ppp.pdf.

You Acknowledge the Power of His Word

Throughout your career, laws will be repealed and new laws may be added, and this requires you to stay up-to-date on criminal and traffic laws every year. You cannot enforce laws you are not knowledgeable of, which may result in injustices to victims. Just as you stay current with the laws of your jurisdiction to provide the best service as a law enforcement officer, so knowing God's Word is useful in life for several purposes.

As you acknowledge the power of God's Word in your life, you will begin to see areas where it can be applied daily in every situation. Whether we are alone or in a crowd, there is something for every part of our lives in Scripture. The power of God's Word even applies to our role in life as law enforcement officers, guiding us in integrity, truth, and power. Today, as you see His Word come alive in your own life, think about how it trains you to become a better person, a better law enforcement officer, and a better spouse and parent, thus preparing you for eternity.

Heavenly Father, thank you for giving me understanding of your Word as I read it and for showing me the power and applicability of it in my life. Amen.

All Scripture is God-breathed and is useful for teaching, rebuking, correcting and training in righteousness, so that the servant of God may be thoroughly equipped for every good work.

2 TIMOTHY 3:16–17

You Are at Peace

When we are in a constant state of frustration, we suffer and other people around us, especially those who love us, suffer as well. As we live with unaddressed frustrations, they become like an untreated disease. They never heal on their own, and they lead to terrible results in relationships. As James 4:1 says, "What causes fights and quarrels among you?" As we progress through our career and neglect our own personal care, it is easy to find ourselves living in a constant state of frustration.

Finding a place of peace begins with perspective, knowing most of the things we experience or have frustration about are often beyond our control. If we focus on doing our job, let others focus on doing their job, and trust God to be God, we will begin to find a peace in our lives that previously we did not know. Take comfort today in knowing that you do not have to carry every burden with you throughout life. You have a Comforter in the Holy Spirit. As you release these frustrations to Him, you will find peace in your own life, and your relationships will improve.

> *Heavenly Father, thank you that, today and through all of my future, I am at peace with myself, no longer in strife because of you. Amen.*

What causes fights and quarrels among you?
Don't they come from your desires that battle within you?

JAMES 4:1

You Have a Purpose

Aside from being the shining example of hope for your community, the given purpose of any law enforcement officer is to keep the peace, restore hope, and uphold the pillars of society. Without boundaries, no society can exist. Your purpose is beyond simply arresting someone for a petty theft or a criminal mischief complaint. Sometimes, however, it may seem difficult to see beyond the mundane calls you see on patrol. The reality is that your purpose is significantly broader and deeper than the calls you respond to or the cases you investigate.

Taking into consideration the intersections of your life, there are many relationships and opportunities along the way to invest in the lives of people. You may be passionate about serving the younger generation or the older generation, or maybe somewhere in between. It really doesn't matter if you realize your entire purpose in this life, no matter your profession, is to serve, love, and honor God and lead people to Christ through the way you love and live. Take time today to think about the power of God and how He is working in you to fulfill His good purpose.

Heavenly Father, thank you for working in my life to fulfill your good purpose for your kingdom here on earth. Amen.

*For it is God who works in you to will
and to act in order to fulfill his good purpose.*

PHILIPPIANS 2:13

You Are an Example of Goodness

Too often our society abuses boundaries of good and evil in the name of free speech. Who will establish the example for what is good? Where is the precedence of goodness? Men and women like you, serving their entire lives, are examples of goodness in this world. Regardless of what happens in the rest of the world, there are many people who still abide within the boundaries of goodness and righteousness. We know where our free will comes from, and we know that our freedom and liberty come from God also.

For that reason, in all you do, strive to continue being an example of goodness and righteousness. This is achievable through your words (doing what you say), your actions, and through your professionalism. At the end of each day, at the end of your career, and ultimately at the end of your life, the example of integrity you leave behind will pave the way for many others to come behind you to uphold the standards of goodness and righteousness for generations to come.

> *Heavenly Father, thank you for giving me the position of being an example of goodness. Help me in all I do to be an example of good, to show integrity, and to honor you. Amen.*

In everything set them an example by doing what is good.
In your teaching show integrity, seriousness.

TITUS 2:7

You Are a Sheepdog

There's something that occurs in the brain of a law enforcement officer when a suspect flees on foot. Immediately, the officer is presented with the reality of multiple dangers, potential hazards, the need to consider innocent bystanders, and also to operate within the procedures of the department and state law. Nevertheless, you pursue. Above all the emotions, your feet move to apprehend someone that *no one* else in your community, other than law enforcement, would chase.

This is the calling of a sheepdog—to protect the innocent and helpless, the defenseless and weak, to relentlessly pursue and apprehend the wolves in society. You are the price those who violate the law must face. You are the sheepdog, the herder, the protector, the defender. Today, you have a lot to be proud of. You carry the calling and honor of serving in a capacity few have the courage to do. Honor God, honor your leaders, love people, and watch the backs of those who serve with you. Never stop pursuing.

Heavenly Father, when my body begins to wear down in pursuit, give me breath. Make my feet firm, more swift than those I pursue, and protect me every step. Amen.

The wicked flee though no one pursues,
but the righteous are as bold as a lion.
PROVERBS 28:1

You Are a Leader

Providing good leadership is not limited to those you serve with; it extends to those you serve. Leadership is a topic many often confuse with a position of rank, but in reality it is occupying the field where you are and exuding confidence in humility, leading the way by example, and providing guidance to your peers. Being dependable and reliable to your leadership is a great way to show yourself as a leader to others around you.

Leadership begins with *you*. It begins with you linking arms and working in unity for one mission. Over time, you become seasoned and achieve rank, so providing guidance and acting as an advisor is natural to you. As you look around the leadership structure of your department, you will notice the chain of command has many "advisors," from senior officers, deputies, corporals, sergeants, and lieutenants, all the way down to chief and sheriff. Each of these people provide much-needed leadership, and you are part of that team.

Know that you are a leader, no matter where you are in the process. Continue your development and trust God's timing, and you will see the rewards in due season.

> Heavenly Father, thank you for the position I have been entrusted with. I ask for your favor and blessing and for guidance as I commit every day to you. Amen.

For lack of guidance a nation falls,
but victory is won through many advisers.

PROVERBS 11:14

You Are Honest and True

One of the quickest ways to ruin your career in law enforcement is to lie on the stand while under oath. The news of this will spread quickly among your peers, administrators, judges, and lawyers, and it could lead to criminal charges. While this is an extreme, it is a prime example of how painful dishonesty and false testimony can be to all parties involved. You have likely witnessed the terrible results of these actions, and it caused you to cringe while watching it unfold.

It may seem that the easiest way out is to lie or twist the truth to our favor, but at the end of the day, losing a case, receiving administrative discipline from our superiors, or even losing your career is better than lying. Maintaining your integrity and character go a long way in life, and the simplicity of doing the right thing begins with your heart and your relationship with God. Today, commit to continuing your life of honesty and truthfulness, living as a hope to others who have lost hope in humanity because of the lies of many.

Heavenly Father, thank you for words that are true and right, that they come from a heart that is after you and to please and honor you. Amen.

Like a club or a sword or a sharp arrow
is one who gives false testimony against a neighbor.
PROVERBS 25:18

You Are Alert and of Sound Mind

If you wear a badge, situational awareness is essential for your survival as a law enforcement officer. While you may not go into your shift intoxicated, you may go in distracted, which, as a law enforcement officer, is as good as drunk. Taking the time to ensure your mind is focused and alert, and you are emotionally balanced before duty, means you are prepared for the threats you may face. Having a healthy mind-set, balanced vigilance, and sound perspective will set you on the right foot to begin your day.

Whatever your goals, think about your mind-set today. Are you too relaxed or are you hypervigilant? There's a balance that is healthy, where performance is at an optimum and you can get the most out of your day and are the absolute best version of yourself. There are threats and there is a reality of the dangers in law enforcement, but this does not mean we live foolishly or in a way that robs us of our God-given peace.

Heavenly Father, thank you for a constant mind-set that is prepared for the threats of this world, a mind that is sober and alert, but a spirit at total peace from only a source you give. Amen.

*Be alert and of sober mind.
Your enemy the devil prowls around like
a roaring lion looking for someone to devour.*
1 PETER 5:8

You Are *Not* a Quitter

We could spend much time talking about the valiant acts of people who have fought back in the line of fire, men and women who, when they were faced with grave injuries in battle, persevered and took the fight to the enemy. Were they faced with fear? Absolutely. Did they overcome it? You bet they did. We read of stories of officers who have been stabbed, shot, and assaulted by individuals and vehicles, but who did not give up the fight.

We are called to be peacemakers. As believers of God, we are called to bear the fruits of His Spirit. But do not think that this makes you soft as an officer. Rather, it emboldens you. It solidifies your mind-set and prepares you for battle should that day come. Whatever you face in your life today, plant this thought deep in your mind: *I will never give up, I will never quit, I know my God will lift me up, and I will persevere and take the fight to the enemy.* Embed yourself in the presence of God through prayer and study of His Word today.

> *Heavenly Father, thank you for giving me a mind-set of steel, a spirit of a true warrior, a heart untouchable to this world, and a will that is never broken. I know that with you, I will never quit the fight. Amen.*

LORD, *see how my enemies persecute me!*
Have mercy and lift me up from the gates of death.
PSALM 9:13

You Are an Overcomer

While it may be hard to believe, everything we see is a result of a war between good and evil, "God's side" and the "devil's side": the ripping apart of societies through the eroding of morals, the vanishing consciousness of humanity, the seemingly overwhelming power of hate, and the apparent defeat of love. Any person has the power to overcome evil if he or she will only oppose it with goodness, but few have the courage to face evil in the manner in which you do.

There may be times when the world is chattering with talk that you will be overcome by evil or the plans of the enemy seem too great to defeat. Never allow the threats or presence of the terrible things you deal with to change your mission or who you are as a person, or keep you from fighting for good, for righteousness, for love, and to give peace and hope. Know that the reality of the situation is that you are victorious in Christ, living and expressing love, and opposing evil with good. You are the force that stops the darkness in this world. Keep fighting.

Heavenly Father, thank you for your overcoming power, for the empowering love to face evil, and for courage to do good in the face of evil. Amen.

Do not be overcome by evil,
but overcome evil with good.
ROMANS 12:21

You Are Uniquely Created and Equipped

After hundreds of hours of training, you are prepared for duty as a law enforcement officer. The standards may vary by state, but the goals of training are the same: reduce and eliminate crime, save lives, protect property, and restore order and peace. As believers in Jesus Christ, our equipping does not end with our professional training; we are equipped by God to do everything good for His will.

While many wonder what the will of God is for their life, as a believer your purpose is to use the gifts you have been entrusted with to serve the people of your community, to be a leader of integrity and character, and to honor those in authority. You are to do this as if you are working for God Himself. You have been equipped by His Word to share the love of Jesus through your life. Know your equipping does not end with the gear on your belt, but it is in your heart and in your spirit. You have everything you need to fulfill God's plan for your life.

Heavenly Father, thank you for fully equipping me to fulfill your plan and will for my life. I ask you to help me be a good steward of all that I have been entrusted with. Amen.

May the God of peace ... equip you with everything good for doing his will, and may he work in us what is pleasing to him, through Jesus Christ, to whom be glory for ever and ever. Amen.

HEBREWS 13:21

You Are Courageous

On one occasion, I had a watch commander on my night shift patrol come out to a free-for-all. As a rookie, I made a potentially fatal error and did not remove a suspect from the crowd before questioning or detaining him. Later on, after everything had settled, my lieutenant pulled me aside and sternly reminded me, "Have I not told you in the past to separate them from the crowd? You could've gotten yourself killed!" That conversation was followed by some additional firm and animated scolding, which I was fully deserving and thankful for.

Sometimes our courage comes from moments of error, moments we could learn from, moments we were able to survive and grow from. It is in these lessons that we become stronger and less likely to be discouraged in the fight. There are so many things that you deal with and do not even give a second thought to fear in the moment. Allow your past to become your strength and fuel for your future, not chains that wear you down. You have all you need to prepare you for the fight.

Heavenly Father, thank you for courage, for strength, and for never abandoning me in the fight. Amen.

Have I not commanded you? Be strong and courageous.
Do not be afraid; do not be discouraged,
for the LORD your God will be with you wherever you go.

JOSHUA 1:9

You Bless Those Who Persecute You

Until someone has complained about you "pointing" rudely, it is difficult to understand the level some people will go to in persecuting you or giving you a hard time. The same would apply when we encounter someone on a patrol call or on a traffic stop. Let them talk, cuss, or call you names—it is irrelevant. But as you remain professional and polite, you are setting yourself up for blessings in the supernatural and victory in the natural.

Persecution against Christians in America is nothing like it is in other parts of the world today or like it was many years ago. People are dying in other parts of the world for their faith in Christ, and we simply must make a commitment to live for Him above our own selfish ways. When others persecute you, bless them. Bless them with your words, in prayer, and through actions and deeds. As you do this, you open the windows of opportunity for God's Word to come to life and blessings to flow. Do not speak evil for evil, but bless those who curse you.

Heavenly Father, I ask your blessing over all who have persecuted me, cursed me, or wished harm on me. I declare blessing over their lives, their finances, relationships, families, careers, health, and relationship with you. Amen.

Bless those who persecute you; bless and do not curse.

ROMANS 12:14

You Are an Honorable Person

R ivalries are good for creating healthy competition. Sometimes this can turn nasty in the professional world of law enforcement. Whether it's a colleague or someone you've dealt with on the streets, it takes little effort to create an enemy when you stand up for what is right in a world that is messed up. From backbiting, gossiping, slandering, or old-fashioned bullying, you can face high school–style drama in the adult world. But this can run much deeper and become significantly more serious, from false arrests, false accusations, setups, marital affairs, and much more.

When your enemy stumbles and falls, it may be tempting to initially celebrate and tell the world how faithful God is to vindicate you. While He is faithful to vindicate, we are called to love our enemies. A heart of love for our enemies does not desire to see them fall or stumble; we should not rejoice in their fall. There is power, strength, honor, and confidence in the silence of a vindicated person. Don't take matters into your own hands. Be a person of honor, and let God handle it. And when He does, don't gloat about it.

> *Heavenly Father, I give those who have mistreated me, those who have wronged me or harmed me in any way, to you. I speak blessing over them and ask you to take control. Amen.*

Do not gloat when your enemy falls;
when they stumble, do not let your heart rejoice.

PROVERBS 24:17

You Are Wise

The call may come in as something you dismiss in your mind as low priority, maybe a traffic hazard complaint or a noise complaint. You arrive on scene only to be ambushed by faceless cowards, but you are prepared. Why? You have been trained, you've seen the lives of those who paid the ultimate sacrifice, those who were ambushed and did not make it home. Their lives were not lost in vain. You have become wiser, more vigilant, and more aware. It's no secret there are people who want to harm you through cowardly means, setting traps, or luring you into a setup.

Having the proper mind-set and maintaining situational awareness further prepares us and enlightens us to the tactics of an emboldened enemy. Times are changing and tactics of the enemy are evolving, but their motives are the same. As a child of God, placing your trust and hope in God and leaning on Him for divine help in dealing with humanity will lead you to victory and salvation in times of trouble.

Heavenly Father, thank you for revealing to me the traps of the enemy, the snares set before me, and the ambushes that await, no matter how sweet the honey may seem or how quiet it is. Amen.

They spread a net for my feet;
I was bowed down in distress. They dug a pit in my path—
but they have fallen into it themselves.

PSALM 57:6

You Seek God's Direction

Taking time to pray doesn't have to be a boring, ritualistic behavior that you dread. Once the power of prayer is discovered, it becomes like spending time with a best friend. It's not something you feel you *have* to do out of a performance-based love, but it is a sincere desire to know God on a personal level. We get to know Him through studying His Word and through prayer, whether that takes place in the morning or in the evening, or takes place through whispering prayers throughout the day.

One thing about the darkness we experience as law enforcement officers is that it cannot remain where our light shines. Darkness must flee. It is in darkness that most evil flourishes, but the light of God's Word exposes the darkness for us to see, guiding our path through perilous places. Don't look at spending time reading the Bible as a monotonous task you have to do for God to love you, or praying so God will not send you to hell. No, He loves you—nothing can change that. Read and pray out of a desire to draw closer to God, and watch how your life begins to change.

Heavenly Father, thank you for your perfect Word. I ask you to show me the way. Help me to understand your Word, apply it, and adopt it in my life. Amen.

Your word is a lamp for my feet,
a light on my path.

PSALM 119:105

You Are Strategic

God does nothing by accident. He is a God of order and strategy. When we receive a command to wait, there is a reason for it. As a young officer, I would always try to be the first to a complaint of a fight between two individuals. One day, a seasoned officer said, "Why don't you let them wear down a little bit?" He had a good point. Sometimes we try to rush into things to "fight" when it was never our place to do so—it was God's battle all along.

We cannot take this Scripture as an excuse to do nothing. However, it is a prime example of how we are to recognize the power of God in our lives and understand that He is strategic and orderly and expects us to be the same. There may be times in law enforcement when your best strategy is to wait—it may be rare, but stranger things have happened. In life, give Him the freedom to work instead of trying to fix all your problems. Listen and look today. Is God showing you a place in your life where He wants you to simply be still and let Him handle the situation?

Heavenly Father, thank you for helping me and fighting for me. I ask you to show me when I need to be still and let you fight for me. Amen.

The LORD will fight for you;
you need only to be still.

EXODUS 14:14

You Never Stop Pursuing

With every act of service you perform, you are sowing righteousness and planting seeds of love and goodness in a world that is often overrun with hate. If you have been unproductive, both on the job or in life, break up your unplowed ground and begin to plant seeds. Pursuing God means you are planting seeds of righteousness in every area of your life—home, marriage, relationships, finances, career, and ministry outreach.

For some, this may mean you begin anew with some changes in your marriage, or make some healthy commitments in your finances, health, or fitness. For others, this means having an honest discussion with yourself about where you have been in your career, what you have accomplished, and what you need to do to achieve your goals. Seeking the Lord is not some mystical activity; it is part of our everyday lives. Over time, our pursuit of God will result in a harvest of righteousness, a bounty of goodness and blessings that will overtake us. But it begins today with small steps. Have the courage to take the first step.

Heavenly Father, thank you for giving me the courage to take the necessary steps to begin my pursuit of you, to break up the unplowed ground in my life and sow seeds of righteousness. Amen.

Sow righteousness for yourselves,
reap the fruit of unfailing love,
and break up your unplowed ground;
for it is time to seek the LORD,
until he comes and showers his righteousness on you.
HOSEA 10:12

You Are on the Winning Team

Jesus *is* the Prince of Peace who came to bring peace between humankind and God, but the war between light and darkness has never ceased. It is true that Jesus came to bring salvation to humanity, but He also came to defeat darkness. We know this earth is the devil's playground and the enemy seeks to kill, steal, and destroy, but darkness cannot remain in the light. As a believer in Jesus, you are on the winning team, and as a law enforcement officer, you are in the middle of the fight of good and evil.

Our peace is made perfectly complete through our relationship with Jesus, and we have been commissioned to serve His kingdom, to love God, to love people, and to engage in the battle through His Word and Spirit. On a practical note, in your official capacity as a law enforcement officer, part of restoring peace is, at times, to do battle on behalf of the innocent or defenseless. Sounds familiar, doesn't it? Walk in the truth of God's Word today, knowing you are on the winning team, fully empowered and fully equipped. The battle is already won.

> *Heavenly Father, thank you for the power to defeat darkness, to overcome evil, and to restore peace and order. Amen.*

Do not suppose that I have come to bring peace to the earth. I did not come to bring peace, but a sword.

MATTHEW 10:34

You Are a Watchman

There is glory and suffering as a law enforcement officer. Over the years, you have seen one senseless tragedy after another, a pain that discriminates against no age, no social status, and no race. Tragedy can strike anyone at any time. Yet you stand your watch, relentlessly serving and pursuing those who do evil, which is a never-ending battle. As you gather with other officers, the conversations at times turn dark and someone often wonders if the pain you endure and the burdens you bear are all worth it.

And then you remember: Where would this world be without watchmen on the wall? You stand guard, pursuing those wolves who prey on innocent sheep, protecting those who stray from the flock into harm's way. You know, deep in your soul, if people like you were not on the watch, then this world would have gone to hell a long time ago.

Pursue evil when it comes. Apprehend those who violate the laws. Serve and help those who are helpless. But never relent in your duty as a watchman, for you are part of God's plan, delivering hope to people in need.

> *Heavenly Father, thank you for this honor to serve your people and your kingdom as a watchman—to protect, to serve, and to pursue and apprehend evil. For this there is no greater honor. Amen.*

Listen! Your watchmen lift up their voices;
together they shout for joy.
When the LORD returns to Zion,
they will see it with their own eyes.

ISAIAH 52:8

You Restore Order

Some people live their entire life in disarray—one bad relationship after another, one terrible financial decision after another, parenting problems, and in and out of prison. When you talk to people like this, some tell you none of it is their fault and some honestly tell you they made a lot of bad decisions. But along the way, you will have the opportunity to intervene and have tremendous positive influence in the lives of people.

Restoring order isn't something that began with the inception of the law enforcement profession. Order is in the nature of God; He desires it in our lives, in society, in churches, and throughout the world. While 1 Corinthians 14:40 is a portion of Scripture where the apostle Paul was reproving the Corinthians for disorder in the church, everything we do in life should be done in a "fitting and orderly way" so we honor God. Even amidst the chaos, remember the work you are doing is part of God's plan, it is pleasing to Him, and restoring order in society is nothing to be taken lightly.

Heavenly Father, thank you for showing me the example of order through your Word and using me to restore order in society. Help me to maintain order in my own life. Amen.

But everything should be done
in a fitting and orderly way.
1 CORINTHIANS 14:40

You Are Focused

We may not immediately correlate the words *focus* and *stress* in the same sentence, but it has repeatedly been supported that untreated stress, unhealthy lifestyles, and bad habits lead to chronic fatigue and other issues. As law enforcement professionals, it is understood and an accepted part of the job that there will be odd hours, rotating shifts, high stress, and moments of anxiety. However, if we allow stress and fatigue to go unaddressed, either as law enforcement officers or private citizens, it can lead to much more severe issues.

Developing healthy habits for sleep and nutrition, developing solid relationships with partners on the job and away from work, and having a healthy home life will lend to better patterns of addressing stress and fatigue. When stress dominates our lives, we live in a place of constant defeat, making it difficult to focus on doing excellent work in law enforcement. Today, find healthy ways to rid the stress and build healthy habits in your life. Take time in prayer and reading the Bible, give those things to God, and allow Him to provide you peace. As you take these steps, you will begin to see a massive improvement in your overall focus in life.

Heavenly Father, thank you for taking the burden of my stress, giving me rest, and giving me precision, and for giving me intense focus on you, on duty and in life. Amen.

You will seek me and find me
when you seek me with all your heart.

JEREMIAH 29:13

You Are More Than a Conqueror

There are some people who perform at their prime under pressure and others who crumble at the slightest hint of it. Most law enforcement officers are those who rise to the challenge anytime the pressure is on, performing at their highest levels. Some say it's adrenaline and some say it's genetics, but at the end of the day, it comes down to character. How we respond to adversity has more to do with *who* we are than *what* we are.

At some time in your career, you may find yourself like the psalmist in Psalm 57:4, in the midst of lions, dwelling with ravenous beasts, and in a less-than-pleasant situation. In these moments, when the tension is at a fevered pitch, your heart is pounding and your mind racing, remember you are more than a conqueror in Christ. Not only do you have your faith and not only are you prepared mentally and spiritually, but you are also one of the most well-trained professionals on the street. Affirm that you *are* more than a conqueror. Never let those skills go stale, and never let your relationship with God grow cold.

Heavenly Father, thank you for standing with me in the presence of intense pressure. Thank you for making me more than a conqueror before the battle ever begins; thank you for victory. Amen.

I am in the midst of lions; I am forced to dwell among ravenous beasts—men whose teeth are spears and arrows, whose tongues are sharp swords.

PSALM 57:4

You Restore the Broken

One of the blessings of the work you get to do is serving people who may declare their hate for you, either to their friends or on social media. But when someone breaks into their home or car, or someone assaults them and they become a victim, they call on law enforcement to help. When you respond, it is a wonderful example of love in action. These are opportunities to reveal the true love of Christ through your actions.

When you can take steps to help restore someone's life through helping them get the resources they need or getting them professional assistance, they can see through the propaganda in society and see the humanity of law enforcement, and they see the hearts of the men and women behind the badge. Think about the ways God has used your service to restore the lives of broken people—through words or actions—and how He has strategically positioned you, even in the presence of your enemies, as a minister for His glory.

> *Heavenly Father, may all those I serve see a true reflection of your lovingkindness through my actions and service today, and may you receive my work as an honorable gift back to you. Amen.*

Those who hate me without reason outnumber the hairs of my head; many are my enemies without cause, those who seek to destroy me. I am forced to restore what I did not steal.

PSALM 69:4

You Are Stronger than the Enemy

Our homes are supposed to be safe places, but every year, millions of Americans are victims of burglary, home invasions, and other crimes that rob them of peace in their own homes. There is not one of you who would not defend your property, your family, or your possessions against an intruder, even fighting to the point of death. After healing a possessed man, Jesus used a parable to get the point across to those who were listening.

When we read Luke 11:21–22, it may sound as though Jesus was encouraging us to guard our homes. While there is certainly *nothing* wrong with that, this was not His point. The reference to the "strong man," as consistent with all major commentaries, is satan, and the stronger man is Jesus. Therefore, as you have been empowered with the life and mind of Christ, *you* have been made the stronger person to overtake the enemy, to disarm him, to plunder his spoils, and take rightful possession of what is yours. No longer a victim, no longer a slave, no longer defeated—you are stronger than the enemy.

> *Heavenly Father, thank you for empowering me to defeat the enemy, for filling me with your Spirit, for never leaving me and guiding me all my days. Amen.*

When a strong man, fully armed, guards his own house, his possessions are safe.

LUKE 11:21

You Will Not Be Destroyed

Law enforcement is not for the faint of heart. It's a world that requires you to be resilient, to be able to take a punch and get back up again and stay in the fight, no matter how bad it hurts. Many people have a lot of unanswered questions and may look to you for answers to those difficult, complex questions that we simply cannot answer at times. At any given moment, for a reason not known to us, someone can begin attacking innocent people, causing mass casualties. Your response is the only hope of survival for those involved.

It does not matter how much more evil this world becomes—you can cling to the promise that you will be victorious in Christ. And while we will all leave this life one day, no one can touch our eternal life with Him. You may be surrounded in life from every side, but you will not be defeated. Stand firmly on the promises of God's Word, for it is alive and active. As you apply it in your life, you will see the fingerprints of God throughout your world.

Heavenly Father, thank you for the promise of your protection. I ask for you to surround me with your covering and protection, and that you would guide me with divine wisdom and discernment. Amen.

We are hard pressed on every side, but not crushed;
perplexed, but not in despair; persecuted,
but not abandoned; struck down, but not destroyed.

2 CORINTHIANS 4:8–9

You Adhere to
the Greatest Command

When we consider the greatest command we could issue to an individual, there are many options to choose from. Some may suggest we command others to travel safely, while others may suggest we command others to be vigilant. We all have experienced commands from a superior-ranking officer, and we know what it means to carry out those orders. We do this because of established policy and procedures that tell us how we are to do so.

Much like the policy and procedure manuals we have at work, God's Word spells out how we should respond to various challenges and situations in life. At the end of the day, the greatest command is to love God and love others. It sounds simple, but it is often complex. Loving someone who loves us back is an easy and almost an automatic task. But loving someone who doesn't love us back is difficult. To carry out that command, we must fear God and keep His commandments. Do these things, and you will be on your way to a fruitful life.

Heavenly Father, thank you for loving me before I ever took the step to love you. I pray that you will keep watch over me as I serve your people. Guide my steps to honor your word and keep your commandments. Amen.

Now all has been heard; here is the conclusion of the matter:
Fear God and keep his commandments,
for this is the duty of all mankind.

ECCLESIASTES 12:13